WOKE
RELIGION

WOKE
RELIGION

UNMASKING THE FALSE GOSPEL OF SOCIAL JUSTICE

WES CARPENTER

AMBASSADOR INTERNATIONAL
GREENVILLE, SOUTH CAROLINA & BELFAST, NORTHERN IRELAND

www.ambassador-international.com

Woke Religion

Unmasking the False Gospel of Social Justice

Hardcover ISBN: 978-1-64960-252-7
Paperback ISBN: 978-1-64960-111-7
eISBN: 978-1-64960-161-2

Cover Design by Joshua Frederick
Interior Design by Dentelle Design
Edited by Katie Cruice Smith

Scripture taken from The Holy Bible, English Standard Version. ESV® Text Edition: 2016. Copyright © 2001 by Crossway Bibles, a publishing ministry of Good News Publishers.

AMBASSADOR INTERNATIONAL
Emerald House
411 University Ridge, Suite B14
Greenville, SC 29601, USA
www.ambassador-international.com

AMBASSADOR BOOKS
The Mount
2 Woodstock Link
Belfast, BT6 8DD, Northern Ireland, UK
www.ambassadormedia.co.uk

The colophon is a trademark of Ambassador, a Christian publishing company.

I dedicate this work to my lovely wife who encouraged and helped me with the ideas that led to this book. If there is any profit within these pages it is attributed to her and any error is a result of what is lacking on my part.

TABLE OF CONTENTS

FOREWORD

PASTOR TIMOTHY DECKER

AT THE MOMENT I AM writing this, it's election day, November 3, 2020. The fear that has gripped the nation over Covid-19, the riots, the looting, the potential violence over the election results—in some ways, the concept of Woke religion in the church seems a bit milder today than it did this past summer when I was preaching against it. And yet, much of the Christian disagreement over politics and social issues that have given rise to these fears can be traced back to an embrace of a new system of secular religion advanced in the church—*Woke religion.*

This past summer of 2020, I planned to preach a sermon, maybe two, over the infiltration of critical theory in both society and the Church. The more I studied, the more I realized how big a chomp I bit off. Yet I somehow whittled the series down to five sermons that argued the Woke religion of society was a spiritual battle, rather than simply a cultural fad or phenomenon. All religions seek, in the main, to answer four essential worldview questions: who are we? what's wrong? how do we fix it? and where are we going? Secularism (the religion of non-religionism) and Woke religion have answers to these, all of which are either sub-biblical or flatly contradictory to Scripture.

It became clear to me that the secular religion, with its anti-supernatural worldview and orthopraxy political correctness, had for its orthodoxy critical theory and *Woke theology.* I believe this to be a spiritual battle fought on at least three fronts. It first attacked God as the Creator. This is born out of the fact that in Romans 1, Paul identified the matter of sodomy and homosexuality in terms of idolatry. It is a direct assault against God's creation of male and female in the bonds of marriage. Add to this the transgender movement as also an attack against God's creation and decree, and the invasion is in full force. Secularism and Woke religion sought to answer the first basic religious question (Who are we?) with a resounding anti-biblical response. Man is simply an evolved animal and, therefore, ever and only engages in power struggles. Funny how "survival of the fittest" does not fit into their agenda.

Second, I believe there is a battle for Jesus Christ as Savior. Woke religion is not simply liberation theology repackaged, though that is certainly part of its makeup. It is not simply cultural Marxism applied in the Church. Rather, it is a religious movement to its core that seeks to address perceived sins and offer salvific solutions of redemption either for the oppressed (social justice) or the hegemonic powers that be (e.g. repentance, divestment, and reparation). In this way, the salvation provided in the Woke religion of critical theory is a bankrupt covenant of works. It does not merely say, "Do this and live!" but rather, "Because you are already guilty based on your class/tribe/intersectional hierarchy, you must constantly and perpetually do this; yet you still may not live." It is a graceless system that feigns a promise of forgiveness yet never admits enough penance to achieve absolution. Indeed, Christ Himself would be unable to accomplish atonement under such a covenant of works. This makes this topic critical for the Church, as the Gospel is literally at stake.

Lastly, there is a battle for the Spirit's Church. That this unbiblical philosophy of man has infiltrated the Church has led not only to the loss of the Gospel, but also has undermined the Church's worldview of eschatology as a necessary component for living in "the time between the times." We can suffer injustice and grievances—not because we like them but because we know that there is a future, final, ultimate judgment, where the Judge of the universe will do right! We may demand justice now, but we acknowledge that we may not see it. Yet that runs counter to the Woke religion that requires justice now, even at the expense of ten innocents, because there is no guarantee of tomorrow. That also implies a Marxist, utopian, end-times goal for the Church. That, too, is terribly unbiblical and causes turmoil in society.

That leaves me, then, to the subject of this book by my good friend, Wes Carpenter. He and I have discussed these things and found agreement. Our frustration is that we feel like there are only a few of us in our world. That is why I am glad that works like his *Woke Religion* and others are being written. The church needs them. We are starving ourselves from the wholesome teaching of God's Word while we stuff ourselves with the famishing doctrine of Woke religion. The true Church must cease imbibing from the *zeitgeist*, or spirit of the age, and drink from the fountain of living water. That is what makes a book like *Woke Religion* not only timely but also extremely needed. So drink, Dear Reader. Feast on the hope found in Jesus Christ, not social justice. Take up and read!

PREFACE

AMERICAN SECULARIZATION GOES WOKE

*"For this is why I wrote, that I might test you and know whether you are obedient in everything. Anyone whom you forgive, I also forgive. Indeed, what I have forgiven, if I have forgiven anything, has been for your sake in the presence of Christ, **so that we would not be outwitted by Satan; for we are not ignorant of his designs."***

—2 Corinthians 2:9-11 (emphasis added)

HISTORICAL READINGS OF THE PROMINENT Max Weber's (1864-1920) secularization thesis generally reveal that society has been undergoing a process of religious "disenchantment" as industrialization, technological advancement, and modernization continue to transform the Western world. Lesslie Newbigin says:

> The articulation of the belief is frequently attributed in the first place to Max Weber, who taught that the threefold process of rationalization, industrialization, and bureaucratization was creating a society in which there would necessarily be less and less from for the supernatural, the magical, the transcendent. The modern world, as he saw it, was undergoing a process of disenchantment.[1]

---

1   Lesslie Newbigin, *The Gospel in a Pluralist Society* (Grand Rapids, Michigan: Eerdmans, 1989), 211-212.

The idea that modernity is increasingly secularized has been welcomed because of the negative sentiment toward traditional Christian religion. Charles Taylor argues that secularization has led to greater numbers of people turning away from God and the decline of church attendance: "[S]ecularity consists in the falling off of *religious belief* and practice, in people turning away from God, and no longer going to Church. In this sense, the countries of western Europe have mainly become secular—even those who retain the vestigial public reference to God in public space" (emphasis mine).[2] It is increasingly common for people in Western society to express negative sentiment toward religion, especially Christianity. While Christian church attendance has steeply declined in the past few decades and Christian norms and values are tolerated less in America, it appears that the majority of people are still very religious. The irony is that the distancing from traditional Protestantism in America has, in effect, helped produce the emergence of an alternative religion.

Moreover, doubts have emerged concerning the validity of the secularization thesis, and it is unlikely that religion has declined. Pippa Norris and Ronald Inglehart write:

> Seminal nineteenth-century thinkers predicted that religion would gradually fade in importance with the emergence of industrial society. The belief that religion was dying became the conventional wisdom in the social sciences during most of the twentieth century. The traditional secularization thesis needs updating, however, as religion has not disappeared and is unlikely to do so.[3]

Scholars have widely identified the transcendent nature of religion across history and culture. This was the case for centuries in the pre-modern context, where Christianity and the recognition of the supernatural had significant influence in the Western world. The advent of modernity brought

---

2   Charles Taylor, *A Secular Age* (Massachusetts: Harvard University Press, 2007), 2.
3   Pippa Norris and Ronald Inglehart, *Sacred and Secular: Religion and Politics Worldwide* (Cambridge University Press, 2004), 3-32.

in the separation of Church and State, which may have actually increased religion in America. Taylor writes, "[T]he United States is rather striking in this regard. One of the earliest societies to separate Church and State, it is also the Western society with the highest statistics for religious belief and practice."[4] This phenomenon can partially be explained by the classical liberal, democratic structure of American government, which protects the freedoms of religion, expression, and assembly.

This is a fundamental difference from the paradigm of theocratic monarchs that enforced state religion dating back to Constantine. This democratic phenomenon is expressed through a plurality of Christian denominations in America. These tolerant, democratic principles have contributed to the rise of religious secularism. "Belief in God is no longer axiomatic," says Taylor. "[T]here are alternatives."[5] These alternatives began to solidify by the late twentieth century as American Christianity had nearly dissolved into a fragmented remnant of the moral activism.

In his book, *An Anxious Age: The Post-Protestant Ethic and Spirit of America*, Joseph Buttom argues that the demise of Christianity in America, particularly in Protestantism, has led liberals to transfer their religious practices, values, and beliefs into the political sphere.[6] After all, society does not believe in the biblical prophets, priests, kings, and ideas from the pre-modern world. Moral issues, cultural influence, social solidarity, and new forms of religious activity appear to be more focused on the celebrities, social justice warriors, and political leaders of our time—that mystically resemble traditional religious clergy.

"We live in a spiritual age when the political has been transformed into the soteriological. When how to vote is how our souls are saved," says Buttom.[7] The healing of souls has practically morphed from the ministry of

---

4   Taylor, 2.
5   Taylor, 4.
6   Joseph Buttom, *An Anxious Age* (New York: Crown Publishing Group, 2014).
7   Ibid, 2.

the Church to the function of government. A few days into the controversial aftermath of the 2020 presidential election, vice presidential candidate Kamala Harris wrote on Twitter, "Now the real work begins . . . to heal the soul of our nation. The road won't be easy. But America is ready and so are @JoeBiden and I."[8] Religious elements begin to surface as one examines the secularization of society—progressive, social ethics, such as tolerance, equity, confession of "white guilt" as if it were America's original sin, the rise of cancel culture, and expressions of solidarity with emerging political movements.[9] One wonders if a common thread can be identified in practices such as the lament washing of minorities' feet,[10] protests concerning racial injustices, normalization of transgender eight-year-olds,[11] social unrest associated with riots,[12] testimonies to forsake childbearing (since it is supposedly bad for the environment),[13] attacks against homeschooling,[14] proliferation of pedophilia,[15] discrimination of businesses,[16] university

---

8   Kamala Harris, Twitter Post, November 7, 2020, 8:42 p.m., https://twitter.com/ KamalaHarris/status/1325252289909690372.

9   Sean Collins, "Wokeness: old religion in a new bottle," Spiked-online.com, August 14, 2020, https://www.spiked-online.com/2020/08/14/wokeness-old-religion-in-a-new-bottle.

10   Theresa Braine, "SEE IT: White cops and community members wash black faith leaders' feet at protest," New York Daily News.com, June 9, 2020, https://www.nydailynews.com/news/national/ny-white-cops-community-wash-black-faith-leaders-feet-forgiveness-20200609-yl4gmoau4nclvgndlldgeqlj3y-story.html.

11   Brandon Showalter, "Christian leaders react to Joe Biden's support for 8-y-o kids identifying as transgender," The Christian Post.com, https://www.christianpost.com/news/biden-supports-kids-identifying-as-transgender-christians-react.html (accessed October 16, 2020).

12   Joe Concha, "CNN ridiculed for 'Fiery But Mostly Peaceful' caption with video of burning building in Kenosha," August 27, 2020, https://thehill.com/homenews/media/513902-cnn-ridiculed-for-fiery-but-mostly-peaceful-caption-with-video-of-burning.

13   Erica Gies, "Having kids is terrible for the environment, so I'm not having any," The Washington Post.com, July 14, 2015, https://www.washingtonpost.com/posteverything/wp/2015/07/14/having-kids-is-terrible-for-the-environment-so-im-not-having-any.

14   Liz Mineo, "A warning on homeschooling," The Harvard Gazette online, May 15, 2020, https://news.harvard.edu/gazette/story/2020/05/law-school-professor-says-there-may-be-a-dark-side-of-homeschooling.

15   Cheryl K. Chumley, "Netflix: Pandering to pedophiles everywhere," The Washington Times.com, August 20, 2020, https://www.washingtontimes.com/news/2020/aug/20/netflix-pandering-pedophiles-everywhere.

16   Tim Carman, "Yelp's move to flag restaurants accused of racism could be 'a step in the right direction'—and problematic," The Washington Post.com, October 9, 2020, https://www.washingtonpost.com/food/2020/10/09/yelp-reviews-racism.

webinars to help people recover from being white,[17] small group Bible studies on whiteness,[18] and abortion on demand in the name of "women's rights." The multitude of secular culture's new norms, values, ideas, and practices abound with identifiable religious characteristics as part of a new religion called Woke and Woke social justice.

Given this brief overview of the current state of American society, it is important to discuss the direction of the work ahead. This brief work will demonstrate that the Woke religion functions as an alternative counterfeit religion to Christianity. We will briefly discuss some of the important philosophical shifts that led to the advent of Woke religion. This broadly occurred in three paradigms: pre-modernism to modernism, modernism to postmodernism, and postmodernism to applied postmodernism. Since several works on this subject already detail the complex postmodern and applied postmodern philosophical underpinnings of Woke, this book aims to provide the reading with a balanced, high-level understanding of the transitions and consequences of philosophies that led up to modern-day Woke religion. In conjunction with the philosophical paradigm shifts, a significant theme that ran in parallel was the departure from the Bible as the source of truth in the Western world. This ultimately led to the Woke religion becoming a counterfeit alternative religion to Christianity.

A balance of academic works from critical theory, critical social justice, critical race theory scholars, and popular Woke literature was selected to compare with Christian theology and Scripture. We will systematically compare Woke dogmas to major Christian doctrines.

To assist the reader in understanding the content of this work, the following concepts must be reviewed:

---

17   Phil Shiver, "University of Minnesota offers 12-step AA-based webinar to help people 'recover' from being white," The Blaze.com, October 16, 2020, https://www.theblaze.com/news/university-of-minnesota-12-step-whiteness-recovery.

18   Diane Gaskins, "Thabiti Endorses 'Whiteness 101'—Black Liberation Theology for Small Groups," PulpitandPen.org, October 9, 2019, https://pulpitandpen.org/2019/10/09/thabiti-endorses-whiteness-101-black-liberation-theology-for-small-groups.

Woke epistemology—the determination that oppressed groups have more access to knowledge according to the neo-Marxist hegemony (power structure paradigm).

Woke anthropology—identity determined by societal relation and groups.

Woke hamartiology—the doctrine of sin that determines guilt based upon relationship to the oppressive power structure and skin color.

Woke soteriology—the doctrine of salvation that is realized by becoming awakened to societal injustices and perpetual confession of guilt.

Woke ecclesiology—a doctrine of the Woke church that is realized through social justice activism and revolution.

Woke eschatology—a doctrine of last things that idealizes a deconstruction of Western institutional power structures with the building of an equitable utopia.

These doctrines, along with several others, will be examined in depth. Based upon the incompatible and antithetical nature of Woke doctrine with Christian doctrine, it will be argued that Woke dogmas function as an alternative counterfeit religion to Christianity. While Christians believe in biblical commands such as loving our neighbor and the justice of the moral law, this work shows Wokeness is categorically unbiblical theologically and is, perhaps, a significant aspect of spiritual warfare afflicting the Church in this generation.

We will also discuss the amalgamation of Woke religion with Christianity and the response of selected evangelical leaders. It is apparent that evangelical leaders that are otherwise orthodox in their theology have, in varying degrees, united this religion with the Gospel. We grieve when false teaching is merged with Christianity within the Church, and we ought to show compassion to those who are being led into error and call them to the true Gospel of Jesus Christ. As discussed in this work, this is presently seen through formal denominational resolutions, sermons, scholarly works, interviews, books, and various other forms of communication. I understand that not all evangelicals will respond favorably to this discussion because some of the content is not popular in secular culture and portions of evangelicalism. I aim to approach sensitive matters of injustice, social turmoil, and ethnic tensions with compassion and empathy for the oppressed. Some may criticize this work as an unloving attempt to deny ethnic minorities, turn a blind eye to injustice, approach the issues "the wrong way," or smear those making "progress" for social justice. That is to misunderstand what this work is about.

I, too, am a minority of mixed ethnicity and appeal to the sufficiency of Scripture to address genuine concerns for the oppressed, injustice, and the false teaching in the evangelical midst. It is a fallacy that the Church needs to embrace Woke social justice to address issues of injustice, oppression, and sin. The whole counsel of God and the true Gospel of Jesus Christ already do. I fear that increasing numbers of evangelical leaders—out of the genuine concern and love for our neighbors—have mistakenly embraced secular ideology, including Woke social justice, to address injustice instead of relying solely on the Word of God. I contend that if this continues, the syncretism of Woke social justice into Christian teaching will not solve matters of injustice and will, at best, erode the purity of the Church or, at worst, result in widespread apostasy and the complete downgrade of the Christian religion in America. Only the true Gospel of Jesus Christ can save sinners, reform the Church, and deliver the oppressed throughout the world.

This book concludes with an admonishment to the Church in this spiritual battle to embrace the true Gospel of Christ and reject the false gospel of Woke social justice. This work is a loving encouragement for the Church to seek biblical justice for the oppressed while rebuking those who embrace teaching antithetical to Christianity (Titus 1:13). We join with those who are warning the Church of a false gospel in the evangelical midst. This warning is rooted in genuine love for God, love for people, and righteous hatred toward what is evil. While we lovingly empathize with those who have been treated unfairly and seek to combat the real evil injustices in the world, we cannot join ourselves with the world in order to do so (2 Cor. 6:15).

Those who love the Church will seek to protect the Bride of Christ from false teachers and false doctrine. Some claim that portions of social justice, postmodernism, and critical theory doctrine ought to be tolerated within the Church. I recognize there is a wholesome desire to display love, compassion, and solidarity with the oppressed. I, too, share this biblical desire. However, to do so while embracing false teaching does not "speak the truth in love" (Eph. 4:15). It is not loving to teach people a false gospel or combine false teaching with Christianity. The Law of God calls Christians to "learn to do good; seek justice, correct oppression; bring justice to the fatherless, plead the widow's cause" (Isa. 1:17). However, Christians should never do this with a false gospel from a counterfeit religion or extra-biblical teaching that does not accord with the truth of God's Word.

Scripture is sufficient; Christians do not need the empty philosophies of man to address sin, injustice, ethnic prejudice, or anything else under the sun. Therefore, Christians ought to oppose Woke religion's syncretism with Christianity for the sake of the Gospel of Jesus Christ. Christians ought to be strong in the Lord, stand firm in the battle of spiritual warfare, and defend the faith with the true Gospel (Eph. 6). Christians should not be ashamed of the Gospel (Rom. 1:16) and ought to take heart for "'if the world hates you, know that it has hated me before it hated you'" (John 15:18).

PART ONE
THE FOUNDATIONS OF WOKE RELIGION

WOKE RELIGION

"But even if we or an angel from heaven should preach to you a gospel
contrary to the one we preached to you, let him be accursed."

—Galatians 1:8

WHAT IS WOKE RELIGION?

IT IS IMPORTANT TO CLARIFY what Woke is not before explaining what Woke is. Certain principles can be deduced from the Bible that must not be confused with Woke. Woke is not:

- Striving for peace but "not as the world gives" (John 14:27).
- Seeking Christian unity, for "there is neither Jew nor Greek . . . slave nor free . . . no male and female, for you are all one in Christ Jesus" (Gal. 3:28).
- Trying "to do justice, and to love kindness, and to walk humbly with your God" (Micah 6:8).

Observing sin throughout history, particularly prejudice (Jas. 2:1), does not necessitate being Woke (Isa. 5:20). Loving our neighbors, no matter their cultural background or ethnicity, is not Woke (Luke 10:25-37; Gal. 5:14). The identification of certain ethnic partiality is not Woke (Gal. 2:11-13). Hating evil (Rom. 12:9), recognizing total depravity (Rom. 3:23), defending the rights of the poor and the needy (Prov. 31:8-9), caring for orphans and widows (Jas. 1:27), taking care of our families (1 Tim. 5:8), and adopting children from other ethnicities is not

Woke (Deut. 10:18). Engaging in cultural issues in a true, loving, biblical way (Eph. 4:15), "learn[ing] to do what is good [and to] seek justice" (Isa. 1:17), and showing charity and "rejoic[ing] with the truth" is not Woke (1 Cor. 13:1-13).

Though Woke often uses biblical terms, the definitions, philosophy, and worldview behind them in Woke religion is fundamentally different. Wokeness is an emerging Western religion built upon the philosophical, sociological, and ideological systems of postmodernism, critical theory, social justice, and identity politics that emerged in the late twentieth and early twenty-first century that has been combined with Christianity.

Important to this working definition are the terms below. Brian Duignan states:

> [Postmodernism is] in Western philosophy, a late 20th-century movement characterized by broad skepticism, subjectivism, or relativism; a general suspicion of reason; and an acute sensitivity to the role of ideology in asserting and maintaining political and economic power . . . Postmodernism is largely a reaction against the intellectual assumptions and values of the modern period in the history of Western philosophy (roughly, the 17th through the 19th century).[19]

Stanford Encyclopedia of Philosophy explains, "'Critical Theory' in the narrow sense designates several generations of German philosophers and social theorists in the Western European Marxist tradition known as the Frankfurt School.[20]

Maurianne Adams understands:

> Social justice is both a process and a goal. The goal of social justice is full and equal participation of all groups in a society that is mutually shaped to meet their needs. Social justice includes a vision of society in which the distribution of resources is equitable and all members are psychologically and

---

19   Brian Duignan, *Postmodernism*, https://www.britannica.com/topic/postmodernism-philosophy (accessed October 15, 2020).

20   *Stanford Encyclopedia of Philosophy*, s.v. "Critical Theory," Accessed October 15, 2020, https://plato.stanford.edu/entries/critical-theory.

physically safe and secure . . . as we read and reflect upon the emerging literature on oppression, and as we continually learn through practice the myriad of ways oppression can seduce our minds and hearts or inspire us further learning and activism.[21]

Jennifer L. Eagan helps explain identify politics as "political and social movements that have group identity as the basis of their formation and the focus of their political action. Those movements attempt to further the interests of their group members and force issues important to their group members into the public sphere."[22]

There is a narrow and broad sense in which Woke religion can be understood. Narrowly, to be Woke is to have a heightened "critical consciousness" or acute awareness of the perceived oppressive power structures that make up the world. Belief or faith in the Woke canons results in awakening to the existential reality that all societal relationships are to be understood in relation to the oppressive hegemonic power, which functions like a dualistic, pantheistic force. Broadly, Woke religion tends to incorporate a whole host of ideas that most people in modern culture are familiar with, generally speaking, but may find their roots challenging to identity. Wokeness or "being Woke" are terms and phases meant to generally encompass but not be limited to those who embrace the ideology, philosophy, worldview, and beliefs of social justice, critical social justice, critical race theory, intersectionality, standpoint epistemology[23] or standpoint theory, systemic racism, institutional racism, cultural hegemony,[24] neo-marxism,[25] deconstructionism, decolonization,[26] queer theory,[27] grievance

21 Maurianne Adams, Lee Anne Bell, and Pat Griffin, *Teaching for Diversity and Social Justice: A Sourcebook* (New York: Routledge, 1997), 3.

22 Jennifer L. Eagan, *Encyclopedia Britannica Online*, s.v. "Multiculturalism," accessed October 20, 2020, https://www.britannica.com/topic/multiculturalism#ref1225694.

23 José Medina, *The Epistemology of Resistance: Gender and Racial Oppression, Epistemic Injustice, and the Social Imagination* (New York: Oxford University Press, 2013), 197.

24 Dino Franco Felluga, *Critical Theory: The Key Concepts* (Abingdon: Routledge, 2015), 127-28.

25 Alberto Toscano, "Neo-Marxism," Wiley Online Library, February 15, 2007, https://onlinelibrary.wiley.com/doi/10.1002/9781405165518.wbeosn012.

26 Gurminder Bhambra, et al., *Decolonizing the University* (London: Pluto Press, 2018), 2.

27 Joshua Trey Barnett and Corey W. Johnson, *Encyclopedia of Diversity and Social Justice*, s.v. "Queer," Sherwood Thomson, ed. (Lanham: Rowman and Littlefield, 2015), p. 581.

studies, applied-postmodernism,[28] and liberation theology.[29] Since some of these terms are increasingly understood in different ways, I will provide definitions and explanations of these ideas below to help establish a working framework of Woke religion for the reader.

Ozlem and DiAngelo write:

> While some scholars and activists prefer to use the term social justice in order to reclaim its true commitments, in this book we use the term critical social justice. We do so in order to distinguish our standpoint on social justice from mainstream standpoints. A critical approach to social justice refers to specific theoretical perspectives that recognize that society is stratified (i.e., divided and unequal) in significant and far-reaching ways along social group lines that include race, class, gender, sexuality, and ability. Critical social justice recognizes inequality as deeply embedded in the fabric of society (i.e., as structural), and actively seeks to change this.[30]

Sherwood Thompson defines critical race theory (CRT) as:

> A scholarly and political approach to examining race that leads to a consequential analysis and profound understanding of racism. It argues, as a starting point, that the axis of American social life is fundamentally constructed in race. As a result, the economic, political, and historical relationships and arrangements that social actors have to institutions and social processes are all race based. CRT also argues that, as a whole, this idea has been purposefully ignored, subdued, and marginalized in both the dominant and public discourse and that there are serious repercussions that arise from this structural blindness (Mills, 1997, p. 153) . . . Though times have changed, and overt forms of

---

28   James Lindsay and Helen Pluckrose, *Cynical Theories: How Activist Scholarship Made Everything about Race, Gender, and Identity* (Durham: Pitchstone Publishing, 2020), 48.

29   D.D. Webster, "Liberation Theology," in *Evangelical Dictionary of Theology Second Edition* (Grand Rapids: Baker Academic, 2001), 686-87.

30   Ozlem Sensoy and Robin DiAngelo, *Is Everyone Really Equal?: An Introduction to Key Concepts in Social Justice Education, first edition* (New York: Teacher's College Press, 2012), xviii.

racial violence seem to be atrocities of the past, *CRT emphasizes that overt expressions of racism have gone underground* and are now expressed through insidious and covert methods. One of the important tenets of CRT is the assertion that race is socially constructed, yet it denotes explicitly and implicitly how power is used and appropriated in society [emphasis mine].[31]

Patricia Collins and Sirma Bilge define intersectionality:

A way of understanding and analyzing the complexity in the world, in people, and in human experiences. The events and conditions of social and political life and the self can seldom be understood as shaped by one factor. They are generally shaped by many factors in diverse and mutually influencing ways. When it comes to social inequality, people's lives and the organization of power in a given society are better understood as being shaped not by a single axis of social division, be it race or gender or class, but by many axes that work together and influence each other."[32]

According to Ozlem Sensoy and Robin DiAngelo, "From a critical social justice perspective, the term racism refers to this system of collective social and institutional White power and privilege."[33] The *Glossary of Terms for Diversity, Equity and Inclusion* defines institutional racism as "the ways in which institutional policies and practices create different outcomes for different racial groups. The institutional policies may never mention any racial group, but their effect is to create advantages for Whites and oppression and disadvantage for people from groups classified as People of Color."[34]

---

31   Sherwood Thompson, Ph.D., ed., *Encyclopedia of Diversity and Social Justice* (London: Rowman & Littlefield, 2015), 65.
32   Patricia Hill Collins and Sirma Bilge, *Intersectionality* (Cambridge: Polity Press, 2016), 2.
33   Ozlem Sensoy and Robin DiAngelo, *Is Everyone Really Equal?: An Introduction to Key Concepts in Social Justice Education, first edition* (Teacher's College Press: New York, 2012),101.
34   "Glossary of Terms for Diversity, Equity and Inclusion," Educate Not Indoctrinate. org, Accessed October 14, 2020, https://educatenotindoctrinate.org/glossary-of-terms-for-equity-diversity-inclusion.

The bedrock of Woke religion is deeply connected to the previous centuries' philosophical paradigm shifts that gradually took place. The departure from the pre-modern world left behind the belief that the Scriptures were the source of truth. Existential dilemmas mounted in modernism and ultimately came to a head in the denial of the existence of God. By the nineteenth century, the focus shifted to man, and philosophers grappled with the question, "Who is man?" Limited by hyper-skepticism, postmodernism—a broad school of thought that began around the mid-twentieth century that rejected modernism—was unable to provide a satisfactory answer to this quintessential problem. At best, postmodernists committed to the rejection of modernism have concluded, "We do not know."

Postmodernism drowned in a world of hyper-skeptic despair, so a new system was needed to provide answers to the questions posed in a brave, new world. The last century was plagued with a maze of the agnostic, purposeless reality of existence that led to despair. This primed the stage for a renewed interest in critical theory—one of the dogmas of Wokeness.

Critical theory dogma began in Frankfurt, Germany, and is often associated with Marxism.[35] According to the *Encyclopedia Britannica*, critical theory is a:

> Marxist-inspired movement in social and political philosophy originally associated with the work of the Frankfurt School. Drawing particularly on the thought of Karl Marx and Sigmund Freud, critical theorists maintain that a primary goal of philosophy is to understand and to help overcome the social structures through which people are dominated and oppressed.[36]

In *Live Not by Lies*, Rod Dreher points out the horrific history of Marxism that took the "Russian intellectuals by storm because its evangelists presented

---

35   Timon Cline, "Identity Politics and the Bondage of the Will," *Founders Journal: Critical Theory and Christian Theology*, Fall 2019, https://founders.org/2020/02/10/identity-politics-and-the-bondage-of-the-will.

36   Adam Augustyn, ed., *Britannica*, s.v. "Critical theory," https://www.britannica.com/topic/critical-theory (accessed October 3, 2020).

Marxism as a secular religion for the post-religious age."[37] Is there a secular religion with similar Marxist roots among us today?

Woke employs neo-Marxist critical theory methods that define Western secular society as systemically racist, institutionally unjust, and categorically oppressive. Deconstruction is a key tenant of postmodernism and wokeness, which is a device used to challenge the meaning of literary texts.[38]

The origins of deconstructionism began in the 1960s by Jacques Derrida as a literary, textual, critical device to subvert the meaning of texts. Deconstructionism expanded to challenge the traditional meaning of words, ideas, intuitions, beliefs, and worldviews.[39] The failure of postmodernism to solve important issues of the twentieth century was revived through social justice activism based upon critical theory dogma. Its goal was to liberate the oppressed from (allegedly) unjust societal power structures.[40] Those who are indoctrinated to believe according to critical theory dogma that institutional injustice and oppression are woven into the very fabric of society have an awakening experience. Laura Roy writes, "The notion of 'getting woke' (or staying woke) is defined as being acutely aware of racial and social injustice—not just awareness and acknowledgement of isolated incidents, but awareness from a position of understanding systemic and institutional racism.[41]

Moreover, in Woke dogma, there are only racist and anti-racist individuals. There is no neutrality. One of the most popular critical race theory scholars is Ibram X. Kendi, who says, "The claim of 'not racist' neutrality is a mask

---

37 Rod Dreher, *Live Not by Lies: A Manuel for Christian Dissidents* (New York: Penguin Random House LLC, 2020), 24.

38 James Lindsay and Mike Nayna, "Postmodern Religion and the Faith of Social Justice," New Discourses.com, June 18, 2020, https://newdiscourses.com/2020/06/postmodern-religion-faith-social-justice.

39 Helen Pluckrose, "How French 'Intellectuals' Ruined the West: Postmodernism and Its Impact, Explained," Areo Magazine.com, March 27, 2017, https://areomagazine.com/2017/03/27/how-french-intellectuals-ruined-the-west-postmodernism-and-its-impact-explained.

40 Lindsay and Pluckrose, *Cynical Theories*, 17-18.

41 Laura A. Roy, *Teaching While White: Addressing the Intersections of Race and Immigration* (London: Rowman & Littlefield, 2018), 150.

for racism."[42] He goes on to write, "The most threatening racist movement is not the alt right's unlikely drive for a White ethnostate but the regular American's drive for a 'race-neutral' one."[43] Thus, there is no race-neutral, and for one to become anti-racist, one must become woke.

These historical strands of critical theory have manifested into what Dr. Neil Shenvi and Dr. Pat Sawyer call "contemporary critical theory" and what Dr. James Lindsay and Mike Nayna call "applied postmodernism."[44] Figure 1 conceptualizes the relationship between postmodernism, critical theory, and identity politics that manifested into applied postmodernism. On the one hand, these philosophies and ideological movements narrowly have distinct origins while maintaining functional points of continuity. On the other hand, the broad application of these philosophies and ideological movements amalgamated an increasingly interdependent system called applied postmodernism.

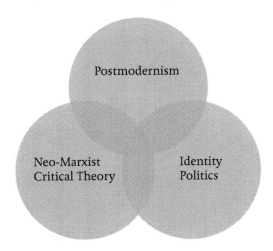

Figure 1: Applied Postmodernism

The fundamental component that effected the transition from postmodernism to applied postmodernism was identity politics. Identity

---

42   Ibram X. Kendi, *How to Be an Antiracist*, (New York: One World, 2019), 9.
43   Ibid, 20.
44   James Lindsay and Mike Nayna, "Postmodern Religion and the Faith of Social Justice," AreoMagazines.com December 18, 2018, https://areomagazine.com/2018/12/18/postmodern-religion-and-the-faith-of-social-justice.

politics were (and still are) viewed as the only way progress toward the founding principle of American equality has been made. DiAngelo writes, "The term identity politics refers to the focus on the barriers specific groups face in their struggle for equality. We have yet to achieve our founding principle, but any gains we have made thus far have come through identity politics."[45]

Scott David Allen rightly connects the counterfeit social justice that has influenced evangelicalism to the "hollow and deceptive" philosophies (Col. 2:8) of critical theory that are traced back to Immanuel Kant, Friedrich Nietzsche, Karl Marx, Antonio Gramsci, and Michael Foucault.[46] More importantly, Allen coins the term *ideological social justice* to demonstrate that social justice is "something much bigger than justice. Rather, it is a comprehensive ideology, or worldview, which helps explain why it is attracting so many adherents."[47] In addition to the fact that social justice or *ideological social justice* is a comprehensive worldview, it is a fundamental element to the Woke religion. Social justice awakens all of these components into the religion of Woke as shown in Figure 2.

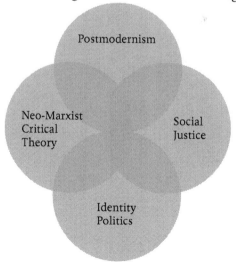

Figure 2: The Foundation of Woke Religion

---

45   Robin DiAngelo. *White Fragility: Why It's So Hard for White People to Talk About Racism* (Boston: Beacon Press, 2018), xiii.

46   Scott David Allen, *Why Social Justice is Not Biblical Justice* (Grand Rapids: Credo House Publishes, 2020), 3.

47   Ibid.

James Lindsay and Helen Pluckrose rightly said, "The *faith* that emerged is thoroughly postmodern, which means that, rather than interpreting the world in terms of subtle spiritual forces like sin and magic, it focuses instead on subtle material forces, such as systemic bigotry, and diffuse but omnipresent systems of power and privilege."[48]

Postmodern despair was revived through social justice and has been melded with identity politics to form Woke religion. In effect, social justice activists proselytized critical theory like it was a faith-like religion in replacement of the traditional religion and traditional democratic structures that make up Western civilization. By the mid-2010s, this phenomenon was understood by many as the social justice movement or Woke. Lindsay and Pluckrose say:

> When they speak of "racism," for example, they are not referring to prejudice on the grounds of race, but rather to, as they define it, a racialized system that permeates all interactions in society yet is largely invisible except to those who experience it or have been trained in the proper "critical" methods that train them to see it. (There are the people sometimes referred to as being "woke," meaning awakened, to it.)[49]

Woke centers around power, language, authority of knowledge, and social relations. The worldview is dominated by cultural strife and societal identity politics of race, sex, and gender. Lindsay and Pluckrose suggest Woke social justice has religious characteristics:

> They bear witness to our repeatedly demonstrated capacity to take up complex spiritual worldview, ranging from tribal animism, to hippie spiritualism to sophisticated global religions, each of which adopts its own interpretive frame through which it sees the entire world. This one just happens

---

48   Lindsay and Pluckrose, *Cynical Theories*, 17-18.
49   Ibid, 15.

to be about a peculiar view of power and its ability to create inequality and oppression.[50]

This is consistent with Buttom's theory that indicates an emphasis on social sins, such as oppression and power, during the twentieth century Social Gospel movement led to religious social activism in the twenty-first century.[51] With these ideas and terms in mind, we will turn our attention to the important question, "Why is Woke a problem?"

---

50   Ibid, 16.
51   Collins, Ibid.

CHAPTER ONE

WHY WOKE IS A PROBLEM

WHEN WE THINK ABOUT WOKE social justice, I'd like to point out something that more people are recognizing—the religious element. What if I told you Woke social justice is being syncretized with Christianity in American evangelicalism? If this is true, what would this mean for the church? How can we make sense of this?

From a biblical perspective of the history of the world, Satan has often used false teaching as a way to confuse people and afflict the people of God. Sometimes, this is referred to in the Bible as spiritual warfare. One wonders if there is a connection between spiritual warfare and bad ideas or ideologies that can lead to false religions. It seems possible that critical theory, social justice, postmodernism, and progressive identity politics may be creeping into the Church. When these ideas are connected to religion, how do we understand this in the context of spiritual warfare? This is somewhat difficult to explain because not many people have studied these ideas from that perspective, but it does raise some interesting questions: Can these ideas that we are confronting today be traced from prior centuries? If so, what relationship do they have with biblical Christianity? Is it possible that some of these ideas have made their way into the Church and are being embraced by an increasing number of Christian leaders? These are some of the questions I'd like to explore to help understand if Woke is a problem for us today.

The religious creed of Wokeness has spread far beyond sociopolitical organizations and now infects Church denominations,[52] government,[53] K-12 education,[54] universities,[55] mathematics ("2 + 2 = 5"),[56] medicine,[57] Girl Scouts,[58] and the planet Mars (even though it is not inhabited)[59] and is associated with the "Great Reset."[60] Social justice initiatives are seen as complementary to the "Great Reset" post-pandemic rebuilding. Each day in America, there is an occurrence of someone who was fired from their job, publicly shamed on social media, or "canceled" for something that was viewed as racist, homophobic, sexist, or hate speech. The day after Amy Coney Barrett's hearing for the Supreme Court of the United States, "Merriam-Webster's online dictionary quietly changed the meaning of the word 'preference' and the term 'sexual preference' . . . after a Democratic senator claimed it was an 'offensive and outdated term.'"[61] In most cases, these accusations are baseless and projections of social justice identity politics. This degree

---

52 "On Critical Race Theory and Intersectionality," SBC.net, June 1, 2019, https://www.sbc.net/resource-library/resolutions/on-critical-race-theory-and-intersectionality/.

53 Matthew Schwartz, "Trump Tells Agencies To End Trainings On 'White Privilege' And 'Critical Race Theory,'" NPR.org, Accessed October 2, 2020, https://www.npr.org/2020/09/05/910053496/trump-tells-agencies-to-end-trainings-on-white-privilege-and-critical-race-theory.

54 "1619 Project," New Discourses.com, Accessed October 2, 2020, https://newdiscourses.com/tftw-1619-project.

55 Mark Devine, "Princeton's Woke Letter on Systemic Racism Backfires," The American Spectator.org, Accessed October 2, 2020, https://spectator.org/princeton-racism-letter.

56 "Kareem Carr Explains Why 2+2=5," Harvard.edu, Accessed November 2, 2020, https://www.hsph.harvard.edu/biostatistics/2020/09/kareem-carr-explains-why-225.

57 "Social Justice," The Student Senate.com, Accessed November 17, 2020, https://www.thestudentsenate.com/socialjustice.

58 "The Girl Scouts of Northern California Volunteer Policy for Building Equitable Community for All," Girl Scouts Northern California.org, Board Approved July 18, 2020, https://www.gsnorcal.org/content/dam/girlscouts-gsnorcal/documents/volunteer_resources/volunteer-essentials/volunteering-volunteer-policy.pdf.

59 "Motivation," Decolonizing Mars.org, Accessed October 2, 2020 https://www.decolonizemars.org/motivation.

60 Caroline Casey, "What is intersectionality and how can it help businesses tackle diversity and inclusion?," October 23, 2020, https://www.weforum.org/agenda/2020/10/intersectionality-the-real-talking-point-for-tackling-diversity-and-inclusion-in-business.

61 Josh Christenson, "Merriam-Webster's Dictionary Changes Meaning of 'Preference' Following SCOTUS Hearing," The Washington Free Beacon online, Accessed October 14, 2020, https://freebeacon.com/latest-news/merriam-websters-dictionary-changes-meaning-of-preference-following-scotus-hearing.

of censorship and illiberalism has led to malicious attacks on the founding principles of freedom of religion and liberty of speech protected under the U.S. Constitution. The increase of illiberalism associated with social justice has led to what Lindsay and Pluckrose call "a kind of authoritarianism in our midst."[62] Gad Saad explains it as "illiberal idea pathogens."[63] And Jordan Peterson identifies it as "radical PC authoritarianism."[64] Perhaps Dreher summarizes the emerging Woke culture in the West best by comparing it to the old, hardened Soviet Communism:

> What unnerves those who lived under Soviet Communism is this similarity: Elites and elite institutions are abandoning old-fashioned liberalism, based in defending the rights of the individual, and replacing it with a progressive creed that regards justice in terms of groups. It encourages people to identify with groups—ethnic, sexual, and otherwise—and to think of Good and Evil as a matter of power dynamics among the groups. A utopian vision drives these progressives, one that compels them to seek to rewrite history and reinvent language to reflect their ideals of social justice.[65]

Charges of racism from Woke social justice warriors no longer mean individual prejudice; rather, racism is redefined based on one's identity in the power structure hegemony. Sensoy and DiAngelo support this position, stating, "No individual member of the dominant group has to do anything specific to oppress a member of the minoritized group."[66] Voddie Baucham, Jr., describes this view as Ethnic Gnosticism—the idea that one's identity is rooted in your group and the group can be based on sex, race, or so-called

---

62   Lindsay and Pluckrose, *Cynical Theories*, 15.
63   Gad Saad, *The Parasitic Mind: How Infections Ideas Are Killing Common Sense* (Washington, D.C.: Regnery Publishing, 2020).
64   Andrew Buncombe, "Jordan Peterson: Cambridge University pulls fellowship for controversial philosopher who called women 'crazy harpy sisters,'" Independent.co, Accessed November 30, 2020, https://www.independent.co.uk/news/world/americas/jordan-peterson-cambridge-university-fellowship-philosophy-a8832076.html.
65   Dreher, xi.
66   Sensoy and DiAngelo, 62.

sexual orientation.[67] Baucham argues that Ethnic Gnosticism is rooted in "Cultural Marxism" which "divide(s) the world between those who establish and benefit from cultural hegemony and everyone else."[68] One is an oppressor or "racist" without even knowing it because nearly everything has been categorically redefined according to the orthodoxy of critical theory and practiced in social justice.

Critical race theory, a subset of critical theory, has become such an immense problem that the president of the United States issued an executive order banning it from all Federal employee training programs. A memo to the heads of the Executive departments and agencies reads:

> All agencies are directed to begin to identify all contracts or other agency spending related to any training on "critical race theory/white privilege," or any other training or propaganda effort that teaches or suggests either (1) that the United States is an inherently racist or evil country or (2) that any race or ethnicity is inherently racist or evil. In addition, all agencies should begin to identify all available avenues within the law to cancel any such contracts and/or to divert Federal dollars away from these unAmerican propaganda training sessions.[69]

Furthermore, the rate at which Woke social justice or Woke religion is clearly entering the evangelical Church is particularly alarming. At an accelerating rate, evangelicalism is currently being influenced by, syncretized with, and replaced with this alternative religion. Despite the neo-Marxist roots and antithetical teaching of Woke toward Christianity, the Southern Baptist Convention voted to adopt Resolution 9 in the summer of 2019. This resolution embraced critical race theory and intersectionality as analytical

---

67   Voddie Baucham, "Ethnic Gnosticism," Founders.org, Accessed September 15, 2020, https://founders.org/sermons/ethnic-gnosticism.

68   Jarrod Longshore et al., *By What Standard? God's World . . . God's Rules* (Cape Coral: Founders Press, 2020), 106-7.

69   Russell Vought to the Heads of Executive Departments and Agencies, September 4, 2020, Executive Office of the President, Training in the Federal Government, https://www.whitehouse.gov/wp-content/uploads/2020/09/M-20-34.pdf.

tools subordinate to Scripture. The resolution states, "Analytical tools can aid in evaluating a variety of human experiences."[70] The president of the Southern Baptist convention, J.D. Greear, appears to be influenced by the Woke ideology that hierarchy ought to be torn down—which is not a biblical concept since God ordains hierarchy in Creation (1 Tim. 2:11-15; 1 Tim. 3:2). In a message to Beth Moore, he tweeted, "Hoping that we are entering a new era where we in the complementarian world take all the Word of God seriously–not just the parts about the distinction of roles but also re the tearing down of all hierarchy & his gracious distribution of gifts to all his children!"[71]

Timothy Keller, a professor at Reformed Theological Seminary, retired pastor of Redeemer Presbyterian Church, and co-founder of The Gospel Coalition, said in a question and answer session, "If you have white skin, it's worth $1,000,000 over a lifetime . . . you have to say . . . 'I am the product of and standing on the shoulders of other people who got that through injustice' . . . the Bible says you are involved in injustice, and even if you didn't actually do it.'[72] This almost seamlessly aligns with the claims of critical theory. Robin DiAngelo, a widely famous critical race theory scholar, writes, "Society is structured in ways that make us all complicit in systems of inequality; there is no neutral ground."[73]

Dr. Albert Mohler, the president of Southern Baptist Seminary and proponent of theological conservatism, has taken some issue with critical race theory, particularly in how it is described in the Southern Baptist Convention's Resolution 9. Although, he merely critiqued the origins and consequences of critical race theory (identity politics) but not the theory itself. He rightly says, "The main consequence of critical race theory and

70   "On Critical Race Theory And Intersectionality," Ibid.
71   "J.D. Greear's sloppy theology on gender: Abolishing ALL hierarchy?," Capstone Report.com, Accessed October 14, 2020, https://capstonereport.com/2018/05/06/j-d-greears-sloppy-theology-gender-abolishing-hierarchy/32026.
72   "Grace, Justice, & Mercy: An Evening with Bryan Stevenson & Rev. Tim Keller Q &A, RedeemerCFW, June 3, 2016, YouTube video, 51:32, https://youtu.be/32CHZiVFmB4.
73   Sensoy and DiAngelo, *Is Everyone Really Equal? An Introduction to Key Concepts in Social Justice Education 2nd edition* (New York and London: Teachers College Press, 2017), 4.

intersectionality is identity politics, and identity politics can only rightly be described, as antithetical to the gospel of Jesus Christ."[74] Yet it is puzzling how he wanted Resolution 9 to say more than it did but threads the needle to merely describe the consequences of the theories as antithetical to the Gospel of Christ and not the theories themselves. Referencing a book written by colleagues called *Removing the Stain*, he also argues that racism is, "A stain that we're going to carry as a denomination forever until Jesus comes."[75] Clearly, history cannot be undone; however, this statement is concerning because it clearly echoes the dogma of critical race theory that racism can never be removed or atoned. DiAngelo similarly writes, "Racism is so deeply woven into the fabric of our society that I do not see myself escaping from that continuum in my lifetime."[76]

One of the common errors of critical race theory repeated by evangelicals is the notion of *white privilege.* This almost always leads to the imposition of false guilt upon entire groups of people because of the color of their skin. Evangelical Pastor Matt Chandler clearly utilizes this terminology when he preached, "What is so deceptive about *white privilege* is that it is different from blatant racism or bias . . . A privileged person's heart may be free from racist thoughts or biased attitudes, but may still fail to see how the very privilege afforded to him or her shapes how he or she interprets and understands the situations and circumstances of people without privilege."[77]

The concept of white privilege undoubtedly comes from critical race theory dogma. DiAngelo writes, "Race science was driven by these social and economic interests, which came to establish cultural norms and legal rulings

---

74   "Ideas Have Consequences: Critical Race Theory and Intersectionality in the News from the Southern Baptist Convention," Part III in The Briefing, Albert Mohler.com, Accessed November 9, 2020, https://albertmohler.com/2019/06/14/briefing-6-14-19.

75   "Stain of Mohler 3," TheNewCalvinist, November 25, 2019, YouTube video, 1:04:36, https://www.youtube.com/watch?v=MIlnLU-vt_g.

76   DiAngelo, *White Fragility*, 87.

77   Samuel Smith, "Matt Chandler: Church has mostly 'refused to participate' on race, 'turned over' inheritance," ChristianPost.com, June 10, 2020, https://www.christianpost.com/news/matt-chandler-church-has-mostly-refused-to-participate-on-race-turned-over-inheritance.html.

that legitimized racism and the privileged status of those defined as white."[78] Furthermore, Ashleigh Shackelford, a critical race theory proponent, lectured, "All White people are racist."[79]

Interestingly, John McWhorter highlights the counterfeit religious nature of critical theory dogma, stating, "White privilege is the secular white person's Original Sin, present at birth and ultimately ineradicable. One does one's penance by endlessly attesting to this privilege in hope of some kind of forgiveness."[80] Sadly, the same destructive language, ideas, and philosophy that is taught and practiced in Woke are evidently being preached from the pulpits and seminaries all over America. There has also been increasing reproach mounting for those in the evangelical Church who have not adopted Woke social justice dogma. This includes several professors at a conservative evangelical seminary who were dismissed for their stance against critical race theory.[81] One of the few influential evangelical voices who has not embraced social justice is Pastor Dr. John MacArthur, who says, "It is the greatest danger our nation currently faces."[82]

WOKE IN THE STREETS

Another tragedy of the Woke religion is that it is being popularized in the public square all over America. This is, perhaps, most clearly demonstrated by the Black Lives Matter organization, whose beliefs are based upon critical race theory and practices are consistent with the Woke religion.[83] However,

---

78   DiAngelo, *White Fragility*, 33.
79   "ALL White People are 'Racist Demons' Says BLM Activist & Lecturer at Seminar - Critical Race Theory?," Indicrat, February 7, 2018, YouTube video, 0:55, https://www.youtube.com/watch?v=cRXNaUz5LGY.
80   John McWhorter, "Atonement as Activism," The American Interest.com, Accessed October 2, 2020, https://www.the-american-interest.com/2018/05/24/atonement-as-activism.
81   "Whistleblower: 'Dangerous' theology taught at Al Mohler's SBTS seminary," CapstoneReport.com, Accessed October 2, 2020, https://capstonereport.com/2020/05/18/whistleblower-dangerous-theology-taught-at-al-mohlers-sbts-seminary/34410.
82   John MacArthur, "MACARTHUR: Critical Race Theory, A Sickness That Cannot Be Allowed To Continue," DailyWire.com, Accessed October 2, 2020, https://www.dailywire.com/news/macarthur-a-sickness-that-cannot-be-allowed-to-continue.
83   Soeren Kern. "Black Lives Matter: 'We Are Trained Marxists' - Part I," GatestoneInstitute.org, Accessed October 2, 2020, https://www.gatestoneinstitute.org/16181/black-lives-matter.

the proselytization of the Woke religion is only part of the issue. The real issue is that Black Lives Matter has a problematic spiritual nature, which is embraced by the leaders of the organization.

Celebrated co-founder of the Black Lives Matter movement and self-proclaimed "trained Marxist" Patrisse Cullors unabashedly admits, "We're not just having a social justice movement, this is a spiritual movement."[84] This point was further illustrated during a conversation between Cullors and Melina Abdullah, a professor of African studies at California State University Los Angeles and founder of the Los Angeles chapter of Black Lives Matter. Abdullah stated, "We've become very intimate with the spirits that we call on regularly ... Each of them seems to have a different presence and personality."[85] Cullors further states they are "resurrecting the spirits so they can work through us to get the work that we need to get done."[86]

It is evident from the statements of Black Lives Matter leaders that the organization is not a mere social justice movement—it is part of a religion. The religious practice to invoke dead spirits as practiced by members of Black Lives Matter and is viewed as a core spiritual tenant is strictly condemned by Scripture as wicked. More specifically, Deuteronomy 18:10-12 states, "There shall not be found among you anyone who burns his son or his daughter as an offering, anyone who *practices divination* or tells fortunes or interprets omens, or a sorcerer or a charmer or a medium or a necromancer or one *who inquires of the dead*, for whoever does these things is an abomination to the LORD" (emphasis mine).

This passage of Scripture defines those who practice divination and inquire of the dead to be an abomination to the Lord. Therefore, the actions of Black Livers Matter participants, based on their own description of practices, are partaking in an abominable religion.

---

84   Ryan Foley, "BLM leaders practice 'witchcraft' and summon dead spirits, black activist claims," Christian Post.com, Accessed October 2, 2020, https://www.christianpost.com/news/blm-leaders-practice-witchcraft-and-summon-dead-spirits-black-activist-warns.html.

85   Ibid.

86   Ibid.

Woke social justice is not always easy to identify and is widely only understood in complex philosophical categories; and recent works appear to merely emphasize the historical, sociological, political, and ideological aspects of Woke. Without marginalizing these important components in the defense against Woke, this book seeks to shine the light of truth on the spiritual element that exists and operates at the core of Woke religion since Woke dogma and practice is antithetical to Christianity and founded upon godless philosophy that is not according to Christ.

However, there is a spectrum of influence Woke ideology has upon people as shown in Figure 3. One way to think about it is if someone is part of a cult, they may not know they are being influenced by false teaching. Similarly, some are sympathetic toward Woke but have not fully embraced it. We grieve for them and call them to turn from Woke ideology. Often those sympathetic to Woke religion are ignorant of the designs and counterfeit nature of the religion. They typically have good intentions to advocate for biblical things like justice and help for the oppressed but, sadly, syncretize false teaching into their ministry. We ought to have biblical compassion for those ignorant of the deceptions of Woke. We ought to call them out of darkness into the light of Christ, lest they are taken captive. On the other hand, some people embrace and actively teach the dogmas of the counterfeit religion and are unrepentant of false teaching.

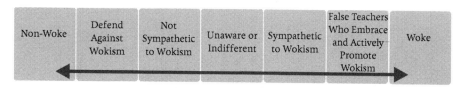

Figure 3: Relationship Between Non-Woke and Woke Influence

False teachers of Woke must be confronted and placed on church discipline according to the steps in Matthew 18. Those who preach the false Woke social justice gospel ought to be confronted at all levels of seminaries, Christian organizations, and parachurch ministries. There is no place for the false religion of Woke social justice in Christianity. Those who merge it with Christianity must be held accountable for the sake of the Gospel of Jesus Christ and purity of the Church. Paul exhorts the Romans to "watch out" and "avoid" those who create obstacles contrary to the doctrine. Paul writes, "I appeal to you, brothers, *to watch out* for those who cause divisions and create obstacles contrary to the doctrine that you have been taught; *avoid them*. For such persons do not serve our Lord Christ, but their own appetites, and by smooth talk and flattery they deceive the hearts of the naive" (Rom. 16:17-18, emphasis mine).

To properly combat Woke, the spiritual nature of the religion must be exposed in conjunction with the historical and philosophical characteristics of this religion. This is not merely a battle over ideas and worldview; this is a cosmic, spiritual war against a real, evil, spiritual enemy. "The LORD is a man of war; the LORD is his name" (Exod. 15:3).

Our duty of Christian spiritual warfare is to fight against these evil spirits in the full armor of God (Eph. 6:10-20). This work aims to help those caught in the deceptions of this counterfeit religion and point them to the Deliverer, the Lord Jesus Christ.

CHAPTER TWO

THE FOUNDATIONAL ERROR OF WOKE RELIGION

THE FOUNDATIONAL ERROR OF WOKE religion is the rejection of truth, namely the Scripture. Woke rejects the doctrine of revelation because it is based upon critical theory, postmodernism, social justice, and progressive identity politics. Woke has false epistemological presuppositions and a system of knowledge that is incompatible with Christianity. Lindsay and Pluckrose explain the background of how the philosophies of Woke Religion work through the discourse of words: "If knowledge is a construct of power, which functions through ways of talking about things, knowledge can be changed and power structures toppled by changing the way we talk about things."[87] In other words, the authority of knowledge is repositioned to man, except not in the mind of man as in modernism, but is based upon man's relations to the societal structures defined by critical theory dogma. "Power and knowledge," says Lindsay and Pluckrose, "are seen as inextricably entwined—most explicitly in Foucault's work, which refers to knowledge as 'power-knowledge.'"[88] This enables power and language to influence societal discourses in an increasingly dangerous way and has been manifested in the development of postcolonial theory, queer theory, critical gender studies, critical race theory, grievance studies, critical fat studies, critical memory

---

87 Lindsay and Pluckrose, *Cynical Theories*, 61.
88 Ibid, 35.

studies, and many other emerging forms of Woke religion that significantly diverge from and are incompatible with Christian categories of knowledge.

Moreover, Woke dogma argues that knowledge and authority is determined by positionality, defined as one's standing with society and not the authority of Scripture.[89] Woke dogma is dominated by a worldview that has determined objective truth and absolutes cannot be obtained; therefore, the truth of God cannot be known. All knowledge in Woke is socially constructed and subjective, and language exists as a construct of social power.[90] Woke teaches critical consciousness defined as a heightened awareness of the power structures in the world.[91] The oppressor group has limited knowledge, and the oppressed group has the most knowledge based on experience. Woke embraces standpoint epistemology, "theories [that] map how a social and political disadvantage can be turned into an epistemological, scientific, and political advantage."[92]

Contrarily, the Bible teaches reality is revealed through Creation (general revelation) and Scripture (special revelation), and God's Word is the authority. John Calvin begins his magnum opus the *Institutes of Christian Religion* with the significant point that we cannot know ourselves without looking to God.

> Our wisdom, in so far as it ought to be deemed true and solid Wisdom, consists almost entirely of two parts: the knowledge of God and of ourselves. But as these are connected together by many ties, it is not easy to determine which of the two precedes and gives birth to the other. For, in the first place, no man can survey himself without forthwith turning his thoughts towards the God in whom he lives and moves; because it is perfectly

---

89   Sensoy and DiAngelo, *Is Everyone Really Equal?*, 29.
90   Lindsay and Nayna, "Postmodern Religion."
91   Mary E. Styslinger, Jennifer Stowe, Nicole Walker and Kayla Hyatt Hostetler, "Becoming Teachers for Social Justice: Raising Critical Consciousness," The Clearing House: A Journal of Educational Strategies, Issues and Ideas, 92, No. 1-2 (2019): 9-14, accessed October 8, 2020, https://www.tandfonline.com/doi/abs/10.1080/00098655.2018.153379 7?journalCode=vtch20&.
92   Sandra Harding, et al., *The Feminist Standpoint Theory Reader: Intellectual and Political Controversies* (New York: Routledge, 2004), 7-8.

obvious, that the endowments which we possess cannot possibly be from ourselves; nay, that our very being is nothing else than subsistence in God alone.[93]

As the Reformers taught, in order to know God, one must look to revelation. Contrary to the skeptical epistemological basis of Woke religion, the metanarrative of biblical revelation provides a consistent, unified framework for knowing Who God is and, therefore, a sufficient basis for knowing who "man" is. Bavinck agrees, stating, "We need revelation to know God and to understand ourselves and our situation before God in his world."[94] Anslem understood the proper order to know God, and thus knowing man as "faith seeking understanding."[95] Augustine appeals to the testimony of revelation for our understanding of what is real in existence and true knowledge of God:

> For if we attain the knowledge of present objects by the testimony of our own senses, whether internal or external, then, regarding objects remote from our own senses, we need others to bring their testimony, since we cannot know them by our own, and we credit the persons to whom the objects have been or are sensibly present. Accordingly, as in the case of visible objects which we have not seen, we trust those who have, (and likewise with all sensible objects) so in the case of things which are perceived by the mind and spirit, i.e. which are remote from our own interior sense, it behooves us to trust those who have seen them set in that incorporeal light, or abidingly contemplate them.[96]

In his defense against the errors of Greek philosophers, Augustine understood that truth was revealed by God to man, and this is the testimony of Scripture. Truth is the key component to the sustainability of civilization and

---

93 John Calvin, Institutes of the Christian Religion (Edinburgh: *Printed for The Calvin Translation Society*, 1845), 81-85, Kindle.

94 Herman Bavinck, *Reformed Dogmatics: Abridged in One Volume* (Grand Rapids, MI: Bakers, 2011), 67.

95 "St. Anslem: Archbishop of Canterbury," Christian Classics Ethreal Library.org, Accessed January 6, 2020, https://www.ccel.org/ccel/anselm.

96 St. Augustine, *The City of God* (New York: Random House Publishing Group, 1999), 7465-69, Kindle.

the purity of the Church. One cannot emphasize enough the significance of Scripture as the source of truth. Likewise, Jesus prays to the Father, "Sanctify them in the truth; your word is truth" (John 17:17). The Word of God trumps the philosophy of man simply because it is Divine revelation from the Spirit.

The Reformed Church taught that knowledge was based upon the Scriptures and that this knowledge was the foundation for true religion. Calvin says, "[T]he testimony of the Spirit is superior to reason." For as God alone can properly bear witness to his own words, so these words will not obtain full credit in the hearts of men until they are sealed by the inward testimony of the Spirit."[97] The key element of deception by the enemy is to reject the truth. This is exactly what Woke religion has done. It is a counterfeit religion based upon epistemological critical theory definitions of sociological power structures and dependent upon a skeptic postmodern rejection of objective truth. For this reason alone, Woke religion ought to never be embraced by Christians

In regards to the doctrine of God and Creation, Woke dogma is dominated by a hyper-emphasis on the neo-Marxist, societal power structure oppressed versus oppressor dualism.[98] Woke religion obsesses over power in the structural hegemony to the degree that power functions as a pantheistic, even panentheistic, god—the god of power is inside of the immanent material forces of society. If the twenty-first century Western world was Tolkien's *Lord of the Rings*, Woke religion would be the ring of power. Woke religion teaches injustice is at the power structure group level; power structures ought to be deconstructed,[99] decolonized—"[to] mak[e] a global infrastructure of anti-colonial connectivity"[100]—dismantled,[101] and overthrown. What Woke

---

97   Calvin, *Institutes of the Christian Religion*, 849-52, Kindle.
98   Sensoy and DiAngelo, *Is Everyone Really Equal?*, 61-62.
99   James Lindsey, "Derridean," New Discourses.com, Accessed October 3, 2020, https://newdiscourses.com/tftw-derridean.
100 Gurminder Bhambra, Kerem Nisancioglu, and Delia Gebrial, eds., *Decolonizing the University* (London: Pluto Press, 2018), 3.
101 Kimberlé Crenshaw, Luke Charles Harris, Daniel Martinez HoSang, and George Lipsitz, eds., *Seeing Race Again: Countering Colorblindness Across the Disciplines* (California: University of California Press, 2019), 15-16.

religion attempts to do is deconstruct sociological systems of power from the epistemology of skepticism, with the center of Wokeness being the invisible nature of power rooted in pagan idolatry.

William G. T. Shedd rightly points out the idolatry of such paganism, "[H]e who has no higher emotions than those of the pantheistic religionist, which are called for by the beauty and splendor of visible nature or the cloudy and mystic awfulness of invisible nature is as really an idolater as the most debased pagan who bows down before a visible and material idol.[102]

The center of Christianity is Jesus Christ.[103] The Christian God is not pantheistic. God is not reduced to a force. God is the Trinity—the Father, Son, and Holy Spirit—one God, three persons (1 John 5:7). God is infinitely holy, just, and omnipotent.[104] God created Heaven and earth and providentially governs creation; and despite sin entering the world at the fall of man, all power structures are not systemically and inherently evil.[105] The ultimate end of Christianity is not changing power structures. Christianity teaches the transformation of *people* by the power of the Gospel of Jesus Christ, not a social revolution that topples power structures.

Woke anthropology is also incompatible to the Christian doctrine of man. Woke religion takes the heart of man and hides it in the social hegemony. The will of man—the identity of man—is erased into the social smog of critical theory dogma. At worst, people are reduced to dehumanized slaves, and at best, the biblical doctrine of man is confused. According to Woke dogma of critical race theory, racism is the ordinary, everyday experience of blacks who are racially oppressed victims of white oppressor power structures.[106]

---

102 William G. T. Shedd, *Dogmatic Theology, Third edition* (Phillipsburg: Presbyterian and Reformed Publishing Company, 2003), 160.
103 Westminster Divines, "The Westminster Confession of Faith (1647)," Ligonier Ministries online, Accessed October 3, 2020, https://www.ligonier.org/learn/articles/westminster-confession-faith.
104 Ibid.
105 Ibid.
106 Richard Delgado, *Critical Race Theory: An Introduction, Second Edition* (New York and London: New York University, 2012), 7.

The very identity of people is, by definition, part of the oppressive or oppressed power structure. In *Critical Race Theory: An Introduction*, Delgado and Stefancic write, "[T]he 'social construction' thesis, holds that race and races are products of social thought and relations. Nor objective, inherent, or fixed, they correspond to no biological or genetic reality; rather, races are categories that society invents, manipulates, or retires when convenient."[107]

Contrarily, Scripture teaches there is one race, and the identity of humanity is not reduced to group power structures.[108] Rather, the identity of people is in the image and likeness of God (Gen. 1:26); the identity of Christians is in Jesus Christ (Gal. 2:20).

Woke religion further maintains a false doctrine of sin and justice. In critical social justice, everyone who is part of the oppressor group is complicit in injustice. Guilt is imputed to nearly everyone in society based on social inequalities and neo-Marxist power structure dogma. This fails to realize the root of true injustice is sin in the heart of man (Jer. 17:9). Justice is not based on artificial social power structure categories. In Christianity, justice is based on the character of God and His law. The Christian doctrine of sin maintains that "all have sinned and fall short of the glory of God" (Rom. 3:23). There is none righteous (Rom. 3:9-12). All fell in Adam (Rom. 5:19). The sin of Adam is imputed to man, and man commits actual sins. Sin is in the flesh and comes from the heart of man.

In Woke religion, "injustices" in the fabric of social structures are categorized by superimposing moral judgment upon groups. Racism is prejudice *plus power structure oppression*. "Oppression is one group's prejudice plus the power to enforce that prejudice,"[109] says Sensoy and DiAngelo. Only whites can be racist because they're part of the oppressive hegemony. "All white people are invested in and collude with racism," says DiAngelo.[110]

---

107 Ibid, 8.
108 "The Westminster Confession of Faith (1647)."
109 Sensoy and DiAngelo. *Is Everyone Really Equal?*, 63.
110 Sensoy and DiAngelo, 62.

According to Scripture, man is not accountable for the sins of others (Ezek. 18:20). All men and women can be ethnically prejudiced or show ethnic partiality (Jas. 2:9). When sin is committed, our "conscience . . . bears witness" to it (Rom. 2:15). Satan tempts man to sin, has power in the world, and causes evil (2 Cor. 4:4; 1 Tim. 2:14). Sin transcends all nations and began at the fall of man.

Contrarily, in Woke religion, there is no category for Satan or spiritual forces of evil, except when social justice dogma is syncretized with Christian doctrine. The scope of injustice and racism is typically American, although racism is thought to be the sole cause of worldwide racial disparities. But it fails to account for why many non-white ethnicities have financial success in America. If white oppression is a totalizing force, how is it that white people are responsible only for African-American disparities but not responsible for African-American virtues? If white power structures dominate minorities, how is it that many white Americans suffer from poverty, such as in the Appalachian Mountains? The question of disparities will be explored in a later chapter.

One of the most significant reasons why Woke religion is antithetical to the Gospel is that there is no Christ in Woke religion. To be Woke is to be Christ-less because Woke teaching does not abide in the teaching of Christ. John writes, "Everyone who goes on ahead and does not abide in the teaching of Christ, does not have God. Whoever abides in the teaching has both the Father and the Son" (2 John 1:9). Shedd explains the fundamental reason for this in all natural religions, stating, "Natural religion (or the religion of justice) can be constructed in a priori manner out of the ideas and laws of human intelligence; but the gospel (or religion of mercy and redemption) can be constructed only out of a special revelation from God."[111] In other words, the reason why false religions do not have the Good News of Jesus Christ is because they are the outworking of carnal minds of men. Even when Woke religion is combined with Christianity, Christ is reduced to a Savior Who

---

111 Shedd, 199.

cannot save anyone from the sin of perpetual social guilt imputed to the oppressive group.

Contrarily, the Bible teaches that Christ is the God-man Who is the Savior of sinners (Rom. 5:8). Christ fulfills the law vicariously (active obedience) as a Substitute and pays the penalty for sin (passive obedience). He has indeed satisfied the wrath of God for the sins of His people. There is no more guilt, and salvation has been perfectly accomplished by Christ (Rom. 3:25).

Woke falls into the Galatian heresy, since works must be carried out through activism, guilt must be perpetually confessed, and sin can never be absolved. In fact, one element of critical race theory is "interest conversion," which means white people only become anti-racist for the self-interest of white elites and not out of a desire to help blacks.[112] Woke religion indoctrinates followers to promote and practice self-righteous virtue signaling, devaluation of white Western beliefs, decolonization, and deconstruction of traditional norms. Woke religion teaches one must become awakened to complicity in institutional and systemic oppression, that relief from racism is virtually impossible, and that intolerant, exclusive solidarity is key to the Woke religion.

Alternatively, in Christianity, salvation is by grace through faith in Christ, not based on works (Eph. 2:8-9). Jesus died for individual people, the elect of all nations (Eph. 1:4). Regeneration is not achieved through the false gnosis of Woke; awakening is brought about by the Spirit of God (John 3:1-21). Through a sovereign work of God, He "remove[s] the heart of stone . . . and give[s] . . . a heart of flesh" (Ezek. 36:26). This spiritual rebirth is essential for the Christian life in this world. Bavinck says, "The foundation, content, and aim of this life is spiritual, and anyone who shares in it is a 'spiritual person' (1 Cor. 2:15; 3:1; Gal. 6:1)—that is, one who is led by the Spirit of God (Rom. 8:4) has the indwelling Spirit (Rom. 8:11) . . . The foundational principle of the spiritual life is the love of God in Christ poured out upon us through the Holy Spirit

---

112   Delgado, *Critical Race Theory*, 8.

(Rom. 5:5)."[113] The spiritual life is distinct from the natural life, stripped of impurity, and the object is God.

Woke is focused on the temporal—the natural, external world—and confession of guilt. "[T]he heartbeat of anti-racism itself is confession," says Ibram Kendi.[114] Devotion to Woke is displayed by continuous group confessions of racism, bowing to minorities, declaring one's positionality, disrupting white comfort (antagonizing white people dining, disturbing the peace in white suburban neighborhoods, etc.), placing one's pronouns in social media profiles, proselytizing Woke literature, engaging in public displays of Woke solidarity, kneeling for the national anthem, and participating in organized protests.[115] Woke religious practice is almost always marked by public denunciation and confessing anti-racism. This involves a personal commitment to the socio-religious revolution of Woke to believe that America is thoroughly racist, since Woke dogma teaches the white racist structures of society must be removed. Further practices include reparations for slaves, hiring of diverse personnel, and increasing support for violence. Since critical race theory contends that racism is everywhere, it follows that nearly all power structures must be restructured based on "justice." This counterfeit religion offers nothing but false hope in a temporal utopia of equal outcome achieved in a revolution by overthrowing power.

Whereas in Christianity, belief in Jesus Christ and repentance of sins are the qualifications ordained by God to become a Christian. Justice is ultimately achieved in the final judgment, whereby Jesus Christ will judge the just and unjust. Judgment is based on deeds and words spoken in the body (Eccl. 12:14). God does not judge us based on our skin color or social group. Biblically, there are only two groups: the federal head of Adam or the federal

---

113   Bavinck, *Reformed Ethics*, 248.
114   Nereida Moreno, "Historian Ibram X. Kendi On 'How To Be An Antiracist,'" NPR. org, Accessed October 8, 2020, https://www.npr.org/local/309/2019/10/30/774704183/ historian-ibram-x-kendi-on-how-to-be-an-antiracist.
115   James Lindsay, "A First-Amendment Case for Freedom from the Woke Religion," News Discourses.com, September 9, 2020, https://newdiscourses.com/2020/09/first-amendment-case-freedom-from-woke-religion.

head of Christ. If one is in Adam, there is only condemnation. If one is in Christ, there is no condemnation because Christ has propitiated the justice of God, and God has set us free from the law of sin (Rom. 8:1-3). God promises to bring about the consummation of the new heavens and new earth, where there will be no injustice and the wicked will be cast into Hell with Satan and the demons (Rev. 19-22).

Woke does not remove sin from the heart of man. It metaphorically rips the heart and soul out of man and hides it in societal relations. Bavinck wrote, "Morality is divorced from God and true virtue becomes impossible."[116] Likewise, Woke appeals to the virtue of justice but apart from God. With God, there is no forgiveness and reconciliation in wokeness because that would destroy the religion. Woke is not good news—it is bad news that all of society is made up of injustices and oppressive power structures. Woke only promises deconstruction, division, and, ultimately, destruction.

The Gospel is Good News. Jesus provides atonement for sin that exists in the heart of man, and He provides true hope. Jesus unites people from all nations in His body that was broken on the cross for the penalty of sin. He extends His righteousness. Woke is a false works righteousness of penance and an earthly purgatory from which one can never escape.

However, there is one way to be delivered from the slavery of the Woke religion. The Gospel of Jesus Christ destroys the false shackles of Woke religion and delivers man from greater injustice that man has committed against God. The Gospel offers true forgiveness to those held captive by the slavery of sin and Satan. The Bible teaches Christians ought to remember the poor, seek justice for the oppressed, and care for orphans and widows. As Christians, we ought to recognize that the world has been full of sin since the Fall, including in the history of America. However, the Bible does not teach us to do that by combining the Gospel with neo-Marxist critical

---

116 Herman Bavinck, *Reformed Ethics: Created Fallen, and Converted Humanity*, Ed. John Bolt (MI: Baker Academic, 2019), 34.

theory, postmodernism, or any other philosophy of man. The Scriptures alone are sufficient for addressing sin, injustice, oppression, and the duty of Christians to obey God's law. It is never justifiable to address sin, injustice, or any transgression of the law of God with the practice and teachings of counterfeit religions, including Woke social justice.

PART TWO

BIBLICAL AND HISTORICAL BACKGROUND OF FALSE RELIGION

CHAPTER THREE

BIBLICAL SKETCH OF SATAN, SPIRITUAL WARFARE, AND FALSE RELIGION

THE SCHOLARS, PASTORS, AND CHURCH leaders who have demonstrated that Woke is a religion are completely accurate in their judgment. Yet Woke, as this work contends, is not merely a religion. Woke is a counterfeit religion in the context of real spiritual warfare. Satan is behind all counterfeit religion in the world and false teaching within the Church. This becomes more apparent through a brief overview of a theology of spiritual warfare. This chapter seeks to biblically observe the existence of Satan, the nature of spiritual warfare, and the devices of Satan to promote counterfeit religion in the world to afflict the Church with false teaching. Once Woke is understood from this perspective, it is impossible to merely reduce Woke to an analytical system, philosophy, or non-spiritual religion. Woke does maintain analytical systems of philosophy and has religious elements. However, Woke is much more than that biblically. It is a counterfeit religion that afflicts the Church with false teaching and is, therefore, Satanic.

SATAN AND DEMONS

Scripture teaches Creation is divided into "things . . . in heaven and on earth, visible and invisible" (Col. 1:16). The apostle Paul says, "For we do not wrestle against flesh and blood, but against the rulers, against the authorities, against the cosmic powers over this present darkness, against the spiritual forces of evil in the heavenly places" (Eph. 6:12). The Church is in a spiritual war that involves cosmic powers and spiritual forces of evil. The Bible provides a true account of angels and demons—their nature as created moral beings or agents, their relationship to God, and their interaction with the world. It is important to have a balanced, biblical approach regarding the nature of spiritual warfare to understand the spiritual nature of Woke religion.

The Reformers balanced their recognition of evil spirits under the sovereignty of God and did not overemphasize Satan's power at work in the world. We must first be sure not to overestimate the power of Satan nor underestimate it. Satan is a fallen angel; he is not God. It is important to pay attention to Scripture's commands concerning the reality of spiritual war. Satan is alluded to directly or indirectly in nine Old Testament books and by every New Testament writer.

Scripture speaks of the kingdom of Satan: "And if Satan casts out Satan, he is divided against himself. How then will his kingdom stand?" (Matt. 12:26). This kingdom of evil spirits (Mark 3:24; Luke 11:17-18) is directly opposed to Christ and the kingdom of God. Satan is the archenemy of God and God's people. The demons are Satan's messengers (Matt. 25:41; 2 Cor. 12:7; Rev. 12:7, 9) and are wicked (Matt. 12:45; Luke 11:26). "Always and everywhere," says Bavinck, "they are the adversaries of God, the opponents of Christ, the deceivers of humans, the accusers of God's children."[117] This deceptive influence upon humanity is a stronghold upon the minds of unbelievers. Owen says, "There is in obstinate unbelievers a darkness that is an effect of the power of Satan on their minds, in blinding them, which makes it impossible for them to behold anything of the glory of Christ."[118]

It was not this way from the beginning of Creation. God created everything good, including the angels (Gen. 1:31), though there are several

---

117 Bavinck, 402.
118 John Owen, *The Glory of Christ* (Pavlik Press, 2012), 2729, Kindle.

places in Scripture where it is clear some of the angels fell from their original position in Creation (2 Peter 2:4, Jude 6). "The Puritans," says Beeke and Jones, "regarded the devil and his minions as angels who were created good by God but fell into sin and misery (2 Peter 2:4)."[119]

The fall of Satan and demons is somewhat of a mystery but partially revealed to us in Scripture (Isa. 14; Ezek. 28; Luke 10:18; Rev. 12). Owen comments:

> Hereon depends the ruin of Satan and his kingdom. His sin, so far as we can conceive, consisted of two parts. 1. *His pride against the person of the Son of God, by whom he was created.* "For by him were all things created that are" (or were when first created) "in heaven, whether they be thrones, or dominions, or principalities, or power," Col. i. 16. Against him he lifted up himself; — which was the beginning of his transgression. 2. Envy against mankind, made in the image of God, of the Son of God the first born. This completed his sin; nothing was now left whereon to act his pride and malice. Unto his eternal confusion and ruin, God, in infinite wisdom, unites both the natures he had sinned against in the one person of the Son; who was the first object of his pride and malice. Hereby his destruction is attended with everlasting shame in the discovery of his folly, wherein he would have contended with infinite wisdom, as well as misery, by the powers of the two natures united in one person.[120]

Satan's pride against the Divine Son of God and his envy against man resulted in his fall. God destroys Satan in the one Person united in the two natures—the God-man Jesus Christ.

Fallen angels are called demons, and they oppose God and His work.[121] Angels and demons are moral, rational beings with a will and intellect (Job 1:6; Zech. 3:1; Matt. 8:28, 18:10, 24:36; 2 Cor. 11:3; Eph. 6:11). According to Schaff, "In defining the mental power and the influence of evil spirits, Thomas Aquinas

---

119   Joel Beeke and Mark Jones, *A Puritan Theology: Doctrine for Life* (Grand Rapids: Reformation Heritage Books, 2012), 7600, Kindle.
120   Owen, 858.
121   Louis Berkhof, *Systematic Theology* (Eerdmans, 2011), 3445-3449, Kindle.

and the other Schoolmen follow Augustine closely, although in elaboration they go beyond him. The demons did not lose their intellectual keenness by their fall."[122]

Bavinck says:

> They are self-conscious and speak (Luke 1:19), desire (1 Pet. 1:12), rejoice (Luke 15:10), worship (Heb. 1:6), believe (James 2:19), lie (John 8:44), sin (1 John 3:8). Great power is ascribed to them (Ps. 103:20; Luke 11:15; Col. 1:16; Eph. 1:21; 3:10; 2 Thess. 1:7; Acts 5:19; Heb. 1:14. Since Satan seduced humanity and brought about its fall (John 8:44; 2 Cor. 11:3; 1 Tim. 2:14; Rev. 12:9, 1—15; 20:2, 10), the world is in his power, lying as it does in the evil one (1 John 5:19). He is the "prince of this world" and the "god of this age" (John 12:31; 16:11; 2 Cor. 4:4) . . . Christ's ministry was open warfare against Satan and his hosts (Matt. 4:1-11; Luke 22:3; John 6:70; 8:44; 13:2, 27), and though it was Satan's hour (Luke 22:53; John 14:20), Christ prevailed in battle (Luke 4:13, 10:18, 11:22; John 12:31, 14:30, 16:11; Col 2:15; Heb. 2:14; 1 John 3:8) and in principle withdrew the domain of the church from his rule (Acts 26:18; Col. 1:13; 1 John 2:13, 4:4; Rev. 12:11).[123]

God has limited the power of these evil spiritual enemies. Puritan Edward Reynolds (1599-1676) wrote: "Satan hath three titles given him in the Scripture, setting forth his malignity against the church of God: a dragon, to denote his malice (Rev. 12:3); a serpent, to denote his subtlety (Gen. 3:1); and a lion, to denote his strength (1 Peter 5:8). But none of all these can stand before prayer."[124] God sovereignly uses Satan for His divine purposes (Job 1-2). The Puritan Ridgley proclaimed, "What would not fallen angels attempt against mankind, were not their sin limited by the providence of God!"[125]

Satan and his minions are no match for the power of the Gospel. God calls people "out of darkness into his marvelous light" through Christ (1 Peter 2:9).

---

122 Philip Schaff, *History of the Christian Church Vol. 5* (Peabody: Hendrickson Publishers, 2011), 471.

123 Bavinck, 389-92.

124 Beeke, 7639-42.

125 Ibid, 7688-91.

John says, "The reason the Son of God appeared was to destroy the works of the devil" (1 John 3:8). Puritan Samuel Rutherford (1600-1661) wrote, "The truth is, Satan's works of sin and hell . . . was a prison house, and a castle of strength, and many strong chains of sin and misery. Christ was manifested to break down and dissolve the house, to break his war-ship, and to set the captives at liberty (Isa. 61:1-2; John 14:30)."[126] John Calvin said, "We are conquerors before we engage with the enemy, for our head Christ has once for all conquered for us the whole world."[127] Since Christ has been victorious over Satan on the cross, the Gospel calls all men everywhere to turn from the power of darkness to Christ (Acts 17:30). In the end, Satan and the demons will be cast into the lake of fire forever.

The Westminster Catechism (Q. 89), states, "On the day of judgment the wicked will 'be punished with unspeakable torments, both of body and soul, with the devil and his angels forever.'"[128] In the end times, Satan will muster all his power against the Church and Christ (Matt. 24; Mark 13; Luke 21; 2 Thess. 2:1-12; Rev. 12) but will be cast into the lake of fire along with the demons (2 Thess. 2:8; 1 Cor. 15:24; Rev. 20:10). "He made his appearance in the Garden of Eden," says Bavinck, "concentrated his power against the incarnate Christ (Matt. 4:24; Acts 16:17-18), and will once again, toward the end of history, be exposed and vanquished (1 Thess. 2:18; 2 Thess. 2:8-11; Rev. 9:1-11; 13:13-15; 19:20)."[129]

SPIRITUAL WARFARE AND FALSE TEACHERS

Since spiritual warfare against Satan is real, God calls Christians to be watchful because Satan's chief means of destroying people is through deception (Gen. 3:1-5, 13; John 8:44; 2 Cor. 11:3; 1 Tim. 2:14; Rev. 12:9).[130] Satan is very deceptive and the corrupted will of man is subject to spiritual attacks.

---

126 Beeke, 7667-71.
127 Ibid, 7681-83.
128 Ibid, 7629.
129 Bavinck, 392.
130 Beeke, 7714-15.

The unregenerate are under the dominion of Satan, says Paul: "And you were dead in the trespasses and sins in which you once walked, following the course of this world, following the prince of the power of the air, the spirit that is now at work in the sons of disobedience" (Eph. 2:1-2). Martin Luther puts it this way, "Satan, is by far the most powerful and crafty prince of this world . . . under the reigning power of whom, the human will, being no longer free nor in its own power, but the servant of sin and of Satan, can will nothing but that which its prince wills."[131]

One of the chief devices of Satan is to lead men astray through false teaching and errors. Spurstowe warned that Satan seduces men into doctrinal error through false teachers (2 Thess. 2:1-2; 2 Peter 2:1). False doctrine is from Satan (Gal. 3:1).[132] Jesus said to the Pharisees, "You are of your father, the devil, and your will is to do your father's desires. He was a murderer from the beginning, and does not stand in the truth, because there is no truth in him. When he lies, he speaks out of his own character, for he is a liar and the father of lies" (John 8:44). Jesus warns His followers of false teaching in Matthew 7:15-16: "'Beware of the false prophets, who come to you in sheep's clothing, but inwardly are ravenous wolves. You will recognize them by their fruits. Are grapes gathered from thornbushes, or figs from thistles?" False teachers are so dangerously deceptive, they appear to be sheep but are actually ravenous wolves.

Calvin believed Satan made pronounced attempts to pervert and obscure the pure doctrine of faith.[133] Even the earliest periods of Israel's history reveal false prophets. Moses warned:

> "If a prophet or a dreamer of dreams arises among you and gives
> you a sign or a wonder, and the sign or the wonder that he tells
> you comes to pass, and if he says, 'Let us go after other gods,'

---

131   Martin Luther, *The Bondage of the Will* (Massachusetts: Hendrickson Publishers, 2008), 3834-36, Kindle.

132   Beeke, 7755-60.

133   Calvin, *Institutes of the Christian Religion*, 2406.

which you have not known, 'and let us serve them,' you shall not listen to the words of that prophet or that dreamer of dreams. For the LORD your God is testing you, to know whether you love the LORD your God with all your heart and with all your soul. You shall walk after the LORD your God and fear Him and keep his commandments and obey his voice, and you shall serve him and hold fast to him. But that prophet or that dreamer of dreams shall be put to death, because he has taught rebellion against the LORD your God" (Deut. 13:1-5).

Jeremiah speaks of false prophets who say, "'Peace, peace,' but there is no peace" (Jer. 6:14). And Peter warns us that "because of them the way of the truth will be blasphemed" (2 Pet. 2:2). These false teachers promote what people want to hear. "For the time is coming when people will not endure sound teaching," says Paul, "but having itching ears they will accumulate for themselves teachers to suit their own passions" (2 Tim. 4:3).

Paul warns of the subtly of the devil's deception: "For such men are false apostles, deceitful workmen, disguising themselves as apostles of Christ. And no wonder, for even Satan disguises himself as an angel of light. So it is no surprise if his servants, also, disguise themselves as servants of righteousness. Their end will correspond to their deeds (2 Cor. 11:13-15). Paul explained to Timothy how to detect the enemy in what doctrine they affirm—"If anyone teaches a different doctrine and does not agree with the sound words of our Lord Jesus Christ and the teaching that accords with godliness (1 Tim. 6:3)." Paul commands Timothy to "charge certain persons not to teach any different doctrine, nor to devote . . . to myths and endless genealogies, which promote speculations rather than the stewardship from God that is by faith" (1 Tim. 1:3-4).

Christians are warned that deceptive heresy is brought into the Church secretly by false teachers who creep in unnoticed (Jude 4). Peter says, "But false prophets also arose among the people, just as there will be false teachers among you, who will secretly bring in destructive heresies, even denying the Master who bought them, bringing upon themselves swift destruction" (2 Peter 2:1).

SPIRITUAL WARFARE AND COUNTERFEIT RELIGION

The primary cause of counterfeit religion is demonic power and influences.

> According to Scripture, the character of pagan religions consists in idolatry. Heathen gods are idols; they do not exist; they are lies and vanity (Isa. 41:29; 42:17; 46:1; Jer. 2:28: Ps. 106:28; Acts 14:15; 19:26; 1 Cor. 8:5; Gal. 4:8). At work in those religions is a demonic power (Deut. 32:17; Ps. 106:28; 1 Cor. 10:20; Rev. 9:20). The Reformers typically traced pagan religions to deception or demonic influences.[134]

The Puritans cite the reason for demonic power in counterfeit religions. According to Owen, "He will endeavor by all ways and means to trouble, discompose, and darken the minds even of them that believe, so as that they shall not be able to retain clear and distinct views of this glory."[135] Paul says, "Now the Spirit expressly says that in later times some will fall away from the faith by devoting themselves to deceitful spirits and teachings of demons" (1 Tim. 4:1). "His original great design, wherever the gospel is preached, is to blind the eyes of men, that the light of the glorious gospel of Christ, who is the image of God, should not shine unto them, or irradiate their minds (2 Cor. iv. 4)," according to Owen.[136]

Wicked practices such as spiritism, theosophy, telepathy, voodoo, necromancy, witchcraft, and unspeakable acts of human cruelty demonstrate the reality of demonic forces. Naturalistic worldviews do not explain such a phenomenon.[137] Scripture also agrees such reality exists (Gen. 41:8, Exod. 7:8-12; Deut. 13:1-2; Matt. 7:22, 24:24; 2 Thess. 2:9; 2 Tim. 3:8; Rev. 13:13-15). The Bible strongly opposes such practices and condemns all such evil (Lev. 19:26,

---

134 Bavinck, 77.
135 Owen, 2793.
136 Owen, 2785.
137 Bavinck, 80.

31, 20:27; Num. 23:23; Deut. 18:10-11; Acts 8:9, 13:6, 16:16, 19:13; Gal. 5:20; Rev. 21:8; 22:15). Counterfeit religions and cults are deceptive by design. They appear to be true in form, but in substance, they deviate from Scripture.

Woke social justice falls into the category of counterfeit religion because Woke dogma deviates from nearly every major doctrine of Scripture and is a works-based religion. Woke is deceptive because Christian terminology is often associated with the Woke dogma. Language such as "justice" and "oppression" are used in both the Bible and Woke. Much like every cult, these terms and others have different definitions in Woke. Pagan religions can mimic Christianity in the forms of sacrifices, priesthood, temple, and prophesy.[138] For this reason, John tells us, "Beloved, do not believe every spirit, but test the spirits to see whether they are from God, for many false prophets have gone out into the world" (1 John 4:1). "Belief in evil spirits occurs among all peoples in all religions," says Bavinck. "Christians must clearly distance themselves from pagan superstitions."[139]

SUBVERSION OF SCRIPTURE

One of the most significant devices of Satan to deceive people into the guise of false teaching and false religion is to subvert Scripture as the source of knowledge. A purposeful replacement of the Word of God as the source of truth has taken place since the Fall. Recall that the devil, said, "Did God actually say, 'You shall not eat of any tree in the garden'?" (Gen. 3:1).

As a result of the Fall, a lack of truth in society has continued to the present. Many people in the Western world understand biblical narratives and Church history as religious stories primarily used in ethics or mythology.140 Paul says, "The god of this world has blinded the minds of the unbelievers" (2 Cor. 4:4). For this reason, maintaining Scripture as the source of truth is extremely significant for the Church to be prepared for

---

138 Ibid.
139 Ibid, 389-92.
140 Newbigin, 68.

spiritual attack. "What have we Bibles for," says Gurnall, "ministers and preaching for, if we mean not to furnish ourselves by them with armor for the evil day?"[141] According to Luther, "The best way to drive out the devil if he will not yield to texts of Scripture, is to jeer and flout him, for he cannot bear scorn."[142] We must stand against him, we must, "be strong in the Lord and in the strength of his might" (Eph. 6:10).

The Church is not given the option to opt out of spiritual warfare or maintain a position of spiritual neutrality. Paul says, "Put on the whole armor of God, that you may be able to stand against the schemes of the devil . . . take . . . the sword of the Spirit, which is the word of God" (Eph. 6:11, 17). Therefore, Christians must fight against Woke social justice with Scripture since it is a scheme of the devil. Gurnall admonishes:

> [We must not be] Christians by halves, but go through with it; the thorough Christian is the true Christian. Not he that takes the field, but he that keeps the field; not he that sets out, but he that holds out in this holy war, deserves the name of a saint. There is not such a thing in this sense belonging to Christianity as an honorable retreat; not such a word of command in all Christ's military discipline, as fall back and lay down your arms; no, you must fall on, and stand to your arms till called off by death.[143]

THE MILITANT CHURCH

The Church must rise and defend against social justice. The apostle Paul warns young Timothy, "For the time is coming when people will not endure sound teaching, but having itching ears they will accumulate for themselves teachers to suit their own passions, and will turn away from listening to the truth and wander off into myths" (2 Tim. 4:3-4). Is not this

---

141 William Gurnall, *The Christian in Complete Armour, or, a Treatise on the Saints war With the Devil: Wherein a Discovery is Made of Policy, Power, Wickedness, and . . . of by That Enemy of God and his People* (Charleston: Andesite Press, 2015), 5918-19, Kindle.

142 C.S. Lewis, *The Screwtape Letters* (San Francisco: HarperOne, 2009), 10, Kindle.

143 Gurnall, 6171-74.

what is happening in churches that promote and teach Woke social justice? Paul's words have rung true in every century; the twenty-first century Church has not been excluded. Paul's last words to the church at Ephesus were, "Therefore be alert" (Acts 20:31).

Likewise, the Church must be on alert against the wiles of Woke. Berkhof says, "The Church in the present dispensation is a militant Church, that is, she is called unto, and is actually engaged in, a holy warfare."[144] The nature of this warfare is to fight against the hostile spiritual forces of darkness, in prayer, by meditation, with the sword of the Spirit, by proclaiming the victorious Gospel of Christ's triumph, through engagement in the battle songs of the cross defeated, and by the Lord crowned.[145] Schaff captures this well:

> Both are books [Daniel and Revelation] of the church militant, and engage heaven and earth, divine, human, and satanic powers, in a conflict for life and death. They march on as "a terrible army with banners." They reverberate with thunderings and reflect the lightning flashes from the throne. But while Daniel looks to the first advent of the Messiah as the heir of the preceding world-monarchies, John looks to the second advent of Christ and the new heavens and the new earth. He gathers up all the former prophecies and sends them enriched to the future. He assures us of the final fulfillment of the prophecy of the serpent-bruiser, which was given to our first parents immediately after the fall as a guiding star of hope in the dark night of sin. He blends the glories of creation and redemption in the finale of the new Jerusalem from heaven.[146]

Satan wars against God's people (Luke 22:31; 1 Cor. 7:5; 2 Cor. 2:11, 11:3, 13-15, 12:7; 1 Thess. 2:18, 3:5; 1 Peter 5:8; Rev. 12:10), so the militant Church is commanded to fight against Him (Matt. 6:13; Eph. 6:12, Rom. 16:20; 1 Peter 5:9; Jas. 4:7; Rev. 12:11). James says, "Submit yourselves therefore to God. Resist

---

144 Berkhof, 14222-24.
145 Ibid.
146 Philip Schaff, *History of the Christian Church Vol. 1* (Peabody: Hendrickson Publishers, 2011), 501.

the devil, and he will flee from you (Jas. 4:7). Christians likewise must resist the false teaching of Woke. Paul says, "For the weapons of our warfare are not of the flesh but have divine power to destroy strongholds" (2 Cor. 10:4). Christians have the weapons to destroy the strongholds of Woke dogma. Thus, Christ prays for His Father to keep us from evil (John 17:15) and that in our warfare, we will be victorious in the armor of God so that we will stand against the wiles of Satan (Eph. 6:11).[147] So, too, we ought to pray for the Church to be protected from Woke. We can take heart; Christ promises that the gates of Hell will not prevail against the Church (Matt. 16:18). Though many Christians are being taken captive by Woke dogma, we trust God knows how to rescue the godly from trials (2 Peter 2:9). The Lord rescued Noah and Lot from a wicked generation; so also will He rescue the righteous (2 Peter 2:5-7) for our God is a mighty fortress (Psalm 46).

---

147 Calvin, 5816.

CHAPTER FOUR

A HISTORICAL SKETCH OF SPIRITUAL WARFARE FROM THE FALL TO THE RESURRECTION

SCRIPTURE PROVIDES VERIFIABLE TESTIMONIES OF God's supernatural intending and predominate will to sovereignly orchestrate events, even the death of His Son according to His redemptive purposes. "[F]or truly in this city there were gathered together against your holy servant Jesus, whom you anointed, both Herod and Pontius Pilate, along with the Gentiles and the peoples of Israel, *to do whatever your hand and your plan had predestined to take place*" (Acts 4:27-28, emphasis mine).

God's providential relationship to creation has not changed. Supernatural powers such as angels and demons did not vanish after the biblical canon was closed. In this historical drama of redemption, God orchestrates all things according to His own will, which includes His sovereign rule over evil spirits to accomplish His purposes in history.

For Augustine, spiritual warfare was real. The devil was seeking to draw worshippers to himself in the pagan temples of the ancient world; and when they were mostly deserted due to the rise of God's kingdom in the advent of Christianity, the evil one used false teachers, heretics, philosophers with diverse opinions, and other means to afflict the Church. A survey of the history of redemption reveals Satan is behind the attacks of God's people.

There is also consistent agreement among the early Church fathers and giants of the faith that counterfeit religion and heresies were a direct result of Satan's attacks against the Church. These observations can be understood as a general rule in the evaluation of spiritual warfare in this brief sketch of the history of redemption. Consistent application of these general principles demonstrates significant plausibility to the fact that Satan continues these attacks similarly through the propagation of counterfeit religion and false teaching. Woke is a false religion that perpetuates false teaching as an extension of Satan's attacks against Christ and the Church that has taken place throughout redemptive history.

The reality of spiritual warfare and devices of Satan to promote counterfeit religion and false teaching through the subversion of Scripture is the main theme that will be observed. This chapter turns to the drama of redemptive history that has been sovereignly orchestrated in a cosmic spiritual war. This chapter aims to broadly overview redemptive history from the Fall to the Resurrection and the following chapter from the Resurrection to the present so that Woke religion can be understood in the historical context of redemptive history. Due to the scope of this work, many swaths of history have to be omitted, and additional histories—particularly the most recent leading up to Woke—have already been produced in other works. Also, the goal of these two chapters is to provide a macro-level context of the history of spiritual warfare and devices of Satan to show the continuity of Woke religion with other attacks of Satan against the Church and Christ in redemptive history.

FROM THE FALL TO THE FLOOD

The prophet Isaiah says, "For the moth shall eat them up like a garment, and the worm shall eat them like wool: but my righteousness shall be forever, and my salvation from generation to generation'" (Isa. 51:8). God will continue His work of salvation from the beginning to the end of the history of the world, deliver the Church from all her enemies, and vanquish the devil's power to thwart the purposes of God through the redemptive work of His Son Jesus Christ. This Divine discourse of redemptive history revealed in the Holy Scriptures is established immediately upon the Fall of man and continues through the entire history of the world, until the consummation of His kingdom in the new heavens and new earth.

Throughout redemptive history, the triune God has purposefully undertaken this grand work in the world through Christ in His offices of Prophet, Priest, and King. According to the covenant of redemption, designed before the foundation of the world through various epochs of redemptive history and extraordinary Divine works, the Father, Son, and the Holy Spirit have been bringing about this one work of glorious grace.

Since the Fall, the soul of man was under condemnation, and the image of God was defaced. The nature of man was corrupted to the degree that man was at enmity with his Creator God and dead in sin. Though by God's grand design, man was to be restored into full reconciliation with God by spiritual regeneration, conversion, sanctification, and glorification in this grand work of salvation revealed throughout redemptive history. This was the purpose and plan of God—to deliver man from his miserable state whereby he rebelled against God and transgressed the law upon which all Adam's posterity was infected with the curse of spiritual death and sin.

The world was placed under a curse, ruined by the Fall, and erupted into generations of chaos provoked by the devil. But God, Who is "rich in mercy" and steadfast love through the mystery of the Gospel of grace (Eph. 2:4), put on display the riches of His love, without which the world and all within would be reduced to everlasting destruction and misery, and affected the design of restoration to bring about the kingdom that will ultimately be established in the new heavens and new earth. "For behold, I create new heavens and a new earth, and the former shall not be remembered or come into mind" (Isa. 65:17). According to the infinite wisdom of God, this grand work of redemption was to destroy the enemies of God. According to Paul, "For he must reign until he has put all enemies under his feet" (1 Cor. 15:25). The predetermined plan of God was ordered such that He would triumphantly defeat the devil—crush the serpent's head by the seed of the woman—Jesus Christ (Gen. 3:15). "The reason the Son of God appeared," writes John, "was to destroy the works of the devil" (1 John 3:8).

Since the promise of Christ's defeat over Satan—through many upheavals, distresses, and hardships—the hand of Providence prepared the way for Christ's grand entrance into the world. God tended to all the affairs of the remnant, spiritual Israel—the Church—making way for the coming of Christ through various circumstances, dispensations of supernatural works, and restraints upon the devil. The mercy of God is gloriously displayed through the Mediator, Jesus Christ, Who was typified in shadows through men of God whom God raised for the establishment of His kingdom on earth. From the fall, Satan was mercifully restrained from destroying man by the intercession of Christ promised in the covenant of grace. "When Satan, the grand enemy, had conquered and overthrown man," says Edwards, "the business of resisting and conquering him was committed to Christ. He thenceforward undertook to manage that subtle powerful adversary."[148]

The first light of the Gospel is the revelation of the covenant of grace; that Christ shall crush the head of Satan was a great blow to the enemy. The deceptive work of Satan was likely praised by the kingdom of darkness as the ultimate victory over God and His work in Creation. Yet the promise of the Gospel was the foundation of the city of God, against which Satan and all the principalities raged. Next, God instituted sacrifices (Gen. 3-4) that found fulfillment in the once-and-for-all sacrifice of the Lamb of God, Who took away the sins of the world (John 1:36). All the pagan nations can be examined to have followed the institution of sacrifices, though according to the kingdom of Satan. All the pagans offered sacrifice to false gods and could

---

148   Jonathan Edwards, *A History of the Work of Redemption* (Ontario: Devoted Publishing, 2020), 295-96, Kindle.

never find atonement for sins. This is, nevertheless, a significant proof of the veracity of Christianity and the falsehood of pagan idolatry.

The world was soon thrown into great wickedness in the ancient world, following the account of the Fall of man; and the people of God were very few, though God preserved a remnant in the Flood on Noah's ark. The wickedness in the world was so severe that God put them all to death, save Noah and his family, by flooding the entirety of the Earth (Gen. 6:9-9:17). Some generations later, the city of the world received another blow at Babel when God dispersed and confused the languages of man for their sin at a time when the Church was being corrupted by the deceptions of Satan and led astray (Gen. 11:1-9).

FROM THE CALLING OF ABRAHAM TO MOSES

By the time of Abraham, the Church of God was severely diminished on earth.

> For Abraham's own country and kindred had most of them fallen off; and without some extraordinary interposition of Providence, in all likelihood, in a generation or two more, the true religion in this line would have been extinct. And therefore God called Abraham, the person in whose family he intended to uphold the true religion, out of his own country, and from his kindred, to a far distant country, that his posterity might there remain a people separate from all the rest of the world; that so the true religion might be upheld there, while all mankind besides were swallowed up in heathenism.[149]

This exemplifies the continuance of God's grand work of redemption to make a covenant with Abraham around two thousand years before the coming of Christ. This promise to Abraham foreshadowed that Christ would come and entailed that his offspring would be as numerous as the stars in the heavens (Gen. 22:17). So then, God would uphold the Church in preserving

---

149 Edwards, 668-71.

the lineage of the patriarchs who lived among the evil men of Canaan and a multitude of enemies. Christ would be of the lineage of Abraham, Isaac, and Jacob, as it was determined and promised according to the purpose of redemption whereby the Church would be preserved through the ages.

God next preserved the family of God by permitting Joseph to be sold into slavery by his brothers, for what they meant was for evil "but God meant it for good" (Gen. 50:20). Joseph was placed at the right hand of the pharaoh through a series of sovereignly orchestrated events that proved to deliver the people of God during the seven-year famine (Gen. 41). The Church was upheld during the Egyptian bondage at the hand of Pharaoh (Exod. 1-12). The people of God were brought out of slavery (Exod. 14), given the moral law at Mount Sinai (Exod. 19-20), and set apart from all the nations of the world until the coming of Christ fifteen hundred years later. Edwards writes:

> About this time was given to the church the first written word of God. This was another great thing done towards the affair of redemption, a new and glorious advancement of the building; which God has given for the regulation of faith, worship, and practice to the end of the world. This rule grew, and was added to from that time, for many ages, till it was finished, and the canon of Scripture completed by the apostle John. It is not very material, whether the first written word was the ten commandments, written on the tables of stone with the finger of God.

From the barren wilderness, God led His people by several miracles into Canaan, a land flowing with milk and honey (Num. 13-36). God gave them the land, overcoming giants and no small amount of trials (Josh. 1-24). Cycles of apostasies (Judges 1-21) were no match for God to preserve the people of God, and worship was maintained whereby the ark, law, priesthood, and people of God were upheld. The Church was gifted with prophets, according to Edwards:

After Samuel was Nathan, and Gad, Iddo, and Heman, Asaph, and others. And afterwards, in the latter end of Solomon's reign, we read of Ahijah; and in Jeroboam and Rehoboam's time we read of prophets; and so continually one prophet succeeded another till the captivity. In the writings of those prophets who are inserted in the canon of Scripture, we read of prophets as being a constant order of men upheld in the land. And even during the captivity, there were prophets still, as Ezekiel.[150]

The chief end of the prophets was to foretell of Christ and the redemptive work He would procure so that the way of His coming would be perfectly prepared. Luke gives an orderly account: "But what God foretold by the mouth of all the prophets, that his Christ would suffer, he thus fulfilled" (Acts 3:18).

FROM DAVID TO BABYLONIAN CAPTIVITY

Upon the establishment of the kingdom of God, Israel was granted a king (1 Sam. 10:9-27)—first Saul, who fell into disobedience (1 Sam. 15), but then David, whose kingdom would never end through the spiritual Seed of Israel (2 Sam. 5). During this period, the tabernacle and previous patterns for worship appointed by God were replaced or more fully realized in the building of the temple in Jerusalem (1 Kings 6).

At the height of the city of God during Solomon's reign, the temple was erected whereby all the nations of the Earth could behold the glory of the true God in Israel. This marked the height of the glory of the Jewish Church. God's people had taken possession of the Promised Land, and in each passing generation, this glory would fade until the coming of Christ. Problems arose within the kingdom. Solomon fell into idolatry (1 Kings 11), and the city of God was divided upon the revolution of ten tribes who separated themselves from the house of David and set up pagan idols (1 Kings 12-16). Half a million men of Israel were killed in battle (2 Chron. 13:17); Baal worship was set up (1 Kings 16:32); and the people of God were led astray through wicked kings

---

150 Edwards, 1197-1200.

who intermarried with pagan nations. God struck down the northern tribes of Israel (2 Kings 17); the temple was destroyed in Judea (2 Kings 23-25); and a small remnant was brought into Babylonian exile. Until the coming of Christ, the Jewish Church would be subject to Babylonian conquerors, kings of Persia, the Grecian monarch, and the Roman Empire. Through Cyrus, God exercised vengeance upon Babylon for the pains they brought upon the Jewish Church as it was foretold in the prophets and erected the Persian kingdom on the ashes of Babylon (Ezra 1-6, Psalm 137, Haggai 1-2, Zech. 1-14).

After seventy years of captivity were ended, God turned the heart of Artaxerxes, a Persian king, to permit a small number of the remnant, along with Ezra and Nehemiah, to return to their once-glorious kingdom and out of the abundance of the Persian treasury, to rebuild the temple (Neh. 2; Ezra 7). Not long after this time, God providentially intervened through Esther to preserve the Jewish Church from destruction (Esther 1-10). True worship of God was rare in these days, though, to the degree that there was not one prophetic word for the four hundred years inter-testimonial period leading up to John the Baptist's preparation of the coming of Jesus Christ (Matt. 3).

The Grecian empire also prepared the way for the kingdom of God to advance rapidly by the establishment of the common Greek language in the greater part of the known world. At the pinnacle of the greatest empire in the world—the Roman monarchy—under one government and one common language, the fullness of time had come—the advent of the incarnation of Christ. At the same time, this marked the rise of Satan's kingdom by the power of Roman military might, the wisdom of men, and a significant decline of the Jewish Church since its height one thousand years prior under Solomon's reign. The philosophy of the heathen world had matured, and the wise men of the Greco-Roman empire had led the world into vanity (1 Cor. 3). Amid the wisdom of the world, God showed the folly of the best heathen philosophers with the Gospel of Christ crucified—foolishness to the world but "the power of God for salvation to everyone who believes" (Romans 1:16).

CHRIST'S INCARNATION TO HIS RESURRECTION

"But when the fullness of time had come, God sent forth his Son, born of woman, born under the law" (Gal. 4:4). God saw fit that Christ did not appear in any other period of the Babylonian captivity, the Persian dynasty, or under the Greeks. It was the purpose of God that Christ should be manifest upon the most powerful of Satan's visible kingdom of the Roman Empire so that the glory of God would be displayed—as in similar fashion over Pharaoh and the Egyptians—in absolute victory over the devil. The mystery of the Gospel was now displayed in the glorious advent of Christ (Eph. 3:1-13), far beyond the wisdom of God's creative work in the beginning; for the Creator had now become a creature—God had put on human flesh (Col. 1:15-19).

Upon the baptism of Jesus in the Jordan (Matt. 3:13-17) and temptation account in the wilderness by the devil, where Christ was greatly exposed to the torments of the evil one (Matt. 4:1-11), Christ assumed His public ministry of obedience whereby He actively procured the one work of salvation for the beloved Church. Jesus preached as One Who had authority, not merely as a prophet who said, "Thus says the Lord," but as God Himself, who declared, "Truly, truly, I say unto you," so that the crowds were astonished at His teaching (Matt. 7:28, 22:33). Jesus performed miracles (John 2:1-11), healed the sick (John 4:43-54), gave sight to the blind (Matt. 20:29-34), exorcised demons (Mark 5:1-20), raised the dead (John 11:1-45), calmed storms (Luke 8:22-25), and thus established His ministry as the true Son of God—the Messiah.

As many as seventy followers of Jesus were sent out to perform the work of the ministry (Luke 10), and twelve disciples were called (Matt. 10:1-4) who would become apostles of the Church, save one—further establishing the kingdom of God on earth (Acts 1-28). These apostles shall sit on the twelve thrones as judges of the twelve tribes of Israel (Matt. 19:28).

Jesus endured much suffering through the course of His ministry and humiliation. Edwards captures this truth when he writes:

He suffered great hatred and reproach. He was despised and rejected of men; one of little account, slighted for his low parentage, and his mean city Nazareth. He was reproached as a glutton and drunkard, a friend of publicans and sinners; was called a deceiver of the people; sometimes was called a madman, and a Samaritan, and one possessed with a devil. (John vii. 20. viii. 48. and John x. 20.) He was called a blasphemer, and was accounted by many a wizard, or one that wrought miracles by the black art, and by communication with Beelzebub. They excommunicated him, and agreed to excommunicate any man that should own him. (John ix. 22.) They wished him dead, and were continually seeking to murder him; sometimes by force, and sometimes by craft. They often took up stones to stone him, and once led him to the brow of a hill, intending to throw him down the precipice, to dash him in pieces against the rocks.[151]

The attacks of Satan upon Christ reached a climatic height at Golgotha, whereby all of redemptive history was centered on the cross of Christ (John 19). The accomplishment of so grand a work of redemption to eternally purchase the salvation of sinners by His precious blood and secure the preservation of the Church in all ages by this work of passive obedience is the most glorious work that has and ever will be done by God. The finished work of Christ is a severe blow to Satan's kingdom and the foundation of the devil's final destruction whereby "the ruler of this world [will] be cast out" (John 12:31).

---

151 Edwards, 2844-46.

CHAPTER FIVE

A HISTORICAL SKETCH OF SPIRITUAL WARFARE FROM THE RESURRECTION TO THE PRESENT

THE CROSS OF CHRIST MARKS the central point of redemptive history. All things prior were for the preparation for it; now, all things that come after the cross of Christ are in spiritual orchestration for the final consummation of the kingdom of God. Isaiah says, "'For behold, I create new heavens and a new earth, and the former things shall not be remembered or come into mind. But be glad and rejoice forever in that which I create; for behold, I create Jerusalem to be a joy, and her people to be a gladness" (Isaiah 65:17-18). Through gradual steps, the ancient world is brought to an end; not one stone is left of the Jewish temple; Satan's kingdom of the Roman Empire falls; and many other events are ordained in order to finalize the eschatological end of this former state of the world to prepare for the heavenly spiritual restoration. The end for which the world was created was, according to Edwards, "to prepare a kingdom for his Son, (for he is appointed heir of the world) which should remain to all eternity."[152]

Of all the earthly kingdoms that were set up before the coming of Christ, none will compare to the heavenly kingdom of Christ. Satan tried to give all the kingdoms of the earthly world to Jesus, and He would not be tempted

---

152 Edwards, 3145-50.

because the purpose for which He came was to establish the eternal kingdom of God (Matt. 4:1-11). "Jesus answered, 'My kingdom is not of this world'" (John 18:36). Upon the resurrection of Christ, this kingdom has been inaugurated, and the consummation of it is brought about through gradual steps from the empty tomb to the final judgment, where the sheep and the goats shall be separated. By an instantaneous act of omnipotence, God could destroy Satan's earthly kingdom. However, by the Sovereign will of the Almighty, Satan is granted to suffer the Church throughout the ages until the end of the world.

In the next place, God appointed apostles to preach the Gospel and commissioned the Church as Jesus commanded: "'Go therefore and make disciples of all nations, baptizing them in the name of the Father and of the Son and of the Holy Spirit, teaching them to observe all that I have commanded you. And behold, I am with you always, to the end of the age" (Matt. 28:19-20).

The preaching of the Gospel displayed the mighty power of God to remove the hearts of stone and give hearts of flesh full of the Spirit according to Christ's promises (Ezek. 36:26). By the proclamation of the Gospel, God unveiled the foolishness of human ideas that sought to exchange the truth for gods of the human imagination.

> Thereby the vanity of human wisdom was shown, and the necessity of the gospel appeared; and hereby a handmaid was prepared to the gospel. An instance of this we have in the apostle Paul, who was famed for his much learning, (Acts xxvi. 24.) being skilled in the learning not only of the Jews, but also of the philosophers. This he improved to subserve the gospel; as he did in disputing with the philosophers at Athens, Acts xvii. 22, &c. By his learning he knew how to accommodate himself in his discourses to learned men, having read their writings; and he cites their own poets. Dionysius, a philosopher, was converted by him, and was made a great instrument of promoting the gospel. And there were many others in that and the following

ages, who were eminently useful by their human learning in promoting the interests of Christ's kingdom.[153]

Satan had received a tremendous blow after the resurrection of Christ and commissioning of the early Church. By the power of the Holy Spirit, many tens of thousands were converted in a relatively short time (Acts 2-4). The kingdom of Christ was much more secure and established through the early Church than in times past, even exceeding the glory of Solomon's kingdom, since the temple became the Church among all nations (1 Cor. 6:19). Gentiles, who formerly were not included in the covenant of God, have now been brought near through the Gospel so that all the nations would be glad (Psalm 67:4; Eph. 2; Rom. 9-11). "'These men who have turned the world upside down have come here also," says Luke the doctor in the Acts of the Apostles (Acts 17:6). Many Gentiles were won to Christ in the city of Ephesus, at the metropolis in Corinth, and in Rome, the greatest city of the first-century world.

SATAN'S AFFLICTION OF THE EARLY CHURCH: PERSECUTION AND HERESIES

Many men were brought out of the kingdom of darkness into the kingdom of light. In even remote cities of the known world, Churches were planted; elders were raised; and the doxology of God's praise could be heard from the lips of Gentiles who praised Jesus's holy name. From this period of the first to the fourth century, the Church encountered great persecutions, deceptive heresies, and philosophies of man. Luke records, "Some of the Epicurean and Stoic philosophers also conversed with him. And some said, 'What does this babbler wish to say?' Others said, 'He seems to be a preacher of foreign divinities'—because he was preaching Jesus and the resurrection" (Acts 17:18). Heresy plagued the early Church throughout the Patristic period. "By the beginning of the third century," says Bavinck, "the foundations of Christian theology had been laid. Against paganism and Judaism, Gnosticism,

---

153   Edwards, 2233-36.

and Ebionitism, the church had deliberately assumed a firm position and rescued the independence of Christianity."[154]

Satan persecuted the early Church in ten periods under heathen Roman emperors. Nero's persecution was the most severe. Peter was crucified after Paul was beheaded in Rome after he writes in prison to Timothy, "For I am already being poured out as a drink offering, and the time of my departure has come. I have fought the good fight, I have finished the race, I have kept the faith" (2 Tim. 4:6-7). Schaff captures the persecutions of Nero against Christians:

> The satanic tragedy reached its climax at night in the imperial gardens on the slope of the Vatican (which embraced, it is supposed, the present site of the place and church of St. Peter): Christian men and women, covered with pitch or oil or resin, and nailed to posts of pine, were lighted and burned as torches for the amusement of the mob; while Nero, in fantastical dress, figured in a horse race, and displayed his art as charioteer. Burning alive was the ordinary punishment of incendiaries; but only the cruel ingenuity of this imperial monster, under the inspiration of the devil, could invent such a horrible system of illumination.[155]

Satan's kingdom of Rome could not stop the multiplying of the Church, and the Gospel prevailed mightily. The Church was unsuccessfully dismantled. Edwards says, "Justin Martyr, an eminent father in the Christian church, says, that in his days there was no part of mankind, whether Greeks or barbarians, or by what name so ever they were called, even the most rude and unpolished nations, where prayers and Thanksgivings were not made to the great Creator of the world, through the name of the crucified Jesus."[156]

The reality of spiritual warfare was evident in the early Church. Schaff says, "The future of the world's history depended on the downfall of heathenism and the triumph of Christianity. Behind the scenes were the powers of the

---

154   Bavinck, 36.
155   Schaff, 235.
156   Edwards, 3596-98.

invisible world, God and the prince of darkness. Justin, Tertullian and other confessors traced the persecutions to Satan and the demons."[157] Irenanus says, "Heretics, in his view, are enemies of the truth and sons of Satan, and will be swallowed up by hell, like the company of Korah, Dathan, and Abiram."[158] Likewise, Terrtullian attributes heresies to the devil.

One of the most dominant heresies of the period was Gnosticism. The Gnostics, according to Schaff, were ruled by Satan:

> The ascetic Gnostics, like Marcion, Saturninus, Tatian, and the Manichaeans were pessimists. They felt uncomfortable in the sensuous and perishing world, ruled by the Demiurge, and by Satan; they abhorred the body as formed from Matter, and forbade the use of certain kinds of food and all nuptial intercourse, as an adulteration of themselves with sinful Matter; like the Essenes and the errorists noticed by Paul in the Colossians and Pastoral Epistles. They thus confounded sin with matter, and vainly imagined that, matter being dropped, sin, its accident, would fall with it. Instead of hating sin only, which God has not made, they hated the world, which he has made."[159]

Heretics in the early Church were despised and often identified with Satan. Church tradition maintains John left a public bath when he saw Cerinthus, the enemy of the truth, fearing that the bath might fall in, and the similar story of Polycarp meeting Marcion and calling him "the first born of Satan." These stories reveal the intense abhorrence with which the orthodox churchmen of those days looked upon heresy.[160]

Satan received a huge blow right after the worst of three hundred years of tormenting the Church. It was not until the miraculous conversion of

---

157   Philip Schaff, *History of the Christian Church Vol. 2* (Peabody: Hendrickson Publishers, 2011), 25.
158   Schaff, *History of the Christian Church Vol. I* (Peabody: Hendrickson Publishers, 2011), 110.
159   Ibid, 282.
160   Schaff, *History of the Christian Church Vol. II* (Peabody: Hendrickson Publishers, 2011), 288.

Constantine in a dream with a cross in his hand that the Church was granted a reprieve from persecutions and widespread martyrdom. Like Moses leading Israel out of bondage, God converted the emperor of Rome; and on the ruins of pagan temples, Christian churches were built. Paganism and false gods (demons) were eradicated, and Christians were elevated to the highest officials in Rome. Heathen temples were torn down, and the Church was established for a time in much prosperity. Since the time of a few dozen followers of Jesus in the first century, the Church had now greatly multiplied in triumph over the heathen kingdom of the world by the power of the Gospel and the blood of martyrs. Despite Satan's attacks through heresies and persecutions, the success of the Gospel through this period gives considerable warrant for the veracity of the Scriptures as the Word of God.

CONSTANTINE TO THE PAPACY

Upon the fall of the heathen Roman world, there was an acceleration of heretical attacks against the Church. God had delivered the Church from persecutions, and the kingdom of Satan in the Roman Empire had been greatly diminished. Yet a more pronounced method of offense entered into the Church through heresies more dangerous than earlier false teachings. Edwards says:

> The Arians began soon aft Constantine came to the throne. They denied the doctrine of the Trinity, the divinity of Christ and the Holy Ghost, and maintained, that they were but mere creatures. This heresy increased more and more in the church, and which threatened to overthrow all, and entirely to carry away the church, insomuch that before the close of the fourth century, the greater part of the Christian church were become Arians.[161]

Athanasius led the charge against the Arians, and the counsel of Nicaea rendered the Arians as heretics. Schaff says:

---

161 Edwards, 3757-60.

Now for a time the strife of the Christians among themselves was silenced in their common warfare against paganism revived. The Arian controversy took its own natural course. The truth regained free play, and the Nicene spirit was permitted to assert its intrinsic power. It gradually achieved the victory; first in the Latin church, which held several orthodox synods in Rome, Milan, and Gaul; then in Egypt and the East, through the wise and energetic administration of Athanasius, and through the eloquence and the writings of the three great Cappadocian bishops Basil, Gregory of Nazianzum, and Gregory of Nyssa.[162]

By the next century, Pelagius had corrupted the Church with the denial of original sin and the work of the Spirit in conversion. Augustine fought against these errors in defense of the orthodox faith. Once these errors of Satan were extinguished, heathen invasions threatened the peace of the Church; and by the fifth century, barbarians sacked the city of Rome. Though these ploys from the evil one brought much destruction and disruption of peace within the Church, they were used for the good propagation of the Gospel in a small period of time among the barbarous nations that conquered the Roman Empire.

Upon the invasion of the Goths, Rome was destroyed in 410, and false religion began to accelerate rapidly. The fall of the Roman Empire is a significant part of redemptive history whereby we observe the saga of spiritual war among men who were part of the city of God and those who were worshippers of the god of this world. Rome had been the greatest empire of the world, exercising dominion for nearly a thousand years, and man presumed it would never fall. How great was the fall of Rome, the darling civilization of the Western world. Who was to blame and how this could have happened occupied the thoughts and minds of those left in the rubble. The pagan gods of which no small number of Romans believed in and

---

162   Philip Schaff, *History of the Christian Church Vol. III* (Peabody: Hendrickson Publishers, 2011), 379.

worshipped could not bear the penalty for this catastrophic demise of Rome. Instead, as history reveals, the Christians were charged with the burden of responsibility for the destruction of Rome, which gave rise to Augustine's defense of the faith in his towering work, *The City of God*.

In this monumental treatise, the glory of Rome and the glory of the City of God stand in striking contrast with one another. The love of God binds the hearts of the citizens of the City of God together in Christ, while the city of the world is founded upon false, self-seeking love, the glory of Rome, and a false system of virtues. "[T]hey who do not belong to this city of God shall inherit eternal misery, which is also called the second death, because the soul shall then be separated from God its [sic] life, and therefore cannot be said to live, and the body shall be subjected to eternal pains," says Augustine.[163]

After Constantine, however, the church was in spiritual decline with many vain, superstitious corruptions, worship of the saints, and idolatrous images. The spiritual knowledge of the laity was reduced to ungodly ignorance, and the clergy, in a large degree, were given to the corruptions of power and wicked, popish errors. The priests better served as stewards of darkness, who oppressed the remnant of God's Church. The sophistry and deception of the Roman Catholic religion increasingly led souls into the mouth of Satan until the dawning of the Reformation. God preserved a portion of the Eastern Church that had not been taken by the Turks and many churches in England, Scotland, and some other places that kept the faith once delivered to the saints.

Satan was permitted to exercise dominion in two chief ways during the Middle Ages: the rise of the papacy and Islam. Edwards writes:

> The Mahometan kingdom is another of mighty power and vast extent, set up by *Satan against the kingdom of Christ*. Mahomet was born in the year of Christ five hundred and seventy, in Arabia. When he was about forty years of age, he began to boast

---

163 Augustine, 15329-31.

that he was the great prophet of God and proceeded to teach his new-invented religion, of which he was to be worshipped as the head next under God [emphasis mine].[164]

According to Schaff, "Sir William Muir concedes his original honesty and zeal as a reformer and warner, but assumes a gradual deterioration to the judicial blindness of a self-deceived heart, and even a kind of *Satanic inspiration* in his later revelations" (emphasis mine).[165] The Turks became followers of this new religion and conquered the Eastern empire. By the year 1300, Europe was invaded and the Turks took Constantinople in the year 1453.[166] The papacy became equally as wicked as the false religion of Islam. Schaff says:

> The papacy itself lost all independence and dignity, and became the prey of avarice, violence, and intrigue, a veritable synagogue of Satan. It was dragged through the quagmire of the darkest crimes, and would have perished in utter disgrace had not Providence saved it for better times. Pope followed pope in rapid succession, and most of them ended their career in deposition, prison, and murder.[167]

The medieval priesthood demonstrates a stronghold of Satanic darkness. Image and saint worship was a problem for the Church in the Middle Ages. Schaff says, "It is a cunning device of Satan to smuggle heathen idolatry into the church under pretext of showing honor to saints. He thus draws men away from a spiritual to a sensual worship."[168]

Satan appears to have been at work during the Crusades. Schaff comments, "Zara was taken Nov. 24, 1202, given over to plunder, and razed to the ground. No wonder Innocent wrote that Satan had been the instigator of this destructive raid upon a Christian people and excommunicated the

---

164 Edwards, 3868-70.
165 Philip Schaff, *History of the Christian Church Vol. IV* (Peabody: Hendrickson Publishers, 2011), 118.
166 Philip Schaff, *History of the Christian Church Vol. II* (Peabody: Hendrickson Publishers, 2011), 3878-81.
167 Schaff, *History of the Christian Church Vol. IV*, 179.
168 Ibid, 293.

participants in it."[169] Many of the measures taken through the Middle Ages to fight heresy were interpreted as a blow against Satan, including burning the books of heretics, banishment, and the death penalty.[170] The belief in spiritual warfare was dominant in the Middle Ages. Schaff states:

> At no point do the belief and experience of our own age differ so widely from the Middle Ages as in the activity of the devil and the realm of evil spirits. The subject has already been touched upon under monasticism and the future state, but no history of the period would be complete which did not give it separate treatment. *For the belief that the satanic kingdom is let loose upon mankind* was more influential than the spirit of monasticism, or than the spirit which carried on the Crusades [emphasis mine].[171]

The truth was ardently defended during these Satanic attacks throughout the Dark Ages, especially on the eve of the Reformation. Over a century before the Reformation, John Wycliffe stood against the popery of Rome, and many of his followers—such as John Huss—endured great persecution.

REFORMATION TO MODERNITY

The sixteenth century marked a major shift in the Western Church, particularly in the Reformation to the biblical foundations of Christianity.[172] The year 1517 is often marked as the advent of the Reformation because of Martin Luther's infamous nailing of the Ninety-five Theses and bold preaching against the corruption among the Catholic clergy. Luther was in many ways a medieval man, who interpreted the world through the lens of spiritual warfare. Schaff says, "The first disturbances broke out at Erfurt in June, 1521, shortly after Luther's triumphant passage through the town on his

---

169   Philip Schaff, *History of the Christian Church Vol. V* (Peabody: Hendrickson Publishers, 2011), 148.
170   Schaff, *History of the Christian Church Vol. V*, 274.
171   Schaff, *History of the Christian Church Vol. V*, 467.
172   Alister E. McGrath, *Historical Theology: An Introduction to the History of Christian Thought* (Oxford: Blackwell, 2013), 156.

way to Worms . . . Luther saw in these proceedings the work of Satan, who was bringing shame and reproach on the gospel."[173] Luther calls Mohammed, "the first-born child of Satan," and believed the pope was worse.[174]

Magisterial reformers such as Mehacthon in Germany, Zuinglius in Switzerland, Knox in Scotland, and Calvin in Geneva (perhaps the most significant) had incalculable roles in furthering the Reformation. Through their efforts and the Protestant contemporaries, God revived the Church again, this time out of the darkness of the Middle Ages and Roman Catholic popery. This did not come without bloodshed over religious disputes and persecution in areas of Poland, Hungary, Germany, and Bohemia.[175]

Calvin describes his struggle with the Patriots and Libertines when he says, "But when Satan had made so many efforts to destroy our Church, it came at length to this, that I, unwarlike and timid as I am, found myself compelled to oppose my own body to the murderous assault, and so to ward it off."[176] Schaff says, "The persecutions of Christians by Christians form the satanic chapters, the fiendish midnight scenes, in the history of the church. But they show also the gradual progress of the truly Christian spirit of religious toleration and freedom."[177]

Many Protestants were burned at the stake under the ruthless Queen Mary of England, and persecution continued until the time of Charles I. After the English civil war, the Puritan divines—such as John Owen, Richard Baxter, and Samuel Rutherford (contemporaries of the first-generation Puritans such as Perkins and Ames)—experienced a short-lived golden age of prosperity and Calvinistic dominance in the English parliament. The Puritans were holy men in Western Europe, contemporaries of the magisterial Reformation who largely sought religious non-conformity from the overreaching Anglican-established Church. "Although the English Reformation initially had a

---

173 Schaff, *History of the Christian Church Vol. VII*, 214.
174 Schaff, *History of the Christian Church Vol. IV*, 116.
175 Jonathan Edwards, 4025-28.
176 Schaff, *History of the Christian Church Vol. VIII*, 299.
177 Schaff, *History of the Christian Church Vol. I*, 11.

strong Reformed tone that lasted into the seventeenth century," says Bavinck, "Anglican luke-warmness led to the Puritan movement."[178] These were devout men who fought for a just cause against tyrants, the freedom of their most sacred rights, and the liberty to worship their God in good conscience. Though they were not a monolithic group, they were deeply devoted to the authority of Scripture as the sole source of truth and fought against the mandated Anglican religious requirements, such as following the use of the Anglican Book of Common Prayer.

In the midst of persecution, the Puritan divines gifted the church with some of the greatest theological volumes, creeds, and confessions of faith in Church history. The construction of theology in the seventeenth century was similar to the Middle Age scholastics; it became less of a biblical theology, evident in Calvin, and more confessional statements in response to the error. Bavinck says:

> Constructive Reformed theology of this sort reached a zenith and a terminus in such confessional statements as the Canons of Dordt (1618-19), the Westminister Confession of Faith and Larger and Shorter Catechisms (1646), and the Helvetic Consensus (1675). However, direct challenges to the Reformed faith also developed. Rationalism, mysticism, subjectivism, Anabaptism, Socinianism, Caresianism, and especially Arminianism reared their heads.[179]

The Westminster Larger Catechism written by the Puritans recognizes Satan as the enemy:

> Thus, people are encouraged to pray for God's mercy (Q. 191), "acknowledging ourselves and all mankind to be by nature under the dominion of sin and Satan, we pray, that the kingdom of sin and Satan may be destroyed . . . that Christ would rule in our hearts here, and hasten the time of his second coming, and our

---

178 Bavinck, *Reformed Dogmatics*, 47.
179 Bavinck, 48.

reigning with him for ever." We must pray for total victory over this enemy (Q. 195).[180]

However, by the mid-eighteenth century, the Puritan movement had died off, in large part due to persecutions such as the Great Ejection and Five Mile Act, where thousands of ministers were forbidden to live within five miles of their parishes by monarchial edict under Charles II. Forthcoming persecutions served to propagate the Gospel into the New World and New England by Protestant Separatists.

Despite modern attempts to demonize the Puritans, they were holy men who engaged in the spiritual conflicts of their time in the context of the seventeenth century European monarchs. Whitefield says, "The Puritans [were] burning and shining lights. When cast out by the black Bartholomew Act, and driven from their respective charges to preach in barns and fields, in the highways and hedges, they in a special manner wrote and preached as men having authority."[181] J.I. Packer explains, "Puritanism was an evangelical holiness movement seeking to implement its vision of spiritual renewal, national and personal, in the church, the state, and the home; in education, evangelism, and economics; in individual discipleship and devotion, and in pastoral care and competence."[182]

The English Puritan non-conformist churches were deeply entrenched in spiritual warfare during the Great Ejection. Religious life in England reached a low point in the early eighteenth century. On every hand, there was profanity, inhumanity, and gross political corruption.[183] Spiritual decline inevitably led to the First Great Awakening, where numerous Reformed Churches, including Welsh Calvinistic Methodists, Calvinistic English Baptists, Scottish Presbyterians, and Dutch Reformed Churches were revived.[184]

---

180 Beeke, 7663-67.
181 George Whitefield, *The Works of the Reverend George Whitefield* (London), Vol. 4, 306-7.
182 J.I. Packer, *An Anglican to Remember—William Perkins: Puritan Popularizer* (London: St. Anthonlin's Lectureship Charity, 1996), 1-2.
183 Engelbrecht, *The Church from Age to Age* (St. Louis: Concordia Publishing House, 2011), 14336-37.
184 Robert Davis Smart and Michael A.G. Haykin, et al. *Pentecostal Outpourings: Revival and the Reformed Tradition* (Grand Rapids: Reformation Heritage Books, 2016), 96-98, Kindle.

Before this period, many parts of the world were held captive in darkness by the devil. This was the case in America, where natives were given to idol worship. During the period before the First Great Awakening, doctrinal errors such as Arminianism, Socinianism, and deism afflicted the Church, and spiritual licentiousness was prevalent. Deism placed the mind of man above Scripture and assumed that truth could be known by reason alone.

By the mid-eighteenth century, the Christian religion was revived through spiritual revivals; America was full of Bibles; and Christ's name was openly proclaimed in many towns. Significant revivals took place during the period among the European and American pietism groups led by men such as Whitefield and the Wesleys. The Pietists' desire to simplify religion led to a spirit of tolerance and religious freedom.[185] "The work of God in converting souls, opening blind eyes, unstopping deaf ears, raising dead souls to life, and rescuing the miserable captives out of the hands of Satan, was begun soon after the fall of man, has been carried on in the world ever since to this day, and will be to the end of the world," says Edwards.[186] These revivals, as one could imagine, may have been the answer to the prayers of their Puritan nonconformist forebearers. These unusual outpourings of God's Spirit renewed emphasis on the Gospel that firmly rested on the truth of Scripture, and many thousands of people were converted.

These awakenings temporarily renewed the Church's emphasis on the cardinal Reformed doctrine of the previous century, *sola scriptura*. Despite Satan's efforts to thwart the plan of God, there was much work done for the kingdom in this period. John Newton, the author of the hymn "Amazing Grace," was a seaman who had been captain of a slave ship but was converted and became a pastor. William Wilberforce led the fight in Parliament to successfully abolish the slave trade in 1807.[187] The rise of the modern

---

185 Engelbrecht, 14498-99.
186 Edwards, 174.
187 Engelbrecht, 14411-15.

missionary movement also took place in the late eighteenth century, perhaps most notably led by William Carey, a Baptist missionary to India.[188]

Through the turn of the nineteenth century, a series of revivals shook college campuses across America, such as Hampden-Sydney College and Yale.[189] Unlike the previous awakening, religious fervor in America's Second Great Awakening lasted for decades. One of the most important figures during this period was Asahel Nettleton, "the forgotten evangelist."[190] He is often overshadowed by Charles Finney, who coined unorthodox revival methods such as "anxious benches" that led to the pragmatic watering down of the twentieth-century evangelicalism.[191]

Spiritual evil undoubtedly plagued the darkest periods of North American Church history, particularly in the grievous complicity of some denominations, such as the Southern Baptist Convention, in slavery, white supremacy, ethnic prejudice, and lack of support for civil rights of African Americans.[192] *The Report of Slavery and Racism in the History of the Southern Baptist Theological Seminary* states, "The seminary's founding faculty all held slaves. James P. Boyce, John A. Broadus, Basil Manly Jr., and William Williams together owned more than fifty persons. They invested capital in slaves who could earn for their owners an annual cash return on their investment."[193]

On the other side of the Atlantic, the Church was strengthened under the ministry of Charles Spurgeon in the nineteenth century; however, the Downgrade Controversy solidified the decline of the Church in Britain. The twentieth century was the bloodiest in history, in part because of the world wars but also because of Stalin's Marxist-Leninism and Mao's communist

---

188 Engelbrecht, 14425-27.
189 Smart, 3204.
190 Ibid, 4193.
191 Smart, 1052.
192 "Report on Slavery and Racism in the History of the Southern Baptist Theological Seminary," (Louisville: The Southern Baptist Theological Seminary), https://sbts-wordpress-uploads.s3.amazonaws.com/sbts/uploads/2018/12/Racism-and-the-Legacy-of-Slavery-Report-v4.pdf, 5-8.
193 Ibid, 5.

regime. The Church was greatly diminished in places dominated by Marxism and communism. Many Christians were persecuted for their faith, and the Church was spiritually weak, mainly due to theological liberalism.

Martyn Lloyd Jones, the "Doctor," led a powerful ministry in England through the mid-twentieth century; but as the Church marched into the twenty-first century, fewer beacons of light remained in the Western world. After the passing of sound men like R.C. Sproul in the midst of the evangelical nominal Christian context of New Left Social Justice Christianity, word of faith prosperity Gospel preaching, the consumerist-seeker church growth movement, the emerging church movement, and the recent threat of false teaching from Woke religion, it is evident the spiritual war in the American Church is raging. One of the remaining influential voices of truth is John MacArthur, the pastor of a church in California who faced several lawsuits and government persecution for meeting as a congregation.

The Church has encountered tremendous affliction from the devil in the world from the time of the Fall until the modern era. Edwards says, "That the church of God and the true religion, which has been so continually and violently opposed, with so many endeavors to overthrow it—and which has so often been brought to the brink of ruin, through the greatest part of six thousand years—has yet been upheld, utmost remarkably shows the hand of God in favor of the church."[194]

In the ancient world, God preserved His people and struck down the ancient kingdoms of the Moabites, Ammonites, and Edomites. He turned the hearts of kings and caused nations to rise and fall. The Babylonians, Persians, Greeks, and Romans were overthrown and altogether destroyed. No other body in the history of the world has endured Satan's relentless attacks, heresies, and the histories of persecutions endured by the Church. Ultimately, Satan's visible kingdom will be overthrown, and all things in this world shall pass away. "[T]hen shall He say also unto them on His left hand," says

---

194 Edwards, 4271-73.

Augustine, "Depart from me, ye cursed, into everlasting fire, prepared for the devil and his angels . . . And these shall go away into everlasting punishment, but the righteous into life eternal."[195] Christ the Judge will render the verdict, "Come, you who are blessed by my Father, inherit the kingdom prepared for you from the foundation of the world" (Matt. 25:34). Christ shall put all His enemies under His feet and triumph over Satan; all the covenant promises of redemption will be completed; and Christ will deliver all things to the Father—that He may be all in all.

This brief survey of redemptive history reveals that spiritual warfare has been ongoing since the Fall of man and will continue until the last day. Countless other historical examples concerning the nature of spiritual warfare among the Church could be provided, and readers are encouraged to investigate the source materials referenced for further study. This humble attempt to identify some of the examples where Satan has afflicted the Church throughout history with counterfeit religion, false teaching, and other forms of spiritual warfare has been provided to help contextualize the present reality of Satan's attacks. Since spiritual warfare has taken place historically in these ways, it is important to understand that it still takes place today. With this understanding, there is significant plausibility that Woke religion is a current form of affliction against the Church and Christ. Parallels are observable between the demonic false teaching that afflicted the Church historically and the false teaching of Woke that plagues the Church today. Throughout history, Satan attacked the Church with heresies and sought to subvert the truth of Scripture. Satan continues to do that today with the counterfeit religion and false teaching of Woke.

---

195 Augustine, 15504.

PART THREE
SKETCH OF THE PHILOSOPHICAL SHIFTS LEADING TO WOKE RELIGION

CHAPTER SIX

PHILOSOPHICAL PARADIGM SHIFTS: PRE-MODERNISM TO MODERNISM

"See to it that no one takes you captive by philosophy and empty deceit, according to human tradition, according to the elemental spirits of the world, and not according to Christ."

—Colossians 2:8

THE APOSTLE PAUL WARNS THE Church at Colossae that one of Satan's tactics is to take the Church captive with the philosophy that is not according to Christ. As it was observed in the previous chapters, false religion and false teaching have historically threatened the Church in a similar way that Woke does presently.

The following chapters will examine how the Scripture as the source of truth was effectively abandoned and replaced with this philosophy in several incremental stages or paradigms. In this way, many were taken captive. These paradigm shifts demonstrate the gradual regression from Scripture as the source of truth and the substitution of this worldly philosophy. This shift has falsely rendered Scripture insufficient, and it has been replaced with sources of philosophical authority. This demonstrates the *philosophical dimension* of the spiritual war. C.S. Lewis said, "Indeed the safest road to Hell is the gradual one—the gentle slope, soft underfoot, without sudden turnings, without milestones, without signposts."[196]

These transitions from pre-modernism to modernism to postmodernism eventually led to the philosophical seedbed for the advent of Woke religion. The paradigms discussed in these chapters are meant to briefly identify some of the important philosophical transitions. None of these paradigms or systems within are monolithic. The systems within each paradigm are not congruous, nor are the categorizations used for each paradigm meant to reduce the complexities of these and other systems that influenced the transitions. Volumes have already been written comprehensively explaining the philosophical nature of each of these systems. Many others could be included, and these philosophies could be systematized and categorized in numerous other ways given the vast periods of thought; however, that would go beyond the scope of this work. Thus, this brief overview of the paradigm shifts will function as a starting point to understand the philosophical transitions that led to the philosophical foundations of Woke.

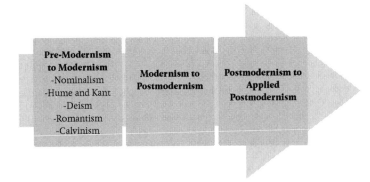

Figure 4: Sketch of Three Major Philosophical Paradigm Shifts

NOMINALISM

Historically, it has been problematic to depend upon philosophical ideas instead of the Bible when constructing a worldview. Many false religions and false teachings have been propagated into the world because people departed from the Scripture as the source of truth. This underscores the importance to develop theology and a worldview upon the Scriptures. Richard Muller demonstrates this specific issue with theology that was too closely knit to Protestant scholasticism. He writes:

> Protestant scholasticism only became intellectually problematic with the passing of the world view to which it was bound as much by historical necessity as by choice. When that world view failed, the orthodox theological system also seemed to fail and rationalism, allied to the new science, appeared as a viable alternative, particularly in the writings of those rationalist philosophers who were not hostile toward theology.[197]

By the late Middle Ages, seeds of error were planted as philosophical categories for universal truth began to be removed. Richard Weaver identifies nominalism as the knockout blow to logical realism in the medieval period as a pivotal historical event. William of Occam's nominalism claimed that universals have no real or true existence. This philosophical juncture led to the belief that transcendent names were merely names and questioned if there was universal truth behind the names. Weaver captures the consequences of the idea: "The practical result of nominalist philosophy is to banish the reality which is perceived by the intellect and to posit as reality that which is perceived by the senses. With this change in the affirmation of what is real, the whole orientation of culture takes a turn, and we are on the road to modern empiricism."[198] The transition from nominalism to empiricism serves as one element of the broader philosophical paradigm shift from pre-modernism to modernism.

---

197 Richard A. Muller, *Post-Reformation Reformed Dogmatics Prolegomena to Theology* (Grand Rapids: Baker, 2003), 144.
198 Richard Weaver, *Ideas Have Consequences* (London: The University of Chicago, 1948), 3.

HUME AND KANT

Another element of the first philosophical paradigm is demonstrated in the philosophy of David Hume and Immanuel Kant. First, Hume is known as the father of modern agnosticism. Agnosticism is similar to pre-modern skepticism, since agnostics do not know if God exists and, in some forms, deny real knowledge of God is possible. Hume believed God could only be known anthropomorphically and that real knowledge of His nature was not possible.[199]

Building upon Hume, Kant affirmed a form of neo-agnosticism which taught only the phenomena can be known, but "the thing itself," or *numina*, is not known.[200] The result was that knowledge of God was impossible. This amounts to nothing less than a modern philosophical form of spiritual deception and attack against the knowledge of God through revelation. Berkhof illustrates this with a quote from Barth: "Romans is a revelation of the unknown God; God comes to man, not man to God. Even after the revelation man cannot know God, for He is always the unknown God. In manifesting Himself to us He is farther away than ever before."[201]

Moreover, the Kantian shift that functionally concluded God was unknowable represents one of the most significant transitions in philosophical departures from Scripture. Bavinck exposes this deceptive error in the following quote: "Since Kant declared God to be unknowable, reason and natural theology were substituted for divine revelation. Morality and religious feeling became the starting point and subject matter of theology; the prolegomena of religious philosophy grew in size and influence in comparison with the content of theology."[202]

After this shift, philosophy was no longer the handmaiden of theology. New complexities arose that began to change the relationship between

---

199 Berkhof, 327-33.
200 Ibid, 334-36.
201 Ibid, 384-88.
202 Bavinck, 25.

theology and philosophy, particularly in the various forms of seventeenth-century rationalism. Incompatibilities appeared between rationalism as a system of knowledge and theology.[203] Many began to recognize the rotten man-centered core of rationalism. "Rationalism rejects any knowledge outside of man himself," says Schaeffer, "especially any knowledge from God."[204] But the damage had already been done to the doctrine of revelation. Since the time of Kant, the traditional view of the Scripture as the source of truth has been under scrutiny and attack. As rationalism was popularized and embraced, this led to a monumental shift in the thinking of the Western world during the eighteenth century.

This had significant impacts on the doctrine of revelation. Muller identifies the departure from Scripture's authority to a synthesis between reason and revelation:

> As orthodoxy faded, rationalism gathered strength and, in the eighteenth century, provided a new philosophical perspective that, even in alliance with theology, proved inimical to the task of creating a large-scale biblical orthodoxy for Protestantism comparable to the broad theological, philosophical, and cultural synthesis offered by earlier generations of Protestant thinkers.[205]

The dogma of the authority of the Scripture that reigned in the Church for millennia, dating back to Augustine, the Fathers, and the apostles, was gradually replaced with the authority of reason—the authority of man. Scripture as the starting point for truth was no longer accepted, and this was a deceptive blow against the Church and the Western world. During the Reformation, the theological debate took place based on the Scripture's authority, but after Kant, the debate took place based on reason. Human reason replaced revelation, according to Bavinck. "Now, reason and historical criticism of Scripture

---

203 Muller, 3166-69.
204 Francis Schaeffer, *How Shall We Then Live?: The Rise and Decline of Western Thought and Culture* (Wheaton: Crossway, 2005), 145-46.
205 Muller, 145.

together served as challenges to the church's dogmas. The conviction took hold that human reason, even apart from faith, could of itself produce all truths of natural theology. Reason not only received its own domain alongside revelation but eventually extended its powers over that of revelation itself."[206]

This led to many other subversions of Scripture in the theological world. Some dogmatic works were structured upon other doctrines instead of on the Bible.[207] The result of the "age of reason" was that the Church effectively dropped her sword and surrendered her right to defend the Truth. One of the main problems this resulted in was the degradation of the moral law. "To reconstruct the moral law through reason is the problem for pagans and more recent moral philosophers. This is a problem for which they think a solution can be found. However, due to the depravity of reason, it is, in fact impossible. Rationalism, supranaturalism, Kant, and the materialists have clearly demonstrated this."[208]

It was impossible to dogmatically claim anything apart from Scripture as the sole source of truth. The moment revelation—the mind of God is given up to the mind of man—that battle was lost. The ability to think God's thoughts after Him is a sheer impossibility, and all that is left is to synthesize man's thoughts after man's thoughts.

Other men alongside Kant contributed to this philosophical shift. Schaeffer identifies four significant men—Jean-Jacques Rousseau, Immanuel Kant, George Wilhelm Hegel, and Soren Kierkegaard.[209] Rousseau contributed to sowing the seeds of contemporary socialism in his *Social Contract*. In different terms than Rousseau, Kant addressed the same problem for man. In Kantian philosophy, there is a dichotomy of knowledge; the noumenal (derived from the Greek word for Spirit) is the realm of value, purpose, and meaning; the phenomenal world can be observed by science and the senses. This dichotomy, or "line of despair," as Schaeffer puts it, is the great divide

---

206 Bavinck, *Reformed Dogmatics*, 25.
207 Ibid, 28.
208 Bavinck, *Reformed Ethics*, 220.
209 Schaeffer, 153-54.

between reason and values.[210] The noumenal realm is unattainable by reason and therefore cannot be known, so nothing real has purpose. Modern man is left in a closed system. This leads to naturalistic materialism with no meaning. Man is stripped of value, dignity, and worth. This philosophical shift was one step closer to the philosophical foundation of Woke and a giant leap away from the sufficiency of Scripture.

DEISM

Deism was another aspect of this paradigm shift. Occam's nominalism, Hume's skepticism, Kant's rationalism, and political turmoil created a vacuum of religious reductionism that led to deism. Deism is the belief that God is not personal and has no sovereign, Providential engagement with creation. This is a false teaching that twists the doctrine of God and was a consequence of the departure of the Scripture as the source of truth. In turn, Orthodox Christianity was stripped down to the mere existence of God and moralism, and the Gospel was corrupted.

"Another thing which has of late exceedingly prevailed among Protestants, and especially in England," says Jonathan Edwards, "is deism."[211] In his work on the history of redemption, he associates Satan's opposition to the Reformation with deism. Deism provided the fertile ground for a concentrated attack on the doctrine of revelation. The philosophical movements of this period landed a powerful blow to the Church and Scripture. By the eighteenth century, the Church was in decline and failed to recognize the sufficiency of Scripture, and Western Christianity was in large part reduced to deistic-rationalism, a false religion.

ROMANTICISM

The fourth element in the pre-modernism to modernism paradigm shift was Romanticism, which sought to place the Divine within the imminence of

---

210 Ibid, 164.
211 Edwards, 4083-87.

humanity—in a similar way to pantheists, except human feelings are ultimate. Bavinck says, "Romanticism of Johann Georg Hamann (1730-88) celebrated the immediate experience of human feeling, the locus of the divine in each person. This trend found its culmination in the theology of Schleiermacher. He considered religion as the enjoyment of God in feeling, a feeling that leads to the desire for community."[212] Schleiermacher's emphasis on feeling is a departure from puritanical intellects such as Jonathan Edwards. It more resembles the hedonism of the ancient Greeks devoid of a basis for enjoyment with God because feelings alone are ultimate. Contrarily, Reformed thinkers believed that enjoyment with God was a result of communion with Him, and the foundation of such enjoyment was *sola scriptura*. For example, John Owen has a profound treatment on loving communion with each person of the Trinity, and much of his framework is built upon the exegesis of Scripture.

CALVINISM

The next element of the paradigm shift from the pre-modern to the modern world is the positive, spiritual influence of Calvinism. Calvinism functions in this paradigm as a counter-movement to the general philosophical stream of history. Since Calvinism had such a major impact upon the Western world during this period, it must be mentioned. The beauty of Calvinism is it is a system built upon the Scriptures as the sole source of truth, contrary to the other philosophical systems discussed. In this way, it provides a consistent, unified system for life and rises above the alternative systems. In the pre-modern world, alternative systems of knowledge that diverge from Scripture as the source of truth had a lower view of God and, as a consequence, had a problematic view of man. Biblical distinctions are removed; roles are lost; and ultimately, the nature of man is destroyed.

Low views of man resulted in the caste system in India and slavery, where man was placed in subjection over man. In sects of Islam, women

---

212 Bavinck, *Reformed Dogmatics*, 46.

were often treated as functional slaves of man with harsh laws. Romanism superimposed hierarchical relationships between man and the Church. All diversity in humanity is destroyed for the sake of absolute uniformity. The Bible repudiates slavery, caste systems, abuse of women, taking advantage of the poor, and the papal hierarchical structure.

In the Middle Ages, the hierarchical church of Rome exercised legalistic dominion over society, commerce, and country. The heavy shackles of Rome drove the masses to protest in reformation within the Church that led, in large part, to the restoration and liberty of domestic life within Western society. Calvinism later flourished in democratic, sociopolitical contexts and furthered the establishment of liberty under the self-evident truth that all men are created equal in the image and likeness of God.

Calvinism upholds the biblical truth that God is separate from man, yet personally communes with man in sovereign redemption through Jesus Christ and the regeneration of the Holy Spirit. God revealed Himself, to put it in Kantian terms, out of the numina into the phenomena. God put on human flesh in the incarnation. This ought to have been the answer to the eighteenth century Kantian conundrum. God can be known personally because He has *revealed* Himself by ultimately becoming man and vindicating His Divinity in His resurrection of the dead.

As the Bible teaches, Calvinism establishes personal communion with God, a communion that has been decreed from eternity. This communion is not merited or worked for, as in Romanism and Islam. It is not an impersonal communion with immanent forces, as in pantheism. It is not a communion with the material world that equates God with the material world as in panentheism, paganism, and Woke, which will be discussed in Part Four. Instead, biblical Calvinism establishes that we exist because the Triune God created us, our communion with Him is unmerited by grace, and our salvation from beginning to end is bound in Him, for the glory of God.

Important to a biblical worldview is that both the unity and diversity of our existence is preserved. Kuyper argues that Calvinism is an all-embracing life system, since it establishes our relation to God, man, and the world. He states:

> For our relation to God: an immediate fellowship of man with the Eternal, independently of priest or church. For the relation of man to man: the recognition in each person of human worth, which is his by virtue of his creation after the Divine likeness, and therefore of the equality of all men before God and his magistrate. And for our relation to the world: the recognition that in the whole world the curse is restrained by grace, that the life of the world is to be honored in its independence, and that we must, in every domain, discover the treasures and develop the potencies hidden by God in nature and in human life. This justifies us fully in our statement that Calvinism duly answers the three above-named conditions, and thus is incontestably entitled to take its stand by the side of Paganism, Islamism, Romanism, and Modernism, and to claim for itself the glory of possessing a well-defined principle and an all-embracing life-system.[213]

While we may not agree with Kuyper on every iota, the success of Calvinism to provide a unified system of life that upholds the diverse and distinctive relation between God, man, and the world is substantiated by the fact that Calvin's dogma rested on the Bible. There is a curious historical set of hypotheticals that demonstrate the significance of Calvinism and thus the necessity of biblical dogma. Kuyper recounts what may have happened without Calvinism:

> In that case Spain would have crushed the Netherlands. In England and Scotland the Stuarts would have carried out their fatal plans. In Switzerland the spirit of half-heartedness would have gained the day. The beginnings of life in this new world would have been of an entirely different character. And as an

---

213   Abraham Kuyper, *Lectures on Calvinism* (Grand Rapids: Eerdmans Publishing Company, 1943), 343-51, Kindle.

unavoidable sequence, the balance of power in Europe would have returned to its former position. Protestantism would not have been able to maintain itself in politics. No further resistance could have been offered to the Romish-conservative power of the Hapsburgs, the Bourbons and the Stuarts; and the free development of the nations, as seen in Europe and America, would simply have been prevented. The whole American continent would have remained subject to Spain. The history of both continents would have become a most mournful one.[214]

Instead, it is equally true that what Calvinism supplanted in the hearts and minds of Western Europe and the New World captivated the conscience by binding it to the Scripture. The dead institutions of the Dark Ages were overthrown by Calvinistic zeal, and the way was paved for constitutional civil liberty. Kuyper writes:

> Simultaneously with this there went out from Western Europe that mighty movement which promoted the revival of science and art, opened new avenues to commerce and trade, beautified domestic and social life, exalted the middle classes to positions of honor, caused philanthropy to abound, and more than all this, elevated, purified, and ennobled moral life by puritanic seriousness.[215]

Calvinism is not to blame for the ills of the modern Western world. It was the force that stood against them because it was based upon the Word of God.

Despite the Calvinistic influence in the Church, the consequences of the prior elements resulted in the paradigm shift from pre-modernism to modernism; reason replaced revelation and spread across the Western world in the nineteenth and twentieth centuries. According to Bavinck:

> When, in addition, Holy Scripture is robbed of its divine authority by historical criticism, it should not surprise us that

---

214 Ibid, 461-73.
215 Ibid, 475-80.

religious life loses its vitality. Faith is no longer sure of itself . . .
Consequently, and partly caused by all this, religious life in the
late nineteenth and early twentieth centuries was dramatically
less vigorous than before.[216]

The subversion of Scripture is the root of twentieth-century nominal
Christendom. Religious formality and forms of theological liberalism began
to dominate the Western Church. Bavinck observed this development as well:
"There may be movement in the domain of religion and the study of religion,
but there is little genuinely religious life. People perhaps believe their
confessions, but they no longer confess their faith."[217] The replacement of
Scripture with the philosophy of man in this paradigm shift was completed.
Much of the Church was taken "captive by philosophy and empty deceit,
according to human tradition, according to the elemental spirits of the world,
and not according to Christ" (Col. 2:8). This was the first step in preparing the
philosophical ground for Woke religion. The Church nearly confessed with
the world and Pontius Pilate, "What is truth?" (John 18:38).

---

216 Bavinck, *Reformed Dogmatics*, 27.
217 Ibid.

CHAPTER SEVEN

PHILOSOPHICAL PARADIGM SHIFTS: MODERNISM TO POSTMODERNISM

"In their case the god of this world has blinded

the minds of the unbelievers,

to keep them from seeing the light of the gospel

of the glory of Christ,

who is the image of God."

—2 Corinthians 4:4

IN MANY WAYS, THESE PHILOSOPHICAL paradigm shifts are a result of what took place in the darkness of the mind being blinded by the god of this world. Owen warns of the deception of sin in the mind. He says:

> Strictly speaking, it is the mind that is deceived. If sin attempts to enter the soul by affections, the mind should be able to put a stop to it. But where the mind, the leading faculty of the soul, is infected, sin is sure to prevail. The mind ought always to guide, direct, choose, and lead; hence deception in the mind is most dangerous. If the light in us is darkness, how great is that darkness.[218]

---

218 John Owen, *Indwelling Sin in Believers* (Edinburgh: Banner of Truth, 2012), 60.

The philosophical paradigm shift from modernism to postmodernism begins where the previous paradigm left off. Humanism, theological liberalism, anti-supernaturalism, pantheism, materialism, and macro-evolution build the substructure for the neo-Marxist philosophical underpinnings of Woke religion.

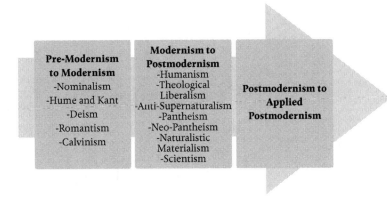

Figure 5: Sketch of Three Major Philosophical Paradigm Shifts

HUMANISM OF THE FRENCH REVOLUTION AND HIGH RENAISSANCE

The first element of the philosophical paradigm shift from modernism to postmodernism is the humanism of the French Revolution and the High Renaissance. "The leaders of the French Revolution," says Kuyper, "not being acquainted with any relation to God except that which existed through the mediation of the Romish Church, annihilated all relation to God, because they wished to annihilate the power of the Church; and as a result of this they declared war against every religious confession."[219]

The humanism of the French Revolution was an attack against the Church and hostility to God in all spheres of society. This was a shift from the Calvinism that in previous centuries flourished in the hearts of Western Europeans. The unbelief in the French Revolution stands in striking contrast

219 Kuyper, 219.

to the pre-modernist world, where faith was expressed in nearly all spheres of society. Bavinck writes:

> People cannot be viewed loosely as mere individuals; human beings are not atoms or numbers. This atomistic view was the error of the French philosophers like Rousseau and is the fundamental error of revolutionary thought. The term "individual" belonged to the revolution and expressed its all-consuming character. Our fathers did not know the word "individualism" because for them there were no mere individuals; to be human was always to be the image of God, a member of the human race. For the revolution, humanity is an aggregate mass of individuals who can be arbitrarily combined, like the random collision of Epicurus's atoms, into state, society, etc.[220]

Contrarily, the faith of the magisterial Reformers, English Puritans, and Pilgrim Separatists was that all of life ought to be lived in the dominion of God's sovereign presence. The French Revolution was entrenched in humanism, a system focused on the autonomy of man rather than the Divine. Schaeffer comments: "In the humanism of the High Renaissance, flowing on to maturity through the Enlightenment, man was determined to make himself autonomous. This flow continues, and by the time we come to modern science man himself is devoured: Man as man is dead. Life is pointless, devoid of meaning."[221]

Humanistic ideas are traceable back to the Middle Ages and infiltrated the Church well before the "Enlightenment." In fact, the Reformation sought to remove many of these humanistic elements from the Church, particularly in the return to *sola scriptura*. However, by the eighteenth century, humanism accelerated and spread rationalistic presuppositions throughout the Church. This had a devastating effect on human relationships. This departure from

---

220 Bavinck, *Reformed Ethics*, 49.
221 Schaeffer, 148.

Scripture as the sole basis for truth by the nineteenth century was known as theological liberalism.

THEOLOGICAL LIBERALISM

Theological liberalism abandoned the orthodox assumption that Scripture was the sole source of truth. Instead, reason and the Bible were syncretized into the foundation for knowledge. Orthodoxy evidently faded into the shadows of antiquity because as a system, theological liberalism lacked a response to modernism and the philosophical presuppositions of the eighteenth and nineteenth century periods. Muller agrees, "The demise of orthodoxy was not so much an obliteration of the form but rather a passing of dominance and a failure to contribute to the ongoing movement and development of theological and philosophical thought."[222]

Theological liberalism has left a dismal mark across scores of dead churches in the past century. Modern philosophers found that if the reason was the starting point, we could not come to the knowledge of God. Beginning with man, one cannot arrive at God. Minds of unbelievers were blinded to the extent that Scripture was subverted and replaced with reason, and God was denied philosophically. As theological liberalism sought to synthesize these ideas from modern philosophy with Christian theology, it inevitably destroyed the foundation of orthodoxy—namely, that the Scriptures are the sole source of truth. Satan blinded the minds of men to deny revelation.

Biblically, revelation must precede reason to arrive at the knowledge of God. The last two hundred years has been a result of this seismic spiritual deception and philosophical shift in the doctrine of revelation—to deny it. "But I am afraid that just as the serpent deceived Eve by his cunning," says Paul, "your thoughts will be led astray from a sincere and pure devotion to Christ" (2 Cor. 11:3). By the cunning of Satan, men were lured and enticed by the ideas of

---

222 Muller, 146.

man to deny the Scriptures. Theological liberalism still wanted to maintain the "historical" Jesus. Theological liberals were ashamed of the Divine Jesus but still wanted to maintain a religious system that was acceptable to the new "gods" of rationalism and modern philosophy. Theological liberals threw Christianity and the Divinity of Jesus out the window as a consequence of rejecting the Scriptures.

Another cardinal false doctrine of theological liberalism is that the world's evil may be overcome by the world's good; presumably, no help is needed from outside the world.[223] This is why liberalism only appeals to what we must do and omits from the Gospel what has been done.

This was the case for the nineteenth and twentieth century Social Gospel movement. The Social Gospel movement laid the foundation of Woke social justice activism in evangelicalism because it hyper-emphasizes works. Christianity, instead, begins with what has been done. "Here is found the most fundamental difference between liberalism and Christianity," says Machen. "Liberalism is altogether in the imperative mood, while Christianity begins with a triumphant indicative; liberalism appeals to man's will, while Christianity announces, first, a gracious act of God."[224] Woke social justice is a call for what to "do" socially without the message of what Christ has "done" already. Woke social justice is a more mature form of the liberalism Machen combated. The source of truth matters. Machen says:

> The important thing is that he tell the truth, the whole truth, and nothing but the truth. If we are to be truly Christians, then, it does make a vast difference what our teachings are, and it is by no means aside from the point to set forth the teachings of Christianity in contrast with the teachings of the chief modern rival of Christianity. The chief modern rival of Christianity is "liberalism." An examination of the teachings of liberalism in

223 J. Gresham, Machen, *Christianity and Liberalism* (Grand Rapids: Eerdmans, 2009), 1782-84, Kindle.
224 Machen, 606-7.

comparison with those of Christianity will show that at every point the two movements are in direct opposition.[225]

ANTI-SUPERNATURALISM

Closely related to theological liberalism is anti-supernaturalism. Anti-supernaturalism is the denial of the supernatural realm. Disbelief in the spiritual world—angels and demons—has declined over the last few centuries. Kant did not directly reject the spiritual realm,[226] although he contributed to the lack of belief in angels and devils in the eighteenth century that led to the lack of distinction between men and animals in the eighteenth century.[227]

For the modernist liberal, there is a disconnection of the historical and the supernatural. Supernaturalism has been replaced with the embrace of naturalism. "A great gulf separates them from those who reject the supernatural act of God," says Machen, "with which Christianity stands or falls."[228] The philosophical movement from supernaturalism to the anti-supernaturalism is similar to what Charles Taylor, in the broader context of the Western world, calls "disenchantment." He says, "Let me start with the enchanted world, the world of spirits, demons, moral forces which our predecessors acknowledged. The process of disenchantment is the disappearance of this world, and the substitution of what we live today: a world in which the only locus of thoughts, feelings, spiritual élan is what we call minds; the only minds in the cosmos are those of humans."[229]

The "disenchanted," liberal Jesus of the twentieth century was *merely* a human. This was nothing less than the old Arian heresy and the older Satanic temptations of "if you are the Son of God" (Matt. 4:6). Machen states, "Yet for modern liberalism a supernatural person is never historical. A problem

---

225 Ibid, 692-94.
226 Otto Zockler, *Geschichte der Beziehungen Zwischen Theologie Und Naturwissenschaft*, (Gutersloh: C. Bertelsmann, 1877-79), II, 69, 249.
227 Bavinck, *Reformed Dogmatics*, 292.
228 Machen, 985-86.
229 Taylor, 30-31.

arises then for those who adopt the liberal point of view, that a supernatural Jesus can never be historical."[230] This is a flat-out denial of what Paul says in Colossians 2:9: "For in him the whole fullness of deity dwells bodily." If you cannot have the supernatural, you cannot have a miracle; you cannot have a resurrection; and you cannot have the triumph of the Christian over the grave in union with Jesus. Instead, in the words of Paul, "If in Christ we have hope in this life only, we are of all people most to be pitied" (1 Cor. 15:19).

Woke religion is hope in this life only because it functionally denies supernaturalism in exchange for a philosophy built upon a naturalistic worldview. Without supernaturalism, we cannot begin to understand, "It is no longer I who live, but Christ who lives in me" (Gal. 2:20). The modernist liberal and Woke followers are blinded to think no external or supernatural help is needed to overcome sin in the heart of man, the fallen condition of humanity. Stripping the Bible of the supernatural events will leave one powerless *to do (law)* and altogether substitute the Gospel for another religion built upon naturalism. Every major doctrine of Scripture must be replaced and reduced to naturalistic dogma. Built upon theological liberalism, this is precisely what happens in the Woke religion. If theological liberalism was the Trojan Horse of the twentieth-century Church, Woke is the Trojan Horse of twenty-first century evangelicalism.

PANTHEISM

While the Trojan Horse of theological liberalism was internally destroying churches in the twentieth century, pantheism was reaping external havoc across Western societies. It is the view that there is no distinction between the natural and supernatural or eminent and transcendent. According to Berkhof, "Pantheism merges the natural and supernatural, the finite and infinite, into one substance. It often speaks of God as the hidden ground of the phenomenal world, but does not conceive of Him as personal, and

---

230 Machen, 1392-93.

therefore as endowed with intelligence and will."[231] Pantheism denies the personal transcendence of a creator and is the opposite extreme of deism. According to Abraham Kuyper, Pantheism was "born from the new German Philosophy and owing its concrete evolution-form to Darwin, claims for itself more and more the supremacy in every sphere of human life, even in that of theology, and under all sorts of names tries to overthrow our Christian traditions, and is bent even upon exchanging the heritage of our fathers for a hopeless modern Buddhism."[232]

The burning embers of ideas from the French Revolution in combination with pantheistic twentieth-century German philosophy amounted to a worldview that was completely divergent from the German Lutheranism of the Magisterial Reformation. The Reformers sought *soli deo gloria*—glory to God alone—while pantheism sought *soli deo hominis*—glory to man alone. Pantheism basically equates God with the creature, similar to paganism. Bavinck makes this point:

> This theistic worldview is sharply opposed by all monisms that reduce reality to a single substance, either matter (materialism) or mind (pantheism). The worldview of theism, by contrast, honors the distinction between God and the world and the distinct physical, psychological, social, and ethical realities of the world. Instead of monistic uniformity, theism aims at unity in diversity, honoring the multiformity of creation itself. While materialism stumbles into psychological phenomena, pantheism cannot find a bridge between thought and existence and does not know what is a mystery and a miracle.[233]

Pantheism cannot maintain the unity of the created order without eliminating diversity. It reduces human beings much lower than they really are ontologically. Similar to pantheism, Woke destroys fundamental distinctions

---

231 Berkhof, 135-37.
232 Kuyper, 143-53.
233 Bavinck, *Reformed Dogmatics*, 84.

between physical, social, and ethical realities in the world. In Woke, humanity is equivocated to social positionality, *and* personal identity is dependent upon the social relations of people in a reductionist pantheist manor. The transcendent and the immanent are fused into a quasi-pantheistic paradigm of social hegemony (i.e., all of reality is some form of the power structure). Appeals for morality cannot be made to the transcendent in Woke because it is reduced to the institutions of the world. Ethics and virtues are determined by the pantheistic force of oppressed and oppressor neo-Marxist dualism. Bavinck says, "Even the greatest evils seeks to cloak itself in the garment of goodness and hide under it."[234] The force of the hegemony is either for you or against you. Society is divided and pitted against one another.

SCHLEIERMACHER'S NEO-PANTHEISM

Pantheism made headway in the Church through Schleiermacher's change in dogmatic theology. Until the nineteenth century, theology first began with theology proper or the doctrine of God. Although, Schleiermacher constructed a new methodology based upon the theological liberalism of this period. Louis Berkhof explains the nature of this significant change:

> The religious consciousness of man was substituted for the Word of God as the source of theology. Faith in Scripture as an authoritative revelation of God was discredited, and human insight based on man's own emotional or rational apprehension became the standard of religious thought. Religion gradually took the place of God as the object of theology. Man ceased to recognize the knowledge of God as something that was given in Scripture, and began to pride himself on being a seeker after God.[235]

His entire dogmatic system began with man and not God, which resulted in a fragmented doctrine of God. Schleiermacher tended to omit the Creator

---

234 Bavinck, *Reformed Ethics*, 233.
235 Berkhof, 34-39.

and creature distinction and blurred the transcendence of God with the immanent. Kuyper explains:

> He completely ignores the transcendent God, and recognizes only a God that can be known by human experience and manifests Himself in Christian consciousness as Absolute Causality, to which a feeling of absolute dependence corresponds. The attributes we ascribe to God are in this view merely symbolical expressions of the various modes of this feeling of dependence, subjective ideas without any corresponding reality.[236]

This type of neo-pantheism in Schleiermacher lowers God's existence to nothing beyond creation. He is criticized to have overemphasized the subjective at the cost of the objective. Revelation was lost under the guise of religion.[237] Barth combated Schleiermacher's theology and attempted to reestablish the transcendence of God but was less than successful.

Moreover, at the turn of the twentieth century, other philosophical issues emerged that further challenged the transcendent nature of God, and that has continued. For example, Berkhof writes, "God is the immanent spirit of the community' (Royce). *'God is the totality of relations constituting the whole social order of growing humanity'* (E. S. Ames)" (emphasis mine).[238] Notice my emphasis on the reduction of God to the relations of social order. This point has more continuity with critical theory dogma in Woke than Christianity.

In Woke, the power structures or social hegemony functions as god, a force of social relations. If the totality of relations is reordered according to Woke dogma, this would result in a utopian, egalitarian metaphysic of equity and deliverance for the oppressed group. This is, in part, why the dogma of Woke religion centers upon power since the pantheistic, hegemonic force is the god of Woke. The problem with a pantheistic, wholly imminent, impersonal God is that this is idolatry.

---

236 Berkhof, 150-53.
237 Ibid, 532-33.
238 Berkhof, 186-89.

NATURALISTIC MATERIALISM

Naturalistic materialism is deeply connected with the anti-supernaturalism and empiricism of the previous paradigms; only now, it is fully mature. In empiricism, perception is the dominant faculty for knowing reality, and man is left to his errant perceptions. "Taken strictly," says Bavinck, "this leads to materialism, because even human consciousness itself including our faculty of knowing, finally has to be reduced to explainable causes in the material, sensory world. The mind is only matter, the matter of the 'physiological brain.'"[239] All of these ideas had deceptive consequences. Pure empiricism led to materialism, which is a full rejection of supernaturalism and revelation as the source of truth. Materialism is a step away from empiricism because there is no acceptance of any reality that is non-material, a more radical view that many eighteenth-century empiricists would not have fully embraced since deism was still dominant.

By the nineteenth century, naturalistic materialism was fully embraced as a philosophy to the detriment of Scripture as the source of truth and the objective reality of anything nonmaterial such as virtue, morality, and objectivity. According to Bavinck:

> It is especially here that modern philosophy and science are most disappointing and need fundamental revision so that we are protected from both materialism and idealism. This reductionism does terrible injustice to the world of nonmaterial things, the world of values, of good and evil, law and custom, religion and morality, all those things that inspire love and hatred in our hearts, lift us up and comfort us or crush and grieve us. This world of the human "spirit," that whole magnificent invisible world, is as much a reality to us as the "real world" that we perceive with our senses.[240]

Materialism is unable to provide a unified system of knowledge, though many attempts have been made to rewrite the traditional meta-narratives

---

239 Bavinck, *Reformed Dogmatics*, 53-54.
240 Ibid, 54.

of Scripture. When these attempts fail, they often have to borrow from Christian theistic categories, in a form of syncretism, because materialism does not allow for consistent knowledge of moral categories.

There was a spiritualist reaction against materialism in the mid-nineteenth century that recognized the existence of dead spirits and possible communication with them by humans.[241] This type of wicked spiritual practice is similar to the practices carried out by the co-founder of Black Lives Matter and others that will be discussed in a later chapter. C.S. Lewis' satire in *The Screwtape Letters* may not be far from the reality of spiritual warfare that takes place all around us. Screwtape, an arch-demon, mentors a less-experienced demon, Wormwood, to guide a man called Patient to the devil.

> Your man [Patient] has been accustomed, ever since he was a boy, to have a dozen incompatible philosophies dancing about together inside his head. He doesn't think of doctrines as primarily "true" or "false", but as "academic" or "practical", "outworn" or "contemporary", "conventional" or "ruthless".[sic] Jargon, not argument, is your best ally in keeping him from the Church. Don't waste time trying to make him think that materialism is true! Make him think it is strong, or stark, or courageous that it is the philosophy of the future. That's the sort of thing he cares about."[242]

Woke is cloaked in manipulative virtues, too. It often emphasizes virtue-signaling or the public expression and sentiment of one's moral, superior, self-righteous character. In reality, Woke religion enslaves man to material power structures through empty promises of liberation for the oppressed through revolution. Marxist-Leninism spoke much about the rights and value of man but on the empty, philosophical foundation of materialism that could not deliver them. The Gulag Soviet forced labor camps ought to remind the reader of the true character beyond the Marxist revolution.[243] Woke also has

---

241 Ibid, 292.
242 Lewis, 36-41.
243 Aleksandr Solzhenitsyn, *The Gulag Archipelago, 1918-1956: An Experiment in Literary Investigation* (New York: Harper & Row, 1985).

no basis for true morality or ethics for humanity. The Woke canon of critical theory operates from closed naturalistic materialism. It is not a coincidence that the critical theory dogma of Woke was founded in the Marxist Frankfort School. If not challenged, the consequences of ideas will be repeated.

SCIENTISM

Many have argued that Christianity is antiquated and unscientific. However, a Christian worldview that presupposes the order of creation provides a basis to do science. "Christianity is the mother of modern science," says Schaeffer, "because it insists that the God who created the universe has revealed Himself in the Bible to be the kind of God he is. Consequently, there is sufficient basis for science to study the universe."[244] What is meant by science is often confused with scientism, which is defined as presupposing a naturalistic materialistic philosophy when conducting the scientific method. Several hundred years ago, scientists began to shift from a worldview that had biblical assumptions to a naturalistic system. Schaeffer points out, "Scientists in the seventeenth and eighteenth centuries continued to use the word God, but pushed God more and more to the edge of their systems. Finally, scientists in this stream of thought moved to the idea of a completely closed system. That left no place for God."[245]

On one hand, as it is more commonly argued, the pre-modernist world of Christian theology actually gave rise to science, citing Galileo and Copernicus. On the other hand, the philosophical paradigm shift toward naturalistic materialism resulted in scientism. Schaeffer provides an accurate explanation of this worldview leap into materialism:

> But equally it left no place for man. Man disappears, to be viewed as some form of determined or behavioristic machine. Everything is a part of the cosmic machine, including people . . . Notice especially that the scientists who gave birth to the earlier great

---

244 Schaeffer, 134.
245 Ibid, 146.

breakthroughs of science would not have accepted this concept. It arose not because of that which could be demonstrated by science, but because the scientists who took this new view had accepted a different philosophic base. The findings of science, as such, did not bring them to accept this view; rather, their world view brought them to this place. They became naturalistic or materialistic in their presuppositions.[246]

Scientism played out in several important ways that are worth mentioning to illustrate how the metanarratives of Scripture were replaced by alternative, problematic understandings of anthropology. Schaeffer states, "Charles Lyell (1797-1875), in his Principles of Geology (1830-1833), was the one who especially opened the door to this by emphasizing the uniformity of natural causes in the field of geology. His idea was that there were no forces in the past except those that are active now."[247]

The same idea was applied to the field of biology, most famously by Charles Darwin (1809-1882) in his theory on the origin of biological life and popularized by Thomas Huxley (1825-1895). Darwin explains in his book *The Origin of Species by Means of Natural Selection* or *The Preservation of Favored Races in the Struggle for Life* (1859), all biological life universally originated from simpler forms. More recently, scholars have distanced themselves from Darwin's theory in part due to the statistical implausibility that purely random chance could result in the incremental complexity between each kind of species.[248] It is also more likely that according to the laws of physics, purely random chance in the universe over eons of time would result in decreasing orders of complexity and a breakdown of biological life. Some try to harmonize creation and evolution by saying that God used evolution to make humans. This is an error simply because it is not consistent with Scripture. How would one interpret Genesis 3:19: "'In the sweat of your face

---

246 Ibid, 147.
247 Schaeffer, 148.
248 Ibid.

you shall eat bread, till you return to the ground, for out of it you were taken; for you are dust, and to dust you shall return'"? If the former state of the human was an animal, then why would God say you are from the dust?

Secondly, Genesis 2:7 clearly says God breathed life into man; he did not evolve. This is affirmed in the book of Job by Elihu when he says, "The Spirit of God has made me, and the breath of the Almighty gives me life" (Job 33:4). God created man out of the ground and breathed life into his soul. Furthermore, man is the crown of God's creation, since God gave man dominion over the earth, including all other creatures. The significance of Scripture is vital as it relates to the doctrine of man, since there is a clear revelation of God in relationship to the rest of creation. From the beginning, the entire human race descended from Adam and Eve. The decree of God was for man to be fruitful and multiply in order for the glory of God's image to be in all the earth. People are not sophisticated chimpanzees. Rather, people are created in the image of God with value, dignity, and worth.

Moreover, the worldview damage had already been done, since Darwinism eventually led to the wide embrace of the philosophy of macroevolution, which teaches different species can change kinds (i.e., parrots can evolve into a horse, or a monkey can incrementally change into a human, given enough time). This worldview was normalized in part due to the indoctrination across nearly all public school systems in the United States during the twentieth century.

Macroevolution is one of the oldest and most simplistic religions in the history of the world. Macroevolution is an inconsistent, non-demonstrable, false theological system. It must assume more miracles and supernatural events than the Christian creation narrative. The problem is not the missing link between kinds or species. It is infinitely more complex than that because macroevolution states that there are subtle evolutionary changes over eons of time, which means there ought to be evidence of every single one. It is a miracle at every point of a fundamental change, which would require millions upon millions of changes and developments in every species. Macroevolution has an infinitely unsustainable problem of countless missing links multiplied by every species. This is multiplied by every subtle change by each species. The only way to solve this issue is to say that an infinite number of miracles happened over eons of time; and somehow, we have no evidence of that, which is an even more astonishing miracle. However, that does not account for the origin of life. Another pillar of miracles is required to explain this, demonstrated by the question: what trait did the non-existent organism have to accumulate itself into the universe? What we ought to see in the fossil record is a countless number of mutations in every species. Yet they simply do not exist.

Other historically traceable factors led to the dominance of this worldview. The phrase "survival of the fittest" was actually first used by Herbert Spencer (1820-1903), who applied Darwin's theory of biological evolution to ethics. In *Physics and Politics: Or, Thoughts on the Application of the Principles of "Natural Selection" and "Inheritance" to Political Science* (1872) by Walter Bagehot (1826-1877) extended the application of this philosophy "to the advance of groups."[249] Schaeffer argues, "These concepts opened the door for racism and the non-compassionate use of accumulated wealth to be sanctioned and made respectable in the name of 'science.'"[250]

The progression of these concepts came to a head in the rise of the Nazi movement in Germany. The philosophy of survival of the fittest produced a fertile seedbed for the racist anti-Semitism historically demonstrated by the leader of the Gestapo, Heinrich Himmler (1900-1945), who stated, "The law of nature must take its course in the survival of the fittest."[251] Hitler applied this concept, since he stated on several occasions, "Christianity and its notion of charity should be 'replaced by the ethic of strength over weakness.'" Sadly, the evolution of these ideas, among other destructive ideas, led to the Nazi

---

249 Ibid, 150.
250 Ibid.
251 Ibid.

death camps. As any student of history knows, multiple complexities of the period led to such destruction of man. Factors such as the weakness of the Christian Church during the period are noteworthy. This was in large part due to the infiltration of liberal theology that exchanged the Bible as the source of truth for rationalism and the influence of a broader, secular, pantheistic, German society. Other scholars have cited that the political and economic circumstances that resulted from World War I, such as hyperinflation, also contributed to the social climate that helped popularize Nazism. These horrific consequences of a failed worldview ought to be the nail in the coffin of macroevolutionary theory and naturalistic materialism. Instead, these worldviews continued to be popularized, impacting broad schools of thought, including neo-Marxist critical theory, a core dogma of Woke. All of the elements of this paradigm shift demonstrate one more step away from Scripture as the source of truth and one step closer to the Woke religion.

CHAPTER EIGHT

PHILOSOPHICAL PARADIGM SHIFTS: POSTMODERNISM TO APPLIED POSTMODERNISM

"No, I imply that what pagans sacrifice they offer to demons and not to God.
I do not want you to be participants with demons."

—1 Corinthians 10:20

THE APOSTLE PAUL SAYS THAT behind pagan rituals is Satan. Christians are not to participate in pagan religion because it is demonic. This includes the battle against empty philosophy and "isms" that lead people into such counterfeit religion. In this final paradigm shift, the spiritual warfare is perhaps the most pronounced because of the surmounted consequences of "isms" from previous paradigms. This final transition from postmodernism to applied postmodernism is the primary structure upon which the Woke religion is framed.

Pre-Modernism to Modernism	Modernism to Postmodernism	Postmodernism to Applied Postmodernism
-Nominalism	-Humanism	-Relativism
-Hume and Kant	-Theological Liberalism	-Skepticism
-Deism	-Anti-Supernaturalism	-Deconstruction
-Romantism	-Pantheism	-Religious Agnostism
-Calvinism	-Neo-Pantheism	- Critical Theory
	-Naturalistic Materialism	-Identity Politics
	-Scientism	

RELATIVISM

Relativism, or moral relativism, is the view that there is no objective morality or absolute truth and that all reality is subjective. Relativism represents one of the most central ideas inherent to postmodernism. It denies the objective and absolutes except for the absolute claim that there are no absolutes. Frederick Moore Vinson (1890-1953), former chief justice of the United States Supreme Court states, "'Nothing is more certain in modern society than the principle that there are no absolutes.' All is relative; all is experience. In passing, we should note this curious mark of our age: The only absolute allowed is the absolute insistence that there is no absolute."[252]

Relativizing morality is a denial of the most basic condition of humanity. In effect, relativism teaches that there is no truth. It is completely divergent from and incompatible with the Bible. Carson argues:

> From the perspective of the Bible, relativism is treason against God and his Word . . . Relativism regularly plays games with language, encourages doctrinal aberration, cultivates duplicity, and pretends to be humble while authorizing astonishing arrogance. Relativism promises freedom but enslaves people: it refuses to acknowledge sin and evil the way the Bible does, and therefore it never adequately confronts sin and evil, and therefore leaves people enslaved by sin and evil.[253]

The Bible shows that relativism as a moral framework is destructive. In the period of Judges, God's people fell into apostasy, and wickedness was everywhere. This is why at the end of the book, it says, "Everyone did what was right in his own eyes" (Judges 17:6). Greek philosophers understood the rudimentary error that relativism made—that is, to deny the objective or universal and turn everything into individual subjectivity. Schaeffer points out this problem: "Plato understood that regardless of what kind of particulars one talks about if there are no absolutes—no universal—then

---

252 Schaeffer, 217.
253 D.A. Carson, *The Intolerance of Tolerance* (Grand Rapids: Eerdmans, 2012), 132-33.

particulars have no meaning. The universal or absolute is that under which all the particulars fit—that which gives unity and meaning to the whole."[254] Relativism, when applied morally to society, is no different.

In the early twentieth century, Jean-Paul Sartre explained the basic problem behind moral relativism. Francis Schaeffer points out, "His concept was that the finite point is absurd if it has no infinite reference point. This concept is most easily understood in the area of morals. If there is no absolute moral standard, then one cannot say in a final sense that anything is right or wrong."[255] Carson describes it like this: "Evil at societal levels, it is an invitation to destruction, for if everyone does that which is right in their own eyes, the end is either anarchic chaos or cultural cries for more laws to establish stability—ultimately even a call for a dictator."[256]

Moreover, the Bible assumes objective, absolute categories in contrast to relativism. The Jews sought to murder Jesus because He spoke in absolutes; He said He was God. "I and the Father are one" (John 10:30). "The Jews picked up stones again to stone him. Jesus answered them, 'I have shown you many good works from the Father, for which of them are you going to stone me?' The Jews answered him, 'It is not for a good work that we are going to stone you but for blasphemy, because you, being a man, make yourself God" (John 10:31-33).

The psalmist also assumes an absolute moral distinction between good and evil. "Keep your tongue from evil and your lips from speaking deceit. Turn away from evil and do good; seek peace and pursue it" (Psalm 34:13-14).The deceptive philosophy of man built upon false sources of knowledge inevitably led to a breakdown of moral categories. "Once the category of evil disappears," says Carson, "our moral discernment has no structure. Strong fiber is reduced to mush; the skeleton of moral reasoning is taken out, and what is left is jelly-like protoplasm. We end up not only with rampant ethical relativism but with the

---

254 Schaeffer, 144-45.
255 Schaeffer, 145.
256 Carson, 132-33.

anemic inability to feel or express moral outrage over pervasive immorality."[257] To appeal to relativism is to appeal to moral confusion.

Scripture has a foundation for moral absolutes that all civilizations must presuppose for human flourishing to be sustainable. From Genesis three to Revelation, the Bible details the reality of moral objectivity. The post-fall human heart is infected with evil. The prophet Jeremiah says, "The heart is deceitful above all things, and desperately sick" (Jer. 17:9). This does not mean the unregenerate cannot do any good whatsoever in any sense. Unregenerate people can certainly do good works because of common grace. However, they cannot do anything spiritually good; unless they are regenerated, they "cannot please God" (Rom. 8:8). Puritan John Owen makes this plain:

> Unbelievers cannot choose good for its own excellence. They only seek good or avoid evil for personal benefit. And these efforts are mostly very weak and languid. Witness the luxury, sloth, worldliness, and security that most men are drowned in. But in believers there is a will of doing good, a habitual disposition and inclination in their wills to what is spiritually good; and where this exists, it is accompanied with answerable effects.[258]

According to the apostle Paul, the sin in the flesh is still warring in the members of the regenerate (Rom. 7). While the power and presence of sin are diminished in believers, sin is nonetheless a universal cancer that pervades across the rest of the entire human race. Sin is deceptive and has been since the Fall in the Garden when the old serpent, the devil, deceived Eve (Gen. 3:13). All transgressions follow this original sin of deception. Augustine and the founding fathers of America recognized the sinful condition of humanity. According to Carson, "A healthy dose of Augustinian realism about sin, as Mark Ellingsen puts it, could make America a better place: indeed, that is why the founding fathers cared so much about checks and

---

257   Ibid, 131.
258   Owen, 3.

balances, about constitutional limitations, above division of powers: they did not trust anyone precisely because the founders had a robust notion of sin."[259]

The founders were right in their diagnoses of sin and the corrupting effect of sin to cause abuse in the exercise of governmental power. The corrupting power of sin was understood in absolutes as depicted in the Puritan's view of the doctrine of sin.

Contrary to moral relativism, the psalmist recounts the goodness of God: "Oh, how abundant is your goodness, which you have stored up for those who fear you and worked for those who take refuge in you, in the sight of the children of mankind" (Psalm 31:19). The basis for morality is the moral law (Psalm 119:141, 160), the nature of God's character, not the subjectivity of the man. Bavinck writes, "This is evident from its content but also in the way that the law does not just show us how we ought to relate to God and to our neighbor. Instead, first and foremost, it shows us how God wants his people to be, contrary to the spirit of the nations that surround them."[260]

However, the new canons of Woke are influenced by relativism because of the postmodernist roots. Like the ancient serpent, critical theory, in effect, says, "For God knows that when you eat of it your eyes will be opened, and you will be like God, knowing good and evil" (Gen. 3:5). In other words, awaken to the knowledge of the evil systemic and institutional power structures. Thus, Woke judges society according to the relativistic standard of critical theory dogma and not the objective, moral standard of God's law. Contrarily, Jesus summarizes the moral law with the command: "'You shall love the Lord your God with all your heart and with all your soul and with all your mind'" (Matt. 22:37). The moral law is spiritual and dependent upon the unchangeable nature of God. In effect, the rejection of the truth of God's Word is to reject God and the glory of Christ, Who alone is Judge (Acts 17:31).

---

259 Carson, 130.
260 Bavinck, *Reformed Ethics*, 221

Moreover, the institutions of the family, Church, and government are, in part, ordained by God to restrain evil. Civil authority is put in place by God for the good of the people and "bears the sword." "For he is God's servant for your good. But if you do wrong, be afraid, for he does not bear the sword in vain. For he is the servant of God, an avenger who carries out God's wrath on the wrongdoer" (Rom. 13:4).

It is a good providence of God that civil laws are not completely built upon relativistic notions of morality. Bavinck says, "Justice must be based on the moral and ought not be in conflict with it, in the terrain of the state and not in the terrain of the inner life."[261] However, as soon as a society treads down the relativistic path, all objective morality is lost, and there is no way to determine right or wrong, good or evil. "Woe to those who call evil good and good evil, who put darkness for light and light for darkness" (Isa. 5:20). If relativism is applied logically, the conclusion is that it is just as right to murder as it is to not murder. There is no basis to say otherwise. The foundation for determining the distinction between goodness and wickedness is removed. Carson writes of the effects of moral relativism in the present Western world:

> These are not abstract issues. A culture that minimizes values such as honor, integrity, valor, self-sacrifice for the sake of other people, truth-telling, and courtesy, while maximizing sexual freedom so strongly that the issues themselves cannot be debated because everything has been decided under the controlling rubric of the new tolerance, is destined in the long haul to pay horrendous costs.[262]

As we have seen in America, relativism is not limited to dictatorial regimes and respects no national boundaries. Postmodern relativism was a dominant worldview throughout the latter portion of the twentieth century.

---

261 Ibid, 225.
262 Carson, 138.

Increased emphasis on hard postmodernism relied heavily upon relativism. Hard postmodernism (differentiated from soft postmodernism) is defined as the following:

> Deconstructive thought that seeks to expose the oppressive power of truth claims and especially of metanarratives. Philosophers such as Jacques Derrdia, Michael Foucault, and Richard Rorty engage in this kind of postmodern philosophy, which seems inevitably relativistic. For them, all truth claims are but masks for will to power. Some critics have described this hard type of postmodern philosophy as "cognitive nihilism." Its main purpose is to relativize truth.[263]

Forms of hard postmodernism were embraced in the increasingly complex social climates of the twenty-first century. This is a highly significant, philosophical foundation for Woke religion.

POSTMODERNIST DECONSTRUCTION, SKEPTICISM, AND RELIGIOUS AGNOSTICISM

By the late twentieth century, Western culture was dominated by postmodernism. Postmodernism denies objective epistemology, rejects meta-narratives, and values subjectivism. The progressive Left abandoned the modernist culmination of Enlightenment thinking and fully embraced postmodernism. Given that postmodernism is a rejection of modernism, there is no category for metanarratives and comprehensive worldviews, such as Christianity, science, and classical democratic liberalism. Knowledge was reduced down to man and the rationalistic thinking of the day.

All the elements of the movement are too expansive to mention here, so only two of the most significant will be briefly identified: deconstructionism and skepticism. The origins of deconstructionism began in the 1960s by Jacques Derrida as a literary, textual, critical device to subvert the meaning of

---

263 Roger E. Olson, *Reformed and Always Reforming: The Postconservative Approach to Evangelical Theology* (Grand Rapids: Baker, 2007), 126-27.

texts. Deconstructionism expanded to challenge the traditional meaning of words, ideas, intuitions, beliefs, and worldviews. If the meaning of words, ideas, concepts, art, symbols, or virtually anything under the sun can be deconstructed or destabilized, then it can be replaced with new meanings and new definitions. Once uncertainty is created around the traditional meaning of ideas, norms, values, and beliefs, then they can be undermined in society and replaced.

Skepticism is equally problematic, especially in the religious context, because of the doubt and uncertainty this scheme casts upon the existence of God. It is a subtly cloaked form of atheism because it appears to be an appeal to humility, and yet within is the fool's heart that says "there is no God" (Psalm 14:1). There is a difference between not knowing while seeking to know the truth and saying that truth cannot exist. The former claim is a faith-seeking agnostic, while the latter is veiled atheism. The cloaked atheist hides behind the appeal to agnosticism while simultaneously making an objective truth claim that God absolutely cannot exist.

In this way, agnosticism is a deceptive ploy of Satan to doubt the existence of God. "[I]n abandoning the embattled walls of the city of God," says Machen, "he has fled in needless panic into the open plains of a vague natural religion only to fall an easy victim to the enemy whoever lies in ambush there."[264] Agnosticism is an ambush of the enemy. The forked tongue of Satan deceptively promises no commitment to certainty about God is required. Yet if one abandons the fortress of the Christian worldview, there is nowhere to go but the wilderness. Infecting the minds of people with doubt and uncertainty has been a deception by Satan since the beginning. "Now the serpent was more crafty than any other beast of the field that the LORD God had made. He said to the woman, 'Did God actually say, *You shall not eat of any tree in the garden*'?'" (Gen. 3:2—emphasis mine).

Moreover, agnosticism maintains continuity with theological liberalism. Both deny the truth of Scripture. The agnostic may only want to distance himself

---

264 Kuyper, 82.

from religion while the theological liberal may want to still claim to be religious with no foundation. Both fall prey to the enemy of skepticism. The agnostic is not off the hook to claim to be uncertain about God. A claim to be uncertain is still a certain claim. However, the skeptic must admit that Christianity is a historical phenomenon beginning around the time of Jesus' death. The skeptic can deconstruct the validity of the message, but the historical message is irrefutable. The question then must be asked, was this historical message concerning Jesus' resurrection true? Were those who saw Jesus telling the truth or not? Jesus claimed to be God—"I am" (John 8:58)—and that all the Scriptures were about Him (Luke 24:25-27). As C.S. Lewis said in his "trilemma," Jesus is a liar, lunatic, or Lord. There are no other options for the skeptic. Skepticism and religious agnosticism are a divisive attack on the basic epistemological assumptions for knowledge in Christian theism. In this way, postmodern skepticism and religious agonistics provided cover fire for the rise of the alternative Woke religion. According to postmodernist skepticism, claims to Christianity cannot be made, and at best, we cannot know if God exists.

Meanwhile, social injustices had not been philosophized away. The postmodernist skeptic deconstructionist still did not solve any of the problems of man. While the moral, ethical, and sociological vacuum widened, scholars looked to critical theory to provide "analytical tools" to address the ills of society. In parallel, the soul's longing for religion was increasingly dissatisfied with postmodernism and driven to despair, since reality had lost meaning, purpose, and certainty.

Moreover, the infamous phrase by Descartes—"*Cogito, ergo sum*" ("I think; therefore, I am")—demonstrates modernism's view in one phrase. Sometime in the late twentieth century, some off-shoots of postmodernism had evolved into "I am oppressed; therefore, I am." Lindsay and Pluckrose put it like this: "I experience oppression, therefore I am . . . so are dominance and oppression."[265] Postmodernism deconstructed epistemology, religion, societal

---

265 Lindsay and Pluckrose, *Cynical Theories*, 52.

structures, and race and offered nothing but despair. It was a colossal failure of a system and may have eventually died off if it was not for critical theory and applied postmodernism.

CRITICAL THEORY

The advent of critical theory is often attributed to the Frankfurt School, founded in the 1920s by German Marxist philosophers in response to communism. Webster says that Marxism "argues that human wholeness can be realized only through overcoming the alienating political and economic structures of society."[266] David Aikman believes Marxism really is, at the core, "the deadly logical consequence of an atheistic, man-centered system of values, enforced by fallible human beings with total power, who believe, with Marx, that morality is whatever the powerful define it to be and, with Mao, that power grows from gun barrels."[267] Friedrich Engels, who coauthored *The Communist Manifesto* with Marx was strongly opposed to Christianity in Britain. Taunton points out, "When asked the name of the person he most detested, Engels' response was unequivocal: 'Spurgeon.'"[268]

However, some suggest there are no direct Marxist connections to all disciplines of critical theory.[269] Critical theory can refer more broadly to several different systems. According to the *Stanford Encyclopedia of Philosophy*, "While Critical Theory is often thought of narrowly as referring to the Frankfurt School that begins with Horkheimer and Adorno and stretches to Marcuse and Habermas, any philosophical approach with similar practical

---

266 Walter Elwell, *Evangelical Dictionary of Theology* (Grand Rapids: Baker Book House, 2001), 686.

267 Lily Rothman, "Why It Took So Long for the World to See How Phnom Penh Fell," Time.com, April 17, 2015, https://time.com/3814193/anniversary-phnom-penh.

268 Larry Taunton, "Understanding What is Happening in America, Part II: The Pale Marxist Trojan Horse," Larry Alex Taunton.com, August 26, 2020, http://larryalextaunton.com/2020/08/understanding-what-is-happening-in-america-part-ii-the-pale-Marxist-Trojan-horse.

269 Neil Shenvi and Pat Sawyer, "Engaging Critical Race Theory and the Social Justice Movement," *Journal of Christian Legal Thought*, 10, No. 1 (2020): 3.

aims could be called a 'critical theory,' including feminism, critical race theory, and some forms of post-colonial criticism."[270]

Nevertheless, while there are broad applications of critical theory, there is evidence that the origins stem from the Frankfurt School. According to Cline, critical theory "stretches back to the early 20th century ideas of Max Horkheimer, Theodore Adorno, and Herbert Marcuse of the Frankfurt School, the neo-Marxism of Antonino Gramsci, and the postmodernism of Michel Foucault and Jacques Derrida."[271] Taunton explains that Gramsci further developed the idea of hegemonies or power structures.

> Where Marx divided the world into a single hegemony of haves and have-nots, Gramsci divided it into more hegemonies: families, education, government, morality, the church, law, and civil society as a whole. Just as Marx had argued that capitalism was a system designed to keep the haves in a master-slave relationship with the have-nots, Gramsci argued that these additional hegemonies were yet further insulation for the powerful against the masses.[272]

Gramsci's strategy was to advance socialism into all spheres of society. This demonstrates a massive divergence from the Christian worldview. Gramsci writes, "Socialism will triumph . . . by first capturing the culture via infiltration of schools, universities, churches and the media by transforming the consciousness of society."[273] This is an application of Marxism to every traditional institution of society and culture, which is often what is meant by the phrase "cultural Marxism," the socialist Trojan Horse. Embedded in cultural Marxism is a comprehensive approach to overthrowing traditional structures of society, such as marriage, the family unit, traditional morality, education, the Church, and the government. Taunton says, "By the 1980s,

---

270 "Critical Theory," *Stanford Encyclopedia of Philosophy*, March 8, 2005, https://plato. stanford.edu/entries/critical-theory.
271 Cline, Ibid.
272 Taunton, Ibid.
273 Ibid.

Gramsci's ideas had achieved something of a cult status among a generation of Western academics."[274]

This neo-Marxism or cultural Marxist ideology is identifiable in the assumptions of critical theory. The definition of oppression in critical theory is substantively different from the definition in the dictionary, which states oppression is "unjust or cruel exercise of [the] authority of power."[275] Yet in critical theory, oppression is primarily understood by "hegemonic power," upon which one group imposes values or ideas on the rest of society. More specifically, the hegemony is "any relationship between groups that define one another (men/women, able-bodied/disabled, young/old) [and] the dominant group is the group that is valued more highly."[276] The one group dominates the societal norms, reminiscent of the capitalist bourgeoisie in Marxist economic theory, at the cost to the minority, the proletariat working-class group. Shenvi and Sawyer explain:

> In saying that a particular man is an "oppressor" the critical theorist is not saying that the man has personally ever abused his power or, for instance, mistreated women in ways that are traditionally understood as unjust. Rather, the critical theorist is asserting that the group to which the man belongs (men) has imposed its views on society regarding what is normal, expected, and valuable, thus making the man an oppressor.[277]

Liberation seeks to eliminate or restructure the oppressive hegemony and is often described in terms such as "social justice." Social justice seeks to liberate the oppressed group from the interdependent injustices of "person's gender, race, ethnicity, religion, sexual orientation, physical or mental ability, or economic class."[278] According to critical theory, traditional norms and

---

274 Ibid.
275 Shenvi and Sawyer, 4.
276 Ibid, 4-5.
277 Ibid, 5.
278 Ibid, 6.

values such as Christian views of marriage, faith, sexuality, parenting, and gender cause victimization and oppression.

APPLIED POSTMODERNISM

These historical strands of critical theory have manifested into what Shenvi and Sawyer call "contemporary critical theory"[279] and what Lindsay and Nayna call "applied postmodernism."[280] Figure 6 conceptualizes the relationship between postmodernism, Neo-Marxist critical theory, and identity politics that manifested into applied postmodernism. On the one hand, these philosophies and ideological movements narrowly have distinct origins while maintaining functional points of continuity. On the other hand, the broad application of these philosophies and ideological movements amalgamated into an increasingly interdependent system called applied postmodernism.

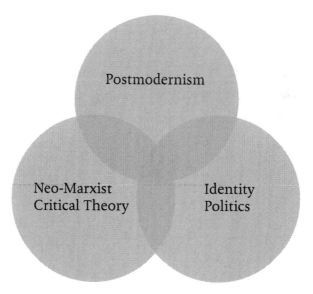

Figure 6: Applied Postmodernism

279 Ibid, 2.
280 Lindsay and Nayna, Ibid.

The fundamental component that affected the transition from postmodernism to applied postmodernism was identity politics. Identity politics were (and still are) viewed as the only way to progress toward the founding principle of equality that has been made. DiAngelo writes, "The term identity politics refers to the focus on the barriers specific groups face in their struggle for equality. We have yet to achieve our founding principle, but any gains we have made thus far have come through identity politics."[281]

Social justice generates the activism that fuses these components into the religion of Woke as shown in Figure 7.

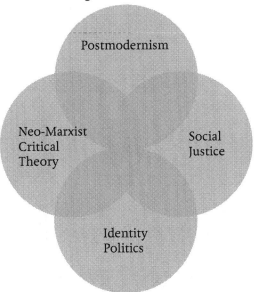

Figure 7: The Foundation of Woke Religion

Lindsay and Pluckrose write, "The *faith* that emerged is thoroughly postmodern, which means that, rather than interpreting the world in terms of subtle spiritual forces like sin and magic, it focuses instead on subtle material forces, such as systemic bigotry, and diffuse but omnipresent systems of power and privilege."[282] In effect, social justice activists proselytize critical theory like it is a faith-like religion in replacement of the traditional religion

---

281 DiAngelo, xiii.
282 Lindsay and Pluckrose, 17-18.

and traditional democratic structures that make up Western civilization. By the 2010s, this phenomenon was understood by many as the social justice movement or Woke.[283]

Woke centers upon the power, language, authority of knowledge, and social relations. The worldview is dominated by cultural strife and societal identity politics of race, sex, and gender. Lindsay and Pluckrose suggest Woke social justice has religious characteristics: "They bear witness to our repeatedly demonstrated capacity to take up complex spiritual worldview, ranging from tribal animism, to hippie spiritualism to sophisticated global religions, each of which adopts its own interpretive frame through which it sees the entire world. This one just happens to be about a peculiar view of power and its ability to create inequality and oppression."[284]

This is consistent with Buttom's theory that indicates emphasis on social sins such as oppression and power during the twentieth century Social Gospel movement led to religious social activism in the twenty-first century.[285]

Through the philosophical paradigm shifts, the Scripture as the source of truth was abandoned and replaced by the ideas of men. On top of the incremental paradigm shifts, the last brick of applied postmodernism was laid. The temple of Woke religion, so to speak, was complete. However, that is not the full story of *why* Woke is a religion. This alone, in all of the traceable historical and philosophical complexities, did not give birth to the religion. That merely built the substructure of ideas and philosophy. Who *really* made Woke a religion? People did because people are inherently religious. Over centuries, the divergence from Truth resulted in postmodernism that left man in spiritual despair. Social justice filled this spiritual void. Advocates of social justice were taken captive by the empty philosophies, according to the elemental spirits of this world and not according to Christ; they are the ones who made Woke a religion.

283 Lindsay and Pluckrose, 15.
284 Ibid, 16.
285 Collins, Ibid.

In summary, over the course of several centuries, the false ideas of man emerged into the counterfeit, pagan religion of Woke. Ultimately, pagan religions have emerged throughout redemptive history as deception and counterfeit worship of Satan (1 Cor. 10:20-21). Given the fact that the philosophical foundation of Woke religion rejects the truth of Scripture and is antithetical to Christianity, it is highly plausible that Woke has manifested into a counterfeit religion. This will be further substantiated by the counterfeit, religious doctrine built upon the carnal philosophy and ideology of the Woke religion. The false doctrine of Woke religion will be discussed in the following chapters and compared with Christian theology.

PART FOUR
WOKE DOGMA

CHAPTER NINE

WOKE EPISTEMOLOGY AND HEGEMONY VS. REVELATION, CHRISTIAN EPISTEMOLOGY, THEOLOGY PROPER, AND CREATION

J.C. RYLE WROTE, "THE MAN who is content to sit ignorantly by his own fireside, wrapped up in his own private affairs, and has no public eye for what is going on in the Church and the world, is a miserable patriot, and a poor style of Christian. Next to our Bibles and our own hearts, our Lord would have us study our own times."[286] With a public eye for what is going on in the Church and the world, one can observe, step-by-step, "ism" by "ism," philosophy by philosophy, theory by theory how Woke became a religion. Woke social justice is made up of several philosophies, ideologies, and religious doctrines. Fundamentally, Woke is a religion because the doctrines demand a drastic change of self-consciousness, the perceived understanding of the world, and an awakening or conversion.

Religions typically "encompass all human relations to God in their entirety."[287] As it will be demonstrated in this part of the book, all human relations, according to Woke doctrine, are to be understood in relationship to the all-encompassing power structures of society. In this way, the power

---

286 J.C. Ryle, *Holiness* (Mulberry: Sovereign Grace Publishers, 2001), 185.
287 Bavinck, *Reformed Ethics*, 54.

structures function similarly to a dualistic, pantheistic force typically defined by the hegemony classes or groups. Awakening to this existential reality is similar to, but not the same as, heightened consciousness or feeling that Schleiermacher observed. Wokeness requires a certain intellectual imperative to put off the old oppressive ways of understanding the world. Woke social justice gives the imperative to confess their identity with and self-revelation of racism that functions like a mystic, religious-political secret hidden within the oppressive societal hegemony. There is a significant emphasis on the new world order to the extent that the future utopia is divine. It is similar to Fitche, who thought, "The moral world order, whose reign we have to advance ethically, is itself God."[288]

Woke social justice is a religion because like nearly all religions, it requires some measure of belief or faith. Belief in the Woke doctrines is required to understand reality in the Woke consciousness. Thus, firm conviction in the teachings of Woke will result in becoming Woke and becoming part of the religion. That begs the question this part of the book will seek to answer: are the dogmas of Woke social justice true?

The Word of God is the only authority for determining the nature of religion. The veracity of any religion can be measured by comparison to the Bible as the source of truth. On the basis of Scripture, this part of the book demonstrates Woke religion is entirely incompatible with Christianity at nearly every point of Christian doctrine. You cannot chew up the meat and spit out the bones without being poisoned by the toxic Woke doctrine. Woke teaching is a false gospel, for what it teaches and also for what it fails to teach, namely biblical Christianity. There is no Christ, no love, no mercy, no grace, no forgiveness, no justice, no righteousness, and hardly a shred of truth that has not been twisted into error in the Woke religion. It is layered in divisive, deceptive, and destructive philosophy that has grown into a counterfeit religion. The substance of Woke religion is built upon anti-Christian canons

---

288 Bavinck, *Reformed Ethics*, 53.

of applied postmodernism dogma and functions as an alternative religion to Christianity as Figures 8 and 9 conceptualize. Connor Wood summarizes some of the important axioms of applied postmodernism:

1. Knowledge and truth are largely socially constructed, not objectively discovered.

2. What we believe to be "true" is in large part a function of social *power*: who wields it, who's oppressed by it, how it influences which messages we hear.

3. Power is generally oppressive and self-interested (and implicitly zero-sum).

4. Thus, most claims about supposedly objective truth are actually power plays, or strategies for legitimizing particular social arrangements (emphasis mine).[289]

Woke dogma is practiced in the context of Western society in the sociopolitical sphere, united in the Church with Christian teaching and/or society at large as a religion. Contrarily, the doctrines of Christianity are founded upon the Scripture and practiced by the Church.

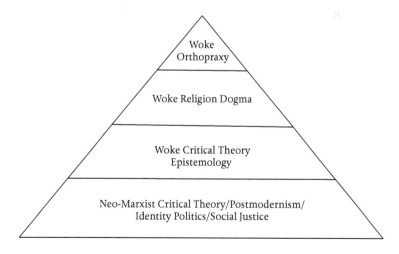

Figure 8: Woke Religion

289 Lindsay and Nayna, Ibid.

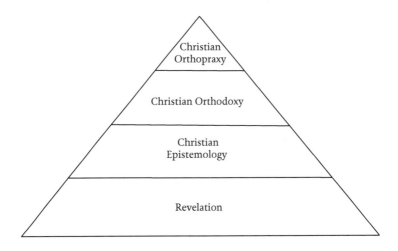

Figure 9: Christian Religion

Christianity is built upon revelation, particularly Scripture (special revelation) as the source of truth. Shedd writes, "The Scriptures, then, as an inspired sum total, are to be referred to God as their author . . . The infallibility and authority which distinguish the scriptures from all other books are due to divine authorship."[290] Some of the many Scripture proofs for this are:

- "All Scripture is breathed out by God" (2 Tim. 3:16).
- "Long ago, at many times and in many ways, God spoke . . . to us by his Son" (Heb. 1:1-2).
- "Men spoke from God as they were carried along by the Holy Spirit" (2 Peter 1:21).

Contrarily, Woke religion is built upon the philosophy of applied postmodernism and social justice as it was sketched in Part Three. Woke dogmas function as a system of beliefs extremely dissimilar in substance to Christianity.

From critical theory emerged critical social justice. These ideas originated with the Frankfurt School that has been associated with Marxism. Sensoy and

---

290 Shedd, 113.

DiAngelo state, "Our analysis of social justice is based on a school of thought know as Critical Theory. Critical Theory refers to a body of scholarship that examines how society works, and is a tradition that emerged in the early part of the 20th century from a group of scholars at the Institute for Social Research in Frankfurt, Germany."[291]

Critical social justice has an epistemology. Figure 10 provides a sketch of the wide differences and incompatibilities between Woke epistemology and Christian epistemology.

Woke Cannons and Epistemology

Woke "cannons" are based upon Neo-Marxist Critical Theory/ Postmodernism/Identity Politics/Social Justice

Relation to society determines authority and knowledge.

All knowledge is socially constructed, subjective, skeptical, objective, true, and cannot be known.

Language constructs reality, a construct of power.

Dominant group has limited knowledge; minority has the most authority.

Inconsistently, objective is knowledge claimed through activism. "Believe woke dogma."

Christian Revelation and Epistemology

Revelation is general in creation and special in the Word of God. The Bible is the authority and measure of truth. The Scriptures are innerant, infallable, sufficient, and authoritative.

Knowledge is based upon revelation. Objectives are knowledge, absolutes, and obtainable truth.

True knowledge of God and man can be known. Faith precedes reason.

Reality is revealed through creation and Scripture.

God's Word is the authority.

Figure 10: Woke "Cannons" and Epistemology vs.
Christian Revelation Epistemology

The authority of knowledge is based on sociological relationships in Woke dogma. DiAngelo claims, "Positionality is the concept that our perspectives are

---

based on our place in society. Positionality recognizes that where you stand in relation to others shapes what you can see and understand."[292] One's societal "position" in relation to other people in society determines knowledge and moral culpability. Understanding, perspective, and even authority is determined by social position, according to Woke critical social justice theory. Social *positionality* is a way to redefine authority and objectivity. Critical social justice scholars do not appear to recognize this inconsistency, even though postmodernism rejects absolutes and is relativistic. Critical social justice redefines new absolutes based on sociological phenomenon such as one's relation to other people. Postmodern philosophical presuppositions dominate critical social justice.

Skepticism, deconstruction, and rejection of objectivity are identified by DiAngelo:

> In order to understand the concept of knowledge as never purely objective, neutral, and outside of human interests, it is important to distinguish between discoverable laws of the natural world (such as the law of gravity), and knowledge, which is socially constructed. By socially constructed, we mean that all knowledge understood by humans is framed by the ideologies, language, beliefs, and customs of human societies. Even the field of science is subjective.[293]

Reality is totally subjective; all knowledge ought to be determined by social structures; there are no absolutes; and there is no truth. Common among postmodern philosophy is to reject modernism and even the objectivity of science. The ironic issue with the claim that suggests one ought to view reality with pure subjectivity—in this case, subjective social constructions—is that this claim must also be understood subjectively. Based upon the logic of this claim, it is not possible that it can be true or objective; at best, one can conclude knowledge is uncertain, including socially subjective constructions of knowledge. This claim is tantamount to a universally meaningless

---

292 Ibid, 15.
293 Ibid.

statement. Nevertheless, DiAngleo reveals the strong commitment to this broader system of postmodernism: "One of the key contributions of critical theorists concerns the production of knowledge . . . These scholars argue that a key element of social injustice involves the claim that particular knowledge is objective, neutral, and universal. An approach based on critical theory calls into question the idea that objectivity is desirable or even possible."[294]

One wonders why there is any reason to subscribe to critical social justice since a central element of the system is that knowledge is objectively meaningless. Critical social justice is a system of unknown subjectivity. There's no plausible reason why social justice as a system can achieve anything beyond relative knowledge. Critical theorists remove the foundation of knowledge they need to make any serious claims—much like all postmodern thinkers. According to this perspective, critical social justice then must necessarily be relative and understood according to whatever subjective interpretation one desires or concludes. One wonders why critical social justice and critical theory should be considered as a source of knowledge if at the end of the day, nothing can really be known. This is an unbiblical error. Jesus said, "'Sanctify them in the truth; your word is truth'" (John 17:17). There are objective absolutes. There is truth. Jesus is the Truth. The Word of God has revealed the Truth.

Further subjective elements of postmodernism are identified in critical social justice. "Positionality asserts that knowledge is dependent upon a complex web of cultural values, beliefs, experiences, and social positions," says DiAngelo.[295] This aligns with standpoint epistemology. Sandra Harding writes, "Each oppressed group can learn to identify its distinctive opportunities to turn an oppressive feature of the group's conditions into a source of critical insight about how the dominant society thinks and is structured. Thus, standpoint theories map how a social and political disadvantage can be turned into an epistemological, scientific, and political advantage."[296]

---

294 Ibid, 29.
295 Ibid.
296 Sandra Harding, ed. *The Feminist Standpoint Theory Reader: Intellectual and Political*

This Woke epistemological dogma is unbiblical because knowledge is not based upon the truth of God's Word and is built upon the philosophies of man. True knowledge is grounded in the Word of God (Prov. 2:6). Francis Schaeffer called this "true truth."[297] Yet what this Woke epistemological definition adds is that "social positions" are an element of knowledge—except this still cannot avoid the ultimate problem of subjective knowledge. It is entirely subjective. If knowledge is subjective, based upon subjective social positions, how can the claim be held that there are institutional, systemic, and totalizing social injustices? Critical social justice and critical theory make claims about the reality of society, based on subjective presuppositions, which reject truth, certainty, and objectivity and which cannot be questioned. These assumptions determined "everyone" is complicit in the "systems of inequalities" in society. Since postmodern, anti-objective presuppositions dominate critical social justice dogma, it results in a flawed epistemological system. Knowledge according to critical theory must only be subjective and can never be objective. According to DiAngelo, critical theory "challenges the claim that any knowledge is neutral or objective, and outside of humanly constructed meanings and interests."[298] This commitment reveals critical social justice is, in fact, self-refuting and nonsensical. If critical social justice is a system of knowledge, by definition, it can never be more than a humanly constructed idea and, therefore, cannot make any objective claims about society, anthropology, morality, or any other field of knowledge. Simply put, critical theory is nothing more than a made-up theory that can never be proven, in the universal objective sense, since universal truth does not exist according to the presuppositions of the theory.

Now, critical social justice gets really interesting but not really surprising, based upon the dominant postmodernist presuppositions. According to Sensoy and DiAngelo, "Language is not a neutral transmitter of a universal

---

Controversies (New York: Routledge, 2004), 7-8.

297 Francis Schaeffer, *The God Who is There* (Downers Grove: InterVarsity Press), 121.

298 Sensoy and DiAngelo, 187.

objective or fixed reality.Rather, language is the way we construct reality."[299] Or if you like, the claim you just read in the English language has no objective or real meaning. There is nothing behind the words. There is no truth, no objective reality, no universals behind or in the language. It is just meaningless constructs of the world in a closed system. It is merely words. If language is not fixed reality and merely a construct of reality, why even make that statement? The reason is because words can be used to redefine power structures. Lindsay and Pluckrose point this out: "Thus, applied postmodernism focuses on controlling discourses."[300] This is perhaps most revealed in the political correctness in present society. According to Lindsay and Pluckrose, there is a postmodern political principle—a belief that "society is formed of power and hierarchies, which decide what can be known and how."[301]

To establish the idea of inequality, social structures have to be redefined according to the subjective definitions of critical social justice. Lindsay and Pluckrose say, "If knowledge is a construct of power, which functions through ways of talking about things, knowledge can be changed and power structures toppled by changing the way we talk about things."[302] This is one of the problems with critical social justice dogma. Critical social justice uses language and redefinitions of social structures to reposition the authority of knowledge. This is entirely unbiblical and an error. The source of authority is the eternal Word of God.

The psalmist writes, "Forever, O Lord, your word is firmly fixed in the heavens" (Psalm 119:89). In various periods of history, authority of knowledge was found in the Church (in pre-modern times of Roman Catholicism) or in science (in modernism). Now in this derivative of postmodernism, critical social justice moves the authority to a sociological group according to power structures. Yet the axioms or terms of critical theory and critical social justice function as what I coin as *neo-objectivity*. Critical social justice will not be

---

299 Sensoy and DiAngelo, 70.
300 Lindsay and Pluckrose, 61.
301 Ibid, 59.
302 Ibid, 61.

subject to examination, especially if one is in the "dominant group." Sensoy and DiAngelo reveal this staggering claim of authority: "Dominant groups have the most narrow or limited view of society because they do not have to understand the experiences of the minoritized group in order to survive . . . Minoritized groups often have the widest view of society, in that they must understand both their own and the dominant group's perspective—develop a double-consciousness—to succeed."[303]

What is being claimed here? In neo-objectivity, if one is in the majority, they have little-to-no authority for knowledge and real experience while the minority group determines authority, knowledge, and reality of experience. This is a curious way to philosophize a sociological system that claims inherent inequalities among the power structures. It is like saying, "The power structures are corrupt because of the majority, and if they balk at this, well, it proves it's true because they have limited or no knowledge." This has the potential to destroy free speech in society. It does not matter how much evidence or substantive argumentation is presented if one is part of the majority group because they do not have the experience or "authority" of the oppressed group—neo-objectivity. No matter what the minority group says or does is to be taken as the authority or real knowledge of experience. On reviewing DiAngelo, Neil Shenvi says, "[One] can either admit that he is racist and fragile, or he can demonstrate that he is racist and fragile by denying that he is racist and fragile."[304]

In critical theory, only the minority or oppressed group can speak the truth. On one hand, the system has committed to subjectivity, but on the other hand, objective terms have to be established for the sociological framework to be intelligible. Critical theorists claim that the oppressing group cannot accurately perceive the world and the way things really are. Shenvi and Sawyer puts it this way:

---

303 Sensoy and DiAngelo, 70.
304 Neil Shenvi, "The Worldview of White Fragility – A Review of Robin DiAngelo's White Fragility," Shenvi Apologetics.com, Accessed October 4, 2020, https://shenvi-apologetics.com/the-worldview-of-white-fragility.

Oppressed people therefore have an advantage over oppressors when it comes to understanding reality. To borrow a point of emphasis from Paulo Freire, they are better able to "read the world." Their "lived experience" of oppression gives them special access to truths that are generally concealed from dominant groups, giving them unique authority and insight to lead in the liberation of both themselves and their oppressors.[305]

Taken strictly, objective knowledge and reason is irrelevant, and experiential knowledge of the oppressed group is the standard for truth. According to Anderson and Collin, critical theory rejects objectivity: "The idea that objectivity is best reached only through rational thought is a specifically Western and masculine way of thinking."[306] What is more interesting is that one can have the same ethnicity of the minority group but still be rejected by the minority group as a racist, a sellout to whites, or not really a minority. For example, in reference to the infamous novel *Uncle Tom's Cabin*, where an African American is portrayed as "differential to whites," "News media host Joy Reid used a racial slur . . . against Supreme Court Justice Clarence Thomas, calling him 'Uncle Clarence.'"[307] Critical race theory scholars appear to define this as a "false consciousness: Phenomenon in which oppressed people internalize and identify with attitudes and ideology of the controlling class."[308]

To recap, what's the bottom line of critical social justice? Oppression exists. Oppression is based upon the majority power hegemony. Therefore, oppression exists. This is a flawed, circular argument. Logically, it supposes nothing more than oppression exists because oppression exists. Then critical social justice attempts to establish an epistemological system on this flawed logic, whereby the authority of knowledge is only given to the minority group

---

305 Shenvi and Sawyer, 8.
306 Margaret L. Andersen, *Race, Class, and Gender: An Anthology. 7th Edition* (Belmont: Wadsworth, 2010), 15.
307 David Rutz, "MSNBC's Joy Reid Calls Clarence Thomas 'Uncle Clarence,'" The Washington Free Beacon online, Accessed November 5, 2020, https://freebeacon. com/media/msnbcs-joy-reid-calls-slurs-clarence-thomas-as-uncle-clarence.
308 Richard Delgado and Jean Stefancic, *Critical Race Theory: An Introduction, Third edition* (Manhattan: New York University Press, 2001), 174.

that experiences oppression. All critical social justice is really saying is the majority group causes inequalities to exist because they say so, and you can't question it. In cult-like fashion, Woke critical social justice indoctrinates you with their authoritarian-like epistemological system, and if you diverge from it, you're part of the problem—you're a racist.

This is a logical consequence of abandoning Scripture as the source of truth in society. When there is no basis for God in society and in our politics, and Providence is rejected, there is no ability to justify why one should be richer than another or why there should be authorities in place over subjects. Rather, a godless foundation for knowledge and relationships would result in revolution, such as in the French Revolution. A rejection of the Bible and of God in our relations naturally rejects the power structures of society. Bavinck says:

> Instead, everything has to be made equal, smoothed out, leveled. (And the guillotine is the instrument to accomplish this.) This requires everything to be trimmed and cut away until what remains is equal in all respects. This effort has to reach far back and deep into history. In reality, however, nothing remains. The revolutionary view is false. We have to understand in the relations in which we stand, naturally and historically.[309]

Woke repeats the same error of revolution because the doctrine of knowledge is devoid of God and Scripture as the source of true knowledge. In Christianity, only God determines ultimate truth and moral authority.

WOKE HEGEMONY DOGMA VS. CHRISTIAN THEOLOGY PROPER, CREATION, AND PROVIDENCE

Woke dogma is dominated by power structure and the assumption that nearly all power structures in the Western world are unjust, oppressive, and racist and ought to be deconstructed. As one observes the endless Woke dogma,

---

309 Bavinck, *Reformed Ethics*, 50.

the most emphasized theme is the concept of power. It is almost always framed in the neo-Marxist oppressor and oppressed group dualistic matrix.

Woke obsesses over the lens of power in the temporal world to the extent that it functions as the god of Woke. In Woke theory, the nature of power structures must be reordered, dismantled, and changed. In some ways, social order and power is pantheistic and even panentheistic—the god of power is within the material social structures. Power structures appear to exhibit a functional, ontological nature. They are nearly omnipotent, since oppression and injustice are totalized across all of society from the power structures. This functions as an alternative doctrine to theology proper, creation, and Providence in several important ways, as illustrated in Figure 11.

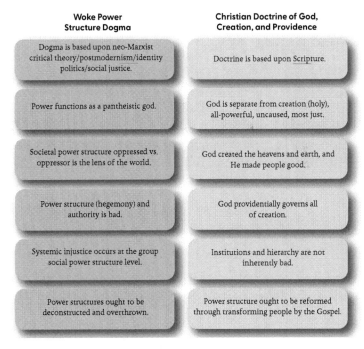

Woke Power Structure Dogma	Christian Doctrine of God, Creation, and Providence
Dogma is based upon neo-Marxist critical theory/postmodernism/identity politics/social justice.	Doctrine is based upon Scripture.
Power functions as a pantheistic god.	God is separate from creation (holy), all-powerful, uncaused, most just.
Societal power structure oppressed vs. oppressor is the lens of the world.	God created the heavens and earth, and He made people good.
Power structure (hegemony) and authority is bad.	God providentially governs all of creation.
Systemic injustice occurs at the group social power structure level.	Institutions and hierarchy are not inherently bad.
Power structures ought to be deconstructed and overthrown.	Power structure ought to be reformed through transforming people by the Gospel.

Figure 11: Woke Power Structure Dogma vs. Creation and Providence

Contrarily, the Bible reveals that God is not pantheistic nor reduced to immanent power. God is the one triune, holy, infinite, eternal, living God and set apart from creation. God is the Creator and had no beginning and has no end. God is infinitely just in His nature and omnipotent. The Westminster Confession summarizes the doctrine of God:

> I. There is but one only, (Deut. 6:4; I Cor. 8:4,6.) living, and true God: (I Thess. 1:9; Jer. 10:10.) who is infinite in being and perfection,(Job 11:7, 8, 9; Job 26:14.) a most pure spirit, (John 4:24.) invisible, (I Tim. 1:17.) without body, parts, (Deut. 4:15, 16; John 4:24, with Luke 24:39) or passions, (Acts 14:11, 15) immutable, (James 1:17; Mal. 3:6) immense, (I Kings 8:27; Jer. 23:23, 24) eternal,(Ps. 90:2; I Tim. 1:17) incomprehensible, (Ps. 145:3.) almighty, (Gen. 17:1; Rev. 4:8.) most wise, (Rom. 16:27.) most holy, (Isa. 6:3; Rev. 4:8.) most free, (Ps. 115:3.) most absolute, (Exod. 3:14.) working all things according to the counsel of His own immutable and most righteous will, (Eph. 1:11.) for His own glory; (Prov. 16:4; Rom. 11:36.) most loving, (I John 4:8, 16.) gracious, merciful, long-suffering, abundant in goodness and truth, forgiving iniquity, transgression, and sin; (Exod. 34:6, 7.) the rewarder of them that diligently seek Him; (Heb. 11:6.) and withal, most just and terrible in His judgments, (Neh. 9:32, 33.) hating all sin, (Ps. 5:5, 6.) and who will by no means clear the guilty. (Nah. 1:2, 3; Exod. 34:7).[310]

Moreover, God created the heavens and the earth and providentially rules His creation. "The LORD has established His throne in the heavens, and his kingdom rules over all" (Psalm 103:19). Woke dogma rejects the biblical doctrine of God and creation. Woke replaces the truth about God and creation with a metaphysic of social power structures. Under every rock is a plot of the oppressors to exercise and maintain power. "All texts are embedded with ideology,"says DiAngelo. "The ideology embedded in most mainstream texts functions to reproduce historical relations of unequal power."[311] Woke tends to diverge from the postmodernism rejection of metanarratives since it maintains a neo-Marxist metanarrative of oppression and power dominance among social structures. This is a common theme among critical race theory,

---

310 Westminster Divines, Ibid.
311 Sensoy and DiAngelo, 210.

a field that emerged out of legal studies in their cynical outlook of the law. Critical race theory scholar John Calmore writes, "Law, of course, is not only an instrument of social control but also a symbolic expression of dominant society."[312] Other CRT scholars agree. Crenshaw says:

> According to Bell, the traditional liberal image of law as the neutral, impersonal mediator of group conflict masks its function in producing and insulating white dominance. From this initial starting point, Bell develops a provocative, overly instrumental account of the ebb and flow of legal decisions about race which explicitly ties each important state of civil rights reform to the long-term interests of whites.[313]

While there are many examples of unfairness and injustice within society, including in the legal system, it is an exaggeration to determine this is in all elements of society. In fact, it is also unhelpful and overlooks many of the complex, interdependent factors that result in disparities and discrimination when social injustice is reduced to the critical race theory paradigm that overemphasizes racism. This is morally cynical, philosophically problematic, and unbiblically dogmatic because it effectively reduces the root cause of injustice to the critical race theory definition of racism instead of the sin. Ethnic prejudice exists, and all spheres of society are flawed because of sin in the heart of man.

Moreover, God has appointed power structures in society, such as the government, to restrain evil. Paul says, "Therefore whoever resists the authorities resists what God has appointed, and those who resist will incur judgment" (Rom. 13:2). The Bible teaches that Christians ought to submit to the authorities that God has appointed. The Bible also teaches that evil has come into the world, and the created order has suffered since the Fall (Gen.

---

312 Cornel West, Kimberle Crenshaw, Neil Gotanda, Gary Peller, and Kendall Thomas, "Critical Race Theory, Archie Shepp, and Fire Music: Securing an Authentic Intellectual Life in a Multicultural World," in *Critical Race Theory: The Key Writings that Formed the Movement* (New York: New York Press, 1995), 323.

313 Ibid, 3.

3:17). As a result, anti-Christian power structures have gained strong dominion in society. Typically, this begins in the academy and the arts. Eventually, it comes down to the public square. For example, the entertainment industry dominates the norms and values for sexuality in ways that are oppressive and exploitative for children and for adults, particularly women. In public schools, the power of the state forces the indoctrination of Darwinistic evolution with no alternative perspectives. The power structure of institutional infanticide not only oppresses unborn babies, but also, millions of babies are systemically murdered them through abortion. Marriage, the family unit, and motherhood have become victims in the public square, cinema, academy, society, etc. The modern socio-political power structure devalues traditional views on marriage, faith, parenting, gender, and sexuality. John MacArthur has made this point:

> Governmental response to the coronavirus pandemic offers more stunning examples of how far our culture has gone in losing its religion. States and counties across the nation have classified places like casinos, abortion clinics, liquor stores, and massage parlors as essential businesses, permitting them to remain open—while churches are commonly categorized as "nonessential" and kept closed. The governor of California and county officials in Los Angeles have shown a determination to keep our church closed, even while encouraging massive political protests by angry people in the streets.[314]

It is fairly certain that the government's desire to continue to keep churches closed while allowing mass riots in the streets in sheer hypocrisy and consistent with the fact that the biblical worldview is no longer the norm and is under attack.[315] Glenn Sunshine agrees:

---

314 John MacArthur, "MACARTHUR: Losing Our Religion," The Daily Wire.com, Accessed October 2, 2020, https://www.dailywire.com/news/macarthur-losing-our-religion.

315 Douglas Axe, William M. Briggs, and Jay W. Richards, *The Price of Panic: How the Tyranny of Experts Turned A Pandemic into a Catastrophe* (Washington, D.C., Regnery Publishing, 2020), 199.

> [D]uring COVID-19 restrictions, churches were prohibited from meeting in direct violation of the First Amendment while Black Lives Matter protests were permitted. In other words, freedom of peaceable assembly applied only to groups promoting approved messages. The regulatory state, on all levels, is thus the biggest threat to liberty and republican government today.[316]

The mainstream media further perpetuates moral destruction through months of lawlessness and riots—in some cases deemed as "mostly peaceful." Illiberal Big Tech censorship is equally as dangerous. In the midst of the 2020 presidential election, extraordinary amounts of conservative content were purged in clear bias, provoking a top national security advisor to describe Tech censorship as a grave threat to national security because of the obstruction of the unalienable right to free speech.[317]

Power structures do exist but not in the definitions of critical theory based upon neo-Marxism. Woke dogma goes too far and totalizes oppression across wide swaths of society. Not all power structures inflict harm upon people. There are power structures in the created order, government, the Church, and practically all forms of societal organization. This provides stability, and they exist for the good of people. Bavinck says:

> The church cannot live without order, regulation, structure, and exercise of power. Generally speaking, it is an undeniable truth that nothing can exist without order and regulation . . . This is generally acknowledged whether one considers families, businesses, armies, societies, or society at large. Anarchy does not work . . . The reality of the incarnation reminds us that Christ came not to remove us from the realities of this world but to save us in them. He came to destroy the works of the devil everywhere and to spark the acknowledgement of the

---

316 Glenn S. Sunshine, *Slaying Leviathan: Limited Government and Resistance in the Christian Tradition* (Moscow: Canon Press, 2020), 173-74.

317 Ryan Saavedra, "Top Homeland Security Official: Tech Censorship Is 'Grave Threat To National Security,'" November 2, 2020, https://www.dailywire.com/news/top-homeland-security-official-tech-censorship-is-grave-threat-to-national-security.

rights and honor of God; his reconciling and renewing activity extends as far as sin has destroyed and corrupted everything. Christ planted his kingdom in that world and made sure that it could exist in it and, like a leaven, have a transforming impact in all areas of life.[318]

It is not true that since power structures exist, they must be oppressive, harmful, or racist. Likewise, it does not mean that power structures can*not* be oppressive, harmful, or racist. Christians ought to do justice and deliver the hand of the oppressed (Jer. 22:3). However, Christians must not do so according to the indoctrination of a counterfeit religion. Woke dogma is designed to deconstruct power structures because it is assumed they *all* are unjust. Woke dogma presupposes the entire fabric of society is oppressive and must be deconstructed. Critical theory wrongly totalizes evil across all traditional power structures and incites revolution against them according to the neo-Marxist paradigm. While there are injustices in Western society that ought to be rectified, there is much good that ought to be preserved. Rebellion against these institutions that God has providentially ordained threatens the peace and civility of society.

The government is ordained from God for the goodwill of the commonwealth. "Let every person be subject to the governing authorities. For there is no authority except from God, and those that exist have been instituted by God" (Rom. 13:1). Governing authorities are God's ministers and do not make laws unto themselves because their rule is not autonomous. There is also a distinction between the authority of the Church and all other powers in society. Bavinck says:

Power and authority, in other areas—family, business, school, society, state—comes from God as the creator of heaven and earth (Romans 13:1), but ecclesiastical power comes directly from God as the Father of our Lord Jesus Christ (1 Cor. 12:28;

---

318 Bavinck, *Reformed Dogmatics*, 672.

Eph. 4:11; Acts 20:28) and is therefore completely free and independent from all other earthly powers. It is, in short, a spiritual power.[319]

There are biblical reasons to not obey governments in certain cases due to the nature of sin in the world. The Church has the authority from the Lord Jesus to disregard unjust governments who institute laws that conflict with the Gospel of Christ and the law of God. In such cases, Christians are commanded to "obey God rather than men" (Acts 5:29). Frederic Bastiat puts it well: "When law and morality contradict each other, the citizen has the cruel alternative of either losing his moral sense or losing respect for the law."[320]

Woke dogma wrongly abandons grace and politicizes nature. This leaves no standard to adequately understand motive, actions, and character as qualities to determine if power is oppressive or not. Bad motives, evil character, and wicked actions help explain why power is used to oppress victims. Power in and of itself does not provide sufficient causality for injustice. Woke critical theory politicizes nature, so it sees nature only in terms of power dominance. It is unfortunate to view all of society through the grim lens of politicized power structures. Critical theory is obsessed with power structures but never recognizes God, Who ordains, preserves, and is sovereign Ruler of power structures. The psalmist says, "For kingship belongs to the LORD, and he rules over the nations" (Psalm 22:28).

The fundamental reason why critical theorists do not recognize God is because their mind is set upon the flesh—earthly power structures. Paul says, "For the mind that is set on the flesh is hostile to God, for it does not submit to God's law; indeed, it cannot" (Rom. 8:7). Woke dogma reduces the hermeneutic for the interpretation of the world to power. It omits the complexities of life, people, culture, sin nature, Satan, and the God Who ordains and rules all power in the world. Critical theory is an unbiblical, simplistic, undiversified

---

319 Ibid.
320 Frederic Bastiat, *The Law* (Hudson: Foundation for Economic Education, 1847/2007), 7.

system of thought hyper-dependent on a narrow view of understanding power structures.

The unbiblical Woke dogma dominated by the natural world omits the spiritual. Scripture maintains consistency between the spiritual and the natural, between grace and the material. "Insomuch as the world consists of heaven and earth," says Bavinck, "and humans consist of soul and body, so also sanctity and glory, virtue and happiness, the moral and the natural world order ought finally to be harmoniously united."[321] The starting point for Woke is nature, and the end is deconstruction of nature. The starting point for Christianity is God; and the end is unity between man and God, whereby the world will be free from sin and the effects of sin, error (John 6:45), death (Luke 20:36), sickness, poverty, suffering (Matt. 5:4; Rev. 7:16-17, 21:4) and corruption (1 Cor. 15:42) through redemption in Christ. John says, "'He will wipe away every tear from their eyes, and death shall be no more, neither shall there be mourning, nor crying, nor pain anymore, for the former things have passed away'" (Rev. 21:4).

---

321 Bavinck, 16636.

CHAPTER TEN

WOKE ANTHROPOLOGY DOGMA VS. CHRISTIAN DOCTRINE OF MAN

FALSE ANTHROPOLOGIES HAVE LED TO much of the errors and confusion of our generation. Dr. Steven Wellum captures the issue provokingly: "Are we creatures of dignity because we are created in God's image? Or are we merely animals, by-products of an impersonal evolutionary process, things that can be, technologically speaking, manipulated and re-fashioned for whatever ends we deem best?"[322]

This chapter will discuss this matter particularly from the Woke anthropology dogma. Not all of the ideologies discussed in this chapter have the same historical origin. However, Woke anthropology has the common neo-Marxist oppressed and oppressor dynamic. This is the most pronounced in critical race theory or critical social justice and can also be observed in feminism, LGBTQIA+, and abortion ideology. This chapter will demonstrate how these ideologies fundamentally diverge from the Christian doctrine of humanity.

---

322 Stephen J. Wellum, "Editorial: The Urgent Need for a Theological Anthropology Today," *Southern Baptist Theological Journal 13, no. 2* (Summer 2009), 2.

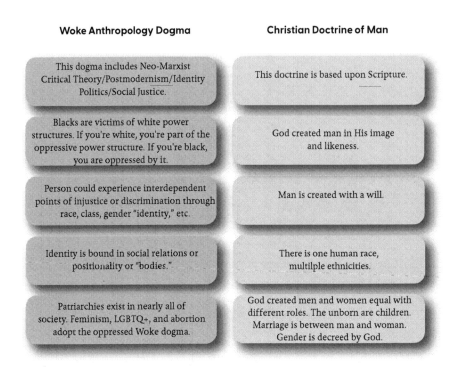

Woke Anthropology Dogma

This dogma includes Neo-Marxist Critical Theory/Postmodernism/Identity Politics/Social Justice.

Blacks are victims of white power structures. If you're white, you're part of the oppressive power structure. If you're black, you are oppressed by it.

Person could experience interdependent points of injustice or discrimination through race, class, gender "identity," etc.

Identity is bound in social relations or positionality or "bodies."

Patriarchies exist in nearly all of society. Feminism, LGBTQ+, and abortion adopt the oppressed Woke dogma.

Christian Doctrine of Man

This doctrine is based upon Scripture.

God created man in His image and likeness.

Man is created with a will.

There is one human race, multilple ethnicities.

God created men and women equal with different roles. The unborn are children. Marriage is between man and woman. Gender is decreed by God.

Figure 12: Woke Anthropology Dogma vs. Christian Doctrine of Man

Humans are one race that has descended from Adam, the one human father. In fact, every human being after the Flood descends from Noah, too, but he does not have the same historical or theological significance as Adam. The failure to affirm this truth has led to ethnic prejudice and ethnic superiority. Beeke and Smalley rightly point out, "If we treat Genesis as a collection of myths or metaphors, then we seriously damage our ability to stand against ethnic prejudice and hatred . . . The answer to this problem is to return to the doctrine of our fundamental unity as one human race descended form one human father, Adam."[323] Modern theories that attempt to address issues of ethnic prejudice are inadequate because they do not affirm this fundamental truth. By the end of the

---

323 Joel R. Beeke and Paul M. Smalley, *Man and Christ, Vol. 2*, Reformed Systematic Theology (Wheaton: Crossway, 2020), 149.

twentieth century, legal scholars had begun to develop critical race theory (CRT). CRT originated from a critique of critical legal studies focused on colorblindness and discrimination. It argues against classical liberalism and claims white people have unequally benefited from civil rights legal casework. Mocombe says:

> Against Critical Legal Studies, CRT theorists recognize the racial, gender, and sexual power dynamics by which Western institutions were constituted, and seek to apply the negative dialectics of critical theory to the intersection of race, law, and power in the pursuit of racial and ethnic equality in Western society.[324]

"Unlike traditional civil rights discourse," says Delgado, "which stresses incrementalism and step-by-step progress, critical race theory questions the very foundations of the liberal order, including equality theory, legal reasoning, Enlightenment rationalism, and neutral principles of constitutional law."[325] Built upon critical legal studies, CRT also stems from radical feminism, civil rights ideas, and cultural empowerment. By this time, the legal scholar Kimberle Crenshaw applied the hegemonic power structure ideas from critical theory to race and taught that black people are victims of the white power structures. She took this a step further in coining the term "intersectionality," meaning that a person could experience interdependent points of injustice or discrimination through race, class, gender, sexual orientation, etc. Robin DiAngelo writes:

> A critical approach to social justice refers to specific theoretical perspectives that recognize that society is stratified (i.e. divided and unequal) in significant and far-reaching ways along social group lines that include race, class, gender, sexuality, and ability. Critical social justice recognizes inequality as deeply embedded in the fabric of society (i.e. as structural), and actively seeks

---

324 Paul Mocombe, "Against Critical Race Theory" *Ethnic studies review*, 37, no. 1 (2017), 1-4.
325 Delgado and Stefancic, 3.

to change this. The definition we apply is rooted in a critical theoretical approach.[326]

In summary, the core problem in critical theory is being part of the hegemony or power structure.

There are several problems with this approach. The first problem is that it removes human responsibility. Inequalities, oppression, and ethnic prejudice do not exist because of institutional "racism," privilege, and the unequal social hegemony. The fundamental reason oppression and ethnic prejudice exist are because of sin. Like all sins, ethnic prejudice and oppression are the consequences of the Fall of man and transcends across all peoples and places. The ancient world is full of examples of oppression, such as the enslavement of the Israelites by the Egyptians detailed in the book of Exodus, the Assyrians in Northern Israel, and the Babylonians in Judah. Solomon wrote, "Again I saw all the oppressions that are done under the sun. And behold, the tears of the oppressed, and they had no one to comfort them! On the side of their oppressors there was power, and there was no one to comfort them" (Eccl. 4:1). Biblically, oppression and injustice transcend the American context, are universal in humanity since the Fall and are sinful.

In Woke dogma, oppression and injustice has a narrower scope (primarily in America), different definitions, and dissimilar solutions. For CRT, *only* whites or the hegemony can be racist. According to the Bible, everyone is a sinner, and ethnic prejudice is a sin. The primary emotions expressed in CRT are guilt and anger. The Christian expresses the fruits of the Spirit—love, joy, peace, etc. (Gal. 5:22-23). The way to unity for CRT is to revolt and build power. The way for Christian unity is through Christ, sanctification, preaching the Gospel in all the earth, and loving our neighbors. The goal of CRT is to revolt and overthrow the hegemony to bring in an equitable utopia by works. The goal of the Gospel is primarily to save sinners from Hell through the redemption in Jesus Christ.

---

326 Sensoy and DiAngelo, xx.

"PRIVILEGE"

Peggy McIntosh was likely one of the first to coin the term "privilege" in 1988 in the context of critical theory and "white privilege." It is part of the critical social justice dogma of humanity. "From a critical social justice perspective," says DiAngelo, "privilege is defined as systemically conferred dominance and the institutional processes by which the beliefs and values of the dominant group are 'made normal' and universal."[327] This definition assumes "dominant" groups exist. This is a subtle way to divide society between dominant and dominated, similar to oppressor and oppressed or majority and minority. All human lives have value"; "people have a right to private property"; "freedom of religion" is essential; "classical democratic norms should be recognized"; "Christianity is still the world's largest religion": these are all considered the dominant beliefs. DiAngelo's claims are contradictory to Scripture.

The Bible does not teach Christianity as an oppressor religion bent on the dominance of the minority. Instead, the Bible teaches God is the Helper to the oppressed. The psalmist says, "The Lord is a stronghold for the oppressed, a stronghold in times of trouble" (Psalm 9:9). Those who are given authority and power by God over others and do what is right ought to be honored, says Peter. "Submit yourselves for the Lord's sake to every human institution, whether it be to the emperor as supreme, or to governors as sent by him to punish those who do evil and to praise those who do good" (1 Peter 2:13-14).

Furthermore, private property must be respected because it helps preserve liberty and goodwill within society. It is a possession that is obtained through work or by gift, such as an inheritance for the purpose of living, prosperity, and stewarding dominion in the earth. Bavinck puts it well: "Some possession is indispensable; otherwise all freedom is lost and no love can be practiced. For loving is giving, and when one has nothing, one can give nothing."[328]

---

327 Sensoy and DiAngelo, 80.
328 Bavinck, *Reformed Ethics*, 231.

IDENTITY

Critical social justice places an incorrect emphasis on societal relations. These philosophies raise socialization to the level of ontology or the identity of one's existence. In Christianity, Christians are children of God led by the Spirit (Rom. 8:14). In Woke religion, people are defined by their social identity. Lindsay and Nayna point this out about social justice. They write, "We are children of society, fashioned by its social constructions and the power dynamics they maintain."[329] This is widely published by critical social justice advocates. DiAngelo states, "Our socialization is the foundation of our identity.Thus to consider that we have been socialized to participate in systems of oppression that we don't condone is to challenge our very sense of who we are."[330]

In a similar way that Derrida deconstructed the meaning of language, Foucault deconstructed knowledge, fusing it to power. Woke anthropology is heavily influenced by Michael Foucault's postmodern concept of "biopower," a political technique to control "bodies" of populations.[331] Connecting Foucault's idea to critical social justice, Lindsay argues:

> This concept, then, is what lies at the heart of the Critical Social Justice use of the term "bodies" in place of "people," from a Theoretical perspective (as opposed merely to a rhetorical one). The view must be, at bottom, that what's relevant about the body is how it is socially constructed so that (sociocultural and political) power might act upon it. Thus, where systemic power is believed to be relevant to the "control" of bodies, including by naming them as they are, the body as a social construct becomes the most relevant object about a person who is being controlled through it.[332]

This social construction in Woke religion actually dehumanizes people because identity is based upon power dynamics and discourses that redefine

---

329 Lindsay and Nayna, Ibid.
330 Sensoy and DiAngelo, 185.
331 Michel Foucault, *The History of Sexuality* (New York: Vintage Books, 1978), 140-44.
332 James Lindsay, "Bodies," New Discourses.com, September 17, 2020, https://newdiscourses.com/tftw-bodies.

people as "bodies." This is where the idea of "spaces" came into vogue. "Black spaces" or "LGBTQIA+ spaces" or "safe spaces" are the Woke application of Foucault's philosophy.

The foundation of the identity of persons is not socialization, societal relationships, or any dimension between peoples. The foundation of the identity of people is the image and likeness of God, since we *are* His image and likeness of God (Gen. 1:26, 9:6; Luke 3:38; Acts 17:28; 1 Cor. 11:7; James 3:9).[333] "When God created man, he made him in the likeness of God" (Gen. 5:1). As Christians, our identity is in Christ, since He was made in our likeness, and we have been conformed to Christ's image, becoming like God again (Rom. 8:29; 1 Cor. 15:49; 2 Cor. 3:18; Phil. 3:21; Eph. 4:24; Col. 3:10; 1 John 3:2).[334] "Now you are the body of Christ and individually members of it" (1 Cor. 12:26-27). As Christians, our identity is so bound to God that our bodies are temples of His Spirit. God purchases Christians by the blood of His Son. Paul says "Or do you not know that your body is a temple of the Holy Spirit within you, whom you have from God? You are not your own, for you were bought with a price. So glorify God in your body" (1 Cor. 6:19-20).

According to postmodern philosophy, "identity" cannot *rise above* man, so it is not surprising that identity would be defined based on the relationships to man. The postmodern man cannot accept this because the Bible has been thrown out the window. In postmodernism, man is merely cells running into each other, nothing more. Yet Woke religion demands "justice." One wonders how a system that demands justice is consistent with a postmodern, naturalist, metaphysical view of reality. Justice is a moral category that is impossible to hold with postmodern skeptic assumptions.

PATRIARCHY

Patriarchy means "father rule," derived from the Greek work πατριάρχης (*patriarches*). According to Zachary Garris, "It describes the practice of men

---

333   Bavinck, *Reformed Dogmatics*, 345.
334   Ibid.

providing for and protecting women and children, as well as men leading in the church and society."[335] However, the patriarchy is a not an acceptable idea in today's society because it is widely misunderstood. It is very common for the biblical patriarchy to be misrepresented as misogynistic or that it subjugates women as ontologically inferior, even though there is no basis for this claim. DiAngelo says, "Patriarchy is the belief in the inherent superiority of men and the creation of institutions based on that belief. Examples of patriarchal ideology worldwide are a male god; the father as the head of the household; males as authority in all social realms such as law, government, religion and culture; women as inherently inferior to men and the property of men."[336]

This definition is problematic because it assumes since men have authority, women are inferior. Male headship does not mean men are superior to women in value. Since men and women are created in the image and likeness of God, they are equal in value, dignity, and worth (Gen. 1:27). Headship is with respect to authority, gender, and roles. Man is not woman, and woman is not man, since they have different genders but the same ontological value created in God's image. Gender is a fixed order in creation, not merely a personal mindset or a social construct.[337]

God has revealed Himself in masculine terms because He has authority over man. In a real sense, God is our Patriarch because He rules over us. The patriarch is revealed in other parts of the Bible. Adam had rule and authority over his wife and was held accountable for the sin of Eve. Beeke and Smalley point out:

> The Lord God came seeking the fallen couple but specifically "called unto Adam, and said unto him, 'Where art thou?' (Gen. 3:9). The first to receive the command was the first to be called to account for breaking it—another sign of leadership. God's

---

335 Zachary M. Garris, *Masculine Christianity* (Santa Clara: Zion Press), 77.
336 Sensoy and DiAngelo, 103.
337 Beeke and Smalley, 210.

punishment on the woman aimed at her roles as a mother and wife, but his punishment on the man brought the more global consequence of a curse upon the ground and death upon mankind (vv. 16-19). It was Adam, not Eve, who stood as the representative of the entire race and whose disobedience brought death and condemnation (Rom. 5:12-19).[338]

Adam was accountable for the entire human race because he had covenant authority. Abraham, Isaac, and Jacob ruled their families. God's leaders in the Old Testament were men, except for a few women prophetesses who did not have formal leadership roles in Israel and did not prophesy publicly but only to small groups.[339] It is important to note how the patriarchy played a role in the family. The tenth commandment assumes male headship, since it states, "'You shall not covet your neighbor's wife" (Exod. 20:17). Husbands were required as the head to provide and protect for their wife (Exod. 21:10). Much forgotten today in the feminist society, fathers had authority over their unmarried daughters, who were under their authority until the headship was transferred in marriage to the husband (Num. 30).

Also common today is to imagine an effeminate Jesus. Jesus, the Son of God, took on a male body, grew into an adult man, and laid down His life for His bride. His resurrected body will always be male in Heaven. Elders and deacons are offices of the Church reserved for qualified men. Their fundamental reason for this is because offices of the Church hold authority.

God has established the patriarchy and created men to rule in the home, church, and society. Garris is correct: "God has given us authority structures in this world, with Himself at the top. He has given civil governments authority over citizens, pastors authority over the church members, husbands authority over wives, and parents authority over children . . . Someone must rule, and God has assigned this task to men."[340]

---

338 Ibid, 212-13.
339 Ibid, 83.
340 Ibid, 101.

Secular society has traded the patriarchy for the matriarchy and egalitarian feminism. The primary role of man is to provide for and protect his family, while the primary role of woman is to be a helper to man.[341] Woman helps man as a companion and bearer children. Adam "called his wife's name Eve, because she was the mother of all living" (Gen. 3:20).

FEMINISM

Feminism is a toxic ideology that is becoming increasingly connected to Woke social justice because it focuses on tearing down the authority structure of the family unit. Zachary Garris is exactly right when he says, "Feminism is the twisted idea that a woman is free when serving her employer but a slave when serving her family. And this has all been to women's detriment."[342] To understand feminist ideology in our contemporary context, we must recognize feminism has a long history typically categorized into three waves beginning in the nineteenth century.

The feminism movement centered on political equality and the social liberation of women and has a strong impact on society today. Egalitarian roots that were later applied to feminism can be traced back to the Jacobin party that carried out the Reign of Terror in 1793-1794 in the French Revolution.[343] The first wave of feminism coined the term in the 1880s and sought to make the economic, social, and political status of men and women equal—most notably the right for women to vote.

There are religious roots to feminism in the Seventh Day Adventist church, founded by Ellen Gould White in 1863, and the Christian Science movement, founded by Mary Baker Eddy in 1879—both unorthodox groups.[344] The second wave of feminism began in the 1960s. "This wave fought for a woman's right to initiate divorce proceedings, no-fault divorce, a woman's

---

341 Ibid, 110-13.
342 Ibid, 24.
343 Ibid, 8.
344 Ibid, 10.

right to abortion and equitable wages,"[345] says Garris. Feminism continued to evolve as secular progressivism influenced the movement. Hoggard-Creegan says, "The twentieth-century movement was undergirded at least in part by a new Marxist inspired understanding of the alienation and oppressiveness of much menial and household work, especially that done by many women."[346] This resulted in the ideology that women need liberation from the oppressive patriarchal structures of society and male-dominated culture norms.

The third wave of feminism began around the 1990s and is more extreme that the previous two waves because it is connected with the push for homosexuality and empowering sexual identity. Garris writes, "Third-wave feminism has certainly succeeded in accomplishing its goals, with the U.S. Supreme Court legalizing same-sex marriage in all 50 states in the 2015 case *Obergefell v. Hodges*, followed by the extension of anti-discrimination laws to homosexuality and transgenderism in the 2020 case *Bostock v. Clayton County* (both of which are entirely lawless rulings)."[347]

Ultimately, the goal of contemporary feminism is to deconstruct the "oppressive" patriarchy into a purely egalitarian society, and the most radical forms have targeted the elimination of family and religion to accomplish this since the two are interconnected.[348] The Bible condemns the abuse and oppression of all human beings, including women, who are created with value, dignity, and worth. Sexual harassment, domestic violence, and the oppression of women are sinful. However, feminism diverges from the authority of Scripture teaching in several ways. First, from the beginning, feminism has maintained anti-Christian positions. Garris argues that "the women's movement, along with its advocacy for women's suffrage, was tied up with a rejection of historic and biblical Christianity."[349] He points out that Elizabeth Cady Stanton, a radical early feminist, rejected passages of the Bible that were deemed unfavorable to

---

345 Ibid, 16.
346 Elwell, 445.
347 Garris, *Masculine Christianity*, 19.
348 Ibid.
349 Ibid, 13.

women, believed Scripture on women's subordination were evil, and thought women had the right to be present at all councils of the Church.[350]

Second, contemporary feminism adds that the male patriarchy ought to be eliminated in many portions of society, including "traditional gender roles in marriage or assumed color preferences in children's nurseries and clothing."[351] Third, large portions of biblical texts are denied, and new theological categories are created.[352] Women are hardly seen as anything other than victims of the male-dominated patriarchy. The source of sin for the critical feminist is males, not the Fall in the Garden. Nor is there recognition or submission to the biblical roles of men and women. Feminism effectively erases the God-ordained roles of distinction between men and women. For the sake of egalitarianism, all diversity and distinction are destroyed. This is an attack against the Word of God, against the roles of men and women in the Church, and against God, Who ordains them.

For example, the Bible explicitly teaches that only men can assume the role of elders (1 Tim. 3; Titus 1). Feminists usurp Scripture's authority here and nearly every other place where men and women's roles are different. Feminist dogma requires the roles must be absolutely the same. It is an error to assume that roles determine value or equality, which they certainly do not. Dignity and worth between men and women are equal based on their ontology, being created in the *imago Dei*. Feminism is a plain departure from biblical truth, given the God-ordained roles of men and women in marriage, that many ought to love their wives like Christ loved the Church and that women ought to respect their husbands.

The near-obsession of critical theory on liberation does not explain why there is little-to-no emphasis on important moral perfections, such as integrity, sexual purity, civility, forgiveness, mercy, and love. The inconsistencies of secular movements tend to influence theology as well. John Frame comments:

---

350 Garris, *Masculine Christianity*, 11-13.
351 Shenvi and Sawyer, Ibid.
352 Elwell, 445.

It is remarkable that theological errors, including errors about God's being and actions, are often reflexes of movements in the secular culture. For example, the concept of libertarian free will has dominated philosophy (both process and analytic schools of thought) in the late twentieth century. Process theology and open theism followed in the wake of that movement. Secular feminism made great gains in the general culture in the 1960s and 1970s. Following that, theologians tried to show that they could be feminists too.[353]

The errors of feminism impacted marriage and the family unit, too. During the first wave of feminism, Theologian B.B. Warfield (1851-1921) said:

[T]he difference in conclusions between Paul and the feminist movement of today is rooted in a fundamental difference in their points of view relative to the constitution of the human race. To Paul, the human race is made up of families . . . To the feminist movement the human race is made up of individuals; a woman is just another individual by the side of the man, and it can see no reason for any difference in dealing with the two.[354]

Beginning in the 1960s, the second wave of feminism further impacted the family unit. "[T]he positive image of the nuclear family was questioned by feminism," says Taylor, "and the new expressive culture and sexual revolution of the 1960s."[355] In the divergence from thousands of years of history, modern secular culture devalues the role of biblical womanhood, particularly in the home as a mother of her children in the context of God-ordained marriage and the family unit. In fact, since people are not meant to live in isolation, the display of virtue in the morality is in the spheres of society. The biblical communion between husband and wife in marriage displays the virtues of love, truth, purity, kindness, sacrifice, honor, and respect.

---

353 John Frame, *The Doctrine of the Christian Life (A Theology of Lordship)* (Phillipsburg: P&R Publishing, 2008), 423.
354 B.B. Warfield, "Paul On Women Speaking in Church," October 30, 1919, *The Presbyterian.*
355 Taylor, 10791.

Likewise, the biblical communion between parents, children, brothers, and sisters functions like a small community, or micro-unit, within society that displays God's moral perfections of justice, righteousness, goodness, and love. One of the quickest ways to undermine civilization is to destroy the moral nature of marriage and the family unit. This takes place through adultery, polygamy, homosexuality, abortion, moral hazard laws, bad policy,[356] and other forms of immorality, which corrupt the moral character of these spheres of society. Instead of children flourishing like olive shoots around the table in the home within the family in society, they are murdered in their mother's womb. In Western society, children are considered inconvenient, and abortion has been normalized to the horrific rate of over a million babies a year, which is genocide (Psalm 139:13; Jer. 1:4-5). Aborting children is no different than sacrificing children in the ancient world to Baal. The deception is still a lie from Satan, and the result is still the murder of babies, except on an unimaginable scale of millions of unborn children.

Furthermore, for women in Western culture, the idea of a successful career is the ideal, and traditional nurturing of children as a stay-at-home mother is looked down upon.[357] Part of this phenomenon can be attributed to the feminism movement and the category errors that roles define value. In secular society heavily influenced by feminism, the social capital of women in a vocational career is much higher than a mother rearing children as a stay-at-home housewife. The goal is to remove the roles to the degree that there is no distinction. There is a cost to this aspect of Woke religion in society—the destruction of the family unit. Children need nurture from their parents—fathers and mothers in the home. Paul writes, "And so train the young women to love their husbands and children, to be self-controlled, pure, working at home, kind, and submissive to their own husbands, that the word of God may not be reviled" (Titus 2:4-5). Bavinck says:

---

356 Garris, *Masculine Christianity*, 22.
357 Ibid, 3.

Community exists next in the family, especially in the love of parents and children. Parents are the givers and their children are the receivers; parental love is the greater. Parents are to nurture their children, initially by requiring unquestioning obedience, but eventually training them to obey freely. Parents have authority and power over the children, who in turn show piety toward their parents.

When parenting is contracted out to the state, then the government assumes the role. This is problematic because the purpose of government is not to nurture children—that is the role of parents (Deut. 6:6-9; Eph. 6:4). According to Zachary Garris, this has had had negative impacts on society:

> Of course, it is not only the family that has suffered. The church and state consist of families, and both institutions are weakened by the breakdown of the family unity. The decline of men has coincided with the rise of the welfare state, as civil government seeks to provide financial assistance—and thus fills the provisionary role of the father—for children born outside of wedlock. Such policies have not only rewarded (and thus encouraged) bad practices, but they have also usurped the charity role traditionally reserved for the church.[358]

Biblically, the government is an agent of justice with the power of the law and the sword to protect the goodwill of the people and constrain evil, so that human flourishing continues (Rom. 13:4). Bavinck writes, "The state compels by force in order to confine sin within the domain of the private life and thus has great moral value. The government is the conscience of the state."[359] Similarly, the Puritan divines wrote, "I. God, the supreme Lord and King of all the world, hath ordained civil magistrates, to be, under Him, over the people, for His own glory, and the public good: and, to this end, hath armed them with the power of the

---

358 Garris, *Masculine Christianity*, 2.
359 Bavinck, *Reformed Ethics*, 233.

sword, for the defense and encouragement of them that are good, and for the punishment of evil doers."[360]

The framers of the Westminster Confession accurately deduce from Scripture that all human authority is derived from God, including civil authority. God is the Source of all authority or ministries on behalf of God, Who ordained them, including the civil magistrate, the Church, and the family unit.[361] Egalitarians reject authority, despise hierarchy, and, therefore, rebel against God, Who has placed authority structures in the world. Garris points out some of the authority structures God has ordained: "Men have authority over their wives in the marriage covenant, parents have authority over their children, elders have authority over the congregation in Christ's church, and civil officials have authority over citizens. Of course, authority can be abused, but this does not change the fact that authority still exists."[362]

Each of these authorities and powers instituted by God has distinct roles designed by God for the good of people. The Confession reminds us of the role of the civil magistrate:

> It is the duty of civil magistrates to protect the person and good name of all their people, in such an effectual manner as that no person be suffered, either upon pretense of religion or infidelity, to offer any indignity, violence, abuse, or injury to any other person whatsoever: and to take order, that all religious and ecclesiastical assemblies be held without molestation or disturbance.[363]

When God's design for these powers, authorities, and institutions are not followed biblically, the result is sin, groaning for the people, and wickedness (Deut. 28:15-68; 2 Chron. 7:14). Christians have a moral obligation toward the State that includes the doctrine of the lesser magistrate, compassion,

---

360 Westminster Divines, Ibid.
361 Toby Sumpter, "A Brief Primer on God's Ordained Spheres of Authority," CrossPolitic. com, Accessed October 29, 2020, https://crosspolitic.com/a-brief-primer-on-gods-or-dained-spheres-of-authority.
362 Garris, *Masculine Christianity*, 8-9.
363 "Of the Civil Magistrate," The Westminster Confession online, Accessed November 1, 2020, https://www.creeds.net/Westminster/c23.htm.

peace, and prayerful supplications. Christians have a duty to obey God when the State commands that which God forbids or forbids what the Bible commands.[364] Christians "must obey God rather than men" (Acts 5:29). Lower-ranking civil authorities have this duty, too. Matthew Trewhella writes, "John Knox for example, in his *Appelation* written to nobles of Scotland in 1558, cites over seventy passages of Scripture to support the doctrine. Knox insisted that the nobles, as lesser magistrates, were responsible to protect the innocent and oppose those who made unjust laws or decrees."[365]

The doctrine of the lesser magistrate declares "that when the superior or higher civil authority makes unjust/immoral laws or decrees, the lessor or lower ranking civil authority has both a right and duty to refuse obedience to that superior authority."[366] Pietism has infected the Church with the idea that Christianity should be a mere private affair and that God's law has no place in government. Steven Ozment is right on this point: "Reform that existed only in pamphlets and sermons, and not also in law and institutions, would remain a private affair, confined to all intents and purposes within the minds of preachers and pamphleteers."[367]

A similar problem occurs when men abandon the family unit and fatherhood. Fathers are commanded, "Fathers, do not provoke your children to anger, but bring them up in the discipline and instruction of the Lord" (Eph. 6:4). Women are left to fulfill the role of the father *and* the role of the mother. This places a massive burden on the mother to provide the nurture required for her children and the resources necessary for their wellbeing that ought to have been provided primarily by the father. The father also provides security and safety and fulfills the role of admonisher in the home. The role of parents is to "train up a child in the way he should go; even when he is old he will not depart

---

364 Exodus 1:15-21; Daniel 6; Matthew 2:1-11; Acts 5:29.
365 Matthew J. Trewhella, *The Doctrine of the Lesser Magistrates: A Proper Resistance to Tyranny and a Repudiation of Unlimited Obedience to Civil Government* (Create Space Independent Publishing Platform, 2013), 3.
366 Ibid, 2.
367 Steven Ozment, *Protestants: The Birth of a Revolution* (New York: Doubleday, 1992), 23.

from it" (Prov. 22:6). These biblical instructions are rooted in the supreme love of God and are to be obeyed through the sanctified desire. Shedd writes:

> When husbands are commanded to "love their wives" (Col. 3:19) and wives to "love their husbands and children" (Titus 2:4), they are commanded to love "in the Lord" . . . The instinctive affection as sanctified by a connection and union with the religion affection of supreme love of God is what is enjoined. The same is true of the love and obedience of children toward their parents (Col. 3:20), of the love and care of parents toward their children (Col. 3:21), of the relation of the citizen to the state (Rom. 13:5; 1 Pet. 2:13-14) . . . None of these are commanded merely as natural instinctive desires and affections, but as sanctified instinctive desires and affections.[368]

Contrarily, pagan feminism has no such transcendent love in view and is instead rooted in natural religion of the unsanctified will. The biblical family unit requires both the father and the mother to fulfill their respective roles. This is not always possible as a result of providential hindrances or the result of sin, but these are not the biblical norm. In the case where a father rejects his roles in the family unit, the mother, most likely, has to rely on either the Church (which is more suited than the State for this role), the State, or private business.

When the culture redefines roles of women and the institution of the family unit, as a general rule, bad consequences follow. The Bible as the source of truth has largely been abandoned, and Woke religion has filled the vacuum of knowledge with error, especially as it relates to the doctrine of man. Woke feminism is, on its face, antithetical to Christianity, and the consequential cost of embracing it has been devastating to the Church and Western civilization as a whole. Garris captures the practical cost well:

> Yet wives working full time means home life is not properly cared for—there are fewer family meals together, daycare and

---

368 Shedd, 511.

public schools become more appealing, and technological devices are given to children as a substitute for parental attention. Further, many men are foregoing marriage because they do not want to marry a woman who acts like a man. They want to marry a woman who will take care of the home and bear children.[369]

Christians must never sacrifice biblical motherhood and the family unit on the altar of feminism. The biblical family unit is essential to the Church and is the cornerstone of Western civilization. Sadly, the Church has become effeminate, which is one of the reasons why evangelicals are increasingly embracing Woke ideology. Woke social justice and feminism both rebel against the authority structures God has ordained in creation. Ultimately, feminism is a destructive ideology, and the Church has failed to address it. Christian men and women ought to embrace their God-ordained roles and biological sex in obedience to God. Christian men, especially pastors, must combat effeminate teaching and practices in the Church.

LGBTQIA+

At a town hall running up to the 2020 presidential election, the former vice president, now-president Joe Biden was asked his views on the subject of transgenderism. Biden responded, "The idea that an 8-year-old child or a 10-year-old child decides to, 'You know, I decided that I want to be transgender, that's what I think I'd like to be, it would make my life a lot easier.' There should be zero discrimination."[370] The 2015 Supreme Court ruling in *Obergefell v. Hodges* that legalized same-sex marriage nationwide has led to the increase of transgender ideology and has become the central matter within LGBT activism. In fact, transgender surgeries to alter sex organs were four times

---

369 Garris, *Christian Masculinity*, 24.
370 Brandon Showalter, "Christian leaders react to Joe Biden's support for 8-y-o kids iden-
     tifying as transgender," Christian Post.com, Accessed October 16, 2020, https://www.
     christianpost.com/news/biden-supports-kids-identifying-as-transgender-christians-
     react.html.

as common in 2014 than in 2000.[371] In the last decade, studies show that gender dysphoria has surged in the United States by one thousand percent.[372] According to Abigail Shrier, the state of California enacted a law that could result in civil punishment for healthcare workers who do not use patients' requested gender pronouns.[373] Similar unconstitutional laws were brought to bear on employers, landlords, and business owners in New York.[374] Having conducted nearly two hundred interviews and discussions with dozens of parents with children being impacted by transgender dysphoria, she explains:

> The Western world has seen a sudden surge of adolescents claiming to have gender dysphoria and self-identifying as "transgender"... Whether or not you have an adolescent daughter, whether or not your child has fallen for this transgender craze, America has become fertile ground for this mass enthusiasm for reasons that have everything to do with our cultural frailty: parents are undermined; experts are over-relied upon; dissenters in science and medicine are intimidated; free speech truckles under renewed attack; government healthcare laws harbor hidden consequences; and an intersectional era has arisen in which the desire to escape a dominant identity encourages individuals to take cover in victim groups.[375]

She makes a clear connection of transgender dysphoria to intersectionality, thus linking it to the broader Woke social justice ideology. In fact, over ninety percent of the parents of girls who are rapidly identifying as transgender are white, demonstrating children have embraced Woke ideology to achieve

---

371 Natalie Rahhal, "Transgender surgeries on the rise as more insurers cover the operations, first-of-its-kind study," The Daily Mail.com, March 2, 2018, finds https://www.dailymail.co.uk/health/article-5455277/Transgender-surgeries-rise-insurers-cover-them.html.

372 M. Goodman and R. Nash, *Examining Health Outcomes for People Who Are Transgender* (Washington, D.C.: Patient-Centered Outcomes Research Institute, 2019), https://doi.org/10.25302/2.2019.AD.12114532.

373 Abigail Shrier, *Irreversible Damage: The Transgender Craze Seducing Our Daughters* (Washington, D.C.: Regnery Publishing, 2020), 3.

374 Ibid.

375 Shrier, 5.

victim status.[376] Transgenderism promises to eliminate discrimination and division under the flag of Woke social justice but instead destroys many young people in America, some irreversibly having surgeries that mutilate their genitals. Transgender women are also given extremely high doses of testosterone that may increase the risk of heart attack significantly.[377] Many Scripture texts reveal the wickedness of the transgender dysphoria that is impacting countless adolescents in America. One in particular that specifically applies to this issue is Paul's warning: "Look out for the dogs, look out for the evildoers, look out for those who mutilate the flesh" (Phil. 3:2). Paul is warning the Philippian church about the circumcision party who "mutilate the flesh." Likewise, there is a direct application today to the Church to watch out for the evildoers who participate in transgenderism, since an increasing practice of transgenderism is to mutilate the flesh.

Carl Truman's book *The Rise and Triumph of the Modern Self* shows that transgenderism and the broader LGBTQIA+ phenomenon is linked to the psychological ideas of men like Nietzsche, Marx, and Darwin. He writes:

> If I am whoever I think I am and if my inward sense of psychological well-being is my only moral imperative, then the imposition of external, prior, or static categories is nothing other than an act of imperialism, and attempt to restrict my freedom or to make me inauthentic. Nietzsche saw this in the nineteenth century. At the same time, Karl Marx and Charles Darwin were also stripping nature of its given metaphysical authority. In this context, transgenderism is merely the latest iteration of self-creation that becomes necessary in the wake of decreation.[378]

---

376 Lisa Littman, "Parent Reports of Adolescents and Young Adults and Perceived to Show Signs of a Rapid Onset of Gender Dysphoria," PLOS ONE 14, no. 3 (August 16, 2018), 6, Table 1, https://journals.plos.org/plosone/article?id=10.1371/journal.pone.0202330.

377 Alzahrani et al., "Cardiovascular Disease Risk Factors and Myocardial Infarction in the Transgender Population," *Circulation: Cardiovascular Quality and Outcomes,* 12, no 4 (April 5, 2019), Figure 1, https://www.ahajournals.org/doi/10.1161/CIRCOUT-COMES.119.005597.

378 Carl R. Trueman, *The Rise and Triumph of the Modern Self: Cultural Amnesia, Expressive Individualism, and the Road to Sexual Revolution* (Wheaton: Crossway, 2020), 363.

For Trueman, transgenderism is the fruit primarily of Nietzsche since it remains in continuity with anti-metaphysical thought rooted in the nineteenth century.[379] The ideas of Freud and Marx were fused with the ideology of the New Left, which resulted in the politicizing of sexual identity, particularly in the transgender movement. Trueman is correct: "[T]he fact that sex is now politics is in large measure the result of this unusual marriage, and the latest iteration of that—the transgender movement—also takes its cue from psychologizing and historicizing of human nature, combined with the now-standard leitmotif of oppression as society's imposition of its own values and norms on the individual."[380]

The marriage between Freud and Marx—or rather, the "psychologizing of oppression and the placing of it at the center of the history of human society"—did give rise to the modern individual understanding of self in the sexual revolution.[381] Kirk and Madsen unabashedly state, "We must forego the temptation to strut our gay pride publically [sic] to such an extent that we undermine our victim image."[382] Victimhood ideology is derived from critical theory, thus establishing it as part of Woke. Kirk and Madsen say as much: "Talk about racism, sexism, militarism, poverty, and all the conditions that oppress the unempowered."[383] Apparently, these relationships go back for some time. Kendi says, "Homophobia cannot be separated from racism. They've been intersected for ages."[384] As the categories of the LGBTQIA+ are intersected with racism, they may become increasingly meaningless. Trueman points out:

> It is, for example, of the nature of intersectionality to make such categories highly volatile and unstable, given its basic assertion

---

379 Ibid, 376.
380 Ibid, 263.
381 Ibid, 267.
382 Marshal Kirk and Hunter Madsen, *After the Ball: How America Will Conquer Its Fear & Hatred of Gays in the 90's* (London: Penguin Group, 1989), 183.
383 Ibid, 180.
384 Ibram X. Kendi, *How to Be an Antiracist* (London: One World, 2019), 193.

that power relations are complex relative to simple taxonomies. The debt such theory owes to Michel Foucault (and therefore to his own inspiration, Friedrich Nietzsche), with his radical questioning of all stable forms of discourse as manipulative bids for power, is evident in the work of influential gender theorists such as Judith Butler.[385]

Thus, it seems high likely that LGBTQIA+ is interconnected to the counterfeit religion of Woke.

The sexual revolution in America has left incalculable damage and carnage, particularly among young people. The average age that a person first views pornography is eleven.[386] Trans-influencers on YouTube have millions of subscribers; one of the most influential has as many as 650,000 alone.[387] As early as kindergarten, the children of America are indoctrinated through the materials, curricula, and training of gender activists.[388] Five-year-olds are introduced to the Gender Unicorn[389] and "Genderbread Person"[390] and are brainwashed that they may have a "girl brain in a boy body" from television shows like *I Am Jazz*.[391] Given that this lucrative industry preys upon America's youth, shrinks play a large role affirming transgenderism, too.[392]

The sexual revolution started in America in the 1960s and has since taken on more pronounced, organized forms. By the late 1980s, the agenda of scholars advocating for the revolution of American culture through gay rights

---

385 Trueman, 362.
386 Jane Randel and Amy Sanchez, "Parenting in the Digital Age of Pornography," Huffington Post Blog, February 26, 2016, https://www.huffpost.com/entry/parenting-in-the-digitalage-of-pornography_b_9301802.
387 Shrier, 60-64.
388 "Health Education Framework: 2019 Revision of the Health Education Framework," California Department of Education, Accessed January 26, 2021, https://www.cde.ca.gov/ci/he/cf.
389 "Gender Unicorn," Trans Student Educational Resources, Accessed January 26, 2021, http://www.transstudent.org/gender.
390 Sam Killermann, "The Genderbread Person Version 2," ItsPronouncedMetrosexual.com, Accessed January 26, 2020, https://www.itspronouncedmetrosexual.com/2012/03/the-genderbread-person-v2-0.
391 Jessica Herthel, *I am Jazz* (New York: Dial Books, 2014).
392 American Psychological Association, "Guidelines for Psychological Practice with Transgender and Gender NonConforming People" *American Psychologist*, 70 (December 2015): 832-33, https://www.apa.org/practice/guidelines/transgender.pdf.

activism was clearly revealed in the call for propaganda campaigns rooted in established principles of psychological manipulation and advertising.[393]

There was a refined strategy among secular academics that was propagated into society. The strategy included "desensitizing" or normalizing homosexuality in culture, entertainment, media, and society.[394] "Jamming" was a more aggressive way to criticize anyone opposed to homosexuality, portrays anyone against homosexuality as a bigot, and was a way for them to experience shame for their opposition. Propagandistic public advertising would depict "homophobic" bigots as shameful, shunned, hated, fearful of social consequences, disliked by the crowd, and "not Christian" through non-logical emotional conditioning.[395] The most significant tactic is "conversion," whereby it makes no difference that the advertising were lies, so long as the net effect was to shame bigots and the public perception of homosexuals was that they are victims. [396]

Thirty years later, this has become so absurd that the category of gender—the very basic biological premise that people are male or female—must be dismantled. *National Geographic* reported the bones of a nine-thousand-year-old woman have been excavated in Peru. Researchers say, "Importantly, the team cannot know the individual's gender identity, but rather only biological sex (which like gender doesn't always exist on a binary). In other words, they can't say whether the individual lived their life 9,000 years ago in a way that would identify them within their society as a woman."[397]

Elimination of gender is rooted in queer theory and originally had presuppositions for the removal of gender ideologically so that it could not result in any social discriminatory inequality. The idea was to effectively

---

393 Kirk and Madsen, xxviii.
394 Kirk and Madsen, 148.
395 Ibid, 151-53.
396 Ibid, 154.
397 Maya Wei-Haas, "Prehistoric female hunter discovery upends gender role assumptions," National Geographic.com, November 4, 2020, https://api.nationalgeographic.com/distribution/public/amp/science/2020/11/prehistoric-female-hunter-discovery-upends-gender-role-assumptions.

erase gender identity so people could not be grouped into categories of gender for "discrimination." This philosophically conflicted with critical theory grouping of people into social categories. On one hand, queer theory sought to remove group categorizations, and critical theory stratifies them based on the neo-Marxist oppressor and oppressed matrix.

Victimization ideology was the bridge between queer theory and critical theory. LGBTQIA+ fused into the oppressed victim categories of critical theory and intersectionality. With the infusion of critical theory dogma, LGBTQIA+ people were very quickly enabled to accomplish the goals of their agenda. Normalization and legalization of LGBTQIA+ happened very quickly because of the victimization ideology of the critical theory dogma. This group could claim they were the most oppressed, victimized group in society because of each intersectional property. A minority has one level of oppressive social chips. But a homosexual minority can claim the whole pot of social victimization chips. As soon as wide swaths of society understood them in the oppressor intersectionality categories, normalization of LGBTQIA+ happened virtually overnight, which was part of their plan.

This ideology has unbiblical definitions for the doctrine of man. The Bible reveals gender is determined by God (Matt. 19:4); homosexuality is a sin (1 Cor. 6:9-10); and all other forms of sexual immortality are wicked (1 Tim. 1:8-10). LGBTQIA+ people in no way whatsoever maintain biblical fidelity and are in rebellion against God. The Bible says, "You shall not lie with a male as with a woman; it is an abomination" (Lev. 18:22). Jesus said, "'Have you not read that he who created them from the beginning made them male and female" (Matt. 19:4). It is a sin against God and rejection of His good intention for sex within the biblical covenant of marriage. Paul describes the nature of LGBTQIA+ people in Romans 1: "For this reason God gave them up to dishonorable passions. For their women exchanged natural relations for those that are contrary to nature; and the men likewise gave up natural relations with women and were consumed with passion for one another, men committing shameless acts with men and receiving in themselves the due penalty for their error" (Rom. 1:26-27).

Alternative worldviews based upon the cultural shifts in the sexual revolution have resulted in multiplied confusion surrounding the doctrine of humanity. Fragmented classifications of gender "identity" are subjective and fall into alignment with postmodernist relativism. This led to teaching children that they should express themselves in how they "identify" their gender in contradiction to and deviation from their biological makeup. This is an example of a rejection of God and the biblical doctrine of man. It is another fruit of the rejection of the Bible as the source of truth. It is wicked to tell a child who is biologically a male that he is not a male as God created him or that the child ought to determine for himself how he wants to identify. This is child abuse and creates psychological, emotional, and spiritual damage in children who are victims of this wickedness. Measures ought to be taken to protect children and preserve minors from this manipulative and destructive ideology.

Moreover, for D.A Cason, traditional values are sacrificed on the alters of "tolerance." Ironically, this is really no tolerance at all because if one disagrees with whatever the current movement says is true, then there is no tolerance. More recently, the word *tolerance* has been almost completely abandoned and rebranded into the terms *diversity* and *inclusion*, though the concepts are very similar in how they are applied. Tolerance really only works one way: submit to the new system of morality or the group striving for power. This new tolerance, or "repressive tolerance," originated in Herbert Marques, who wrote, "Liberating tolerance, then, would mean intolerance against movements from the Right, and toleration of movements from the Left. As to the scope of this tolerance and intolerance: . . . it would extend to the stage of action as well as of discussion and propaganda, of deed as well as of word."[398] The purpose by design is to discriminate tolerance to bring balance (i.e., "restraining the liberty

---

398 Herbert Marques, et al, *A Critique of Pure Tolerance* (Boston: Beacon Press, 1965), 109.

of the Right" for "strengthening the oppressed against the oppressors").[399] This same idea of repressive tolerance is utilized in the Woke religion. If you are part of the oppressor group, there is no tolerance. Diversity and inclusion oftentimes presupposes this idea of intolerance for the oppressed group.

Other parts of the world have recognized the moral decay in Western culture. Carson underscores the fact that "cultures in other parts of the world often see in Western (new) tolerance, not a mature and civilized culture worth emulating, but a childish and manipulative culture that refuses to engage with serious moral issues, and that is a danger to their own worlds owing to the power and reach of digital production."[400] Yet other cultures do not get the final word. God does. "But as for the cowardly, the faithless, the detestable, as for murderers, the sexually immoral, sorcerers, idolaters, and all liars, their portion will be in the lake that burns with fire and sulfur, which is the second death" (Rev. 21:8). Christians ought to pray for those that are held captive by this destructive ideology and practice that they would be delivered by the Gospel of Jesus Christ from this slavery to sin and path toward eternal destruction. Paul writes, "And such were some of you. But you were washed, you were sanctified, you were justified in the name of the Lord Jesus Christ and by the Spirit of our God" (1 Cor. 6:11).

ABORTION

Abortion is also consistent with neo-Marxist Woke dogma. The inability of a woman to have the "choice" to murder her unborn baby is even considered "oppressive" to women, particularly by feminists. Perhaps the most heinous aspect of abortion is the complete disregard and destruction of human life—unborn children. Abortion as an ideology is largely dependent upon the false premise that an unborn child is not a person and that it is the mother's choice to decree if it is a clump of cells if the baby is "unwanted" or

---

399 Ibid, 119-20.
400 Carson, 139.

her child if "wanted." The moral confusion and inconsistency surrounding abortion are staggering.

Marxist atheists and Nazi theorist's views of humanity were also based upon error and likewise led to genocide. D.A. Carson says:

> One dare not forget that the most cruelly oppressive regimes of the twentieth century were not led by Christian believers or by Muslim fundamentalists but by Marxist atheists and Nazi theorists who uncompromisingly embraced secular creeds. They presupposed particular understandings of human beings, and therefore butchered millions of them; they presupposed particular understandings of God, and therefore denied his existence or conscripted him for their party's ends (Christians call that "idolatry"); they presupposed particular understandings of liberty, and therefore crushed it.[401]

It is also notable that these regimes had no tolerance according to their presumptions. If you were a Jew, then according to the Nazi theorists, you were less than human. This is no different today for abortion in what some have called the "culture of death." It is often presupposed that the fetus has no value or worth and is not to be understood as a person. On the other hand, the Bible teaches that conception is the beginning of life (Psalm 139:13). For the pro-abortionist, the question must be asked, then when does the fetus, or child, or whatever term you like, become a person with value, dignity, and worth? Is it when a heartbeat can be recognized, or in the third trimester, or at birth? The moral confusion had led to the view that the personal choice of the mother dominates over top of the value of human life. Carson puts it well when he writes, "Small wonder that we have arrived at the place where our medical experts can help generate life in the womb, and can kill a baby about to emerge from the womb, with no moral differentiation. It is merely a matter of *personal choice*" (emphasis mine).[402] This is a society that deems it lawful to murder their unborn children.

---

401 Carson, 125.
402 Ibid, 131.

More recently, Governor Northam of Virginia commented that the mother and doctors should be able to have discussions about taking the life of a deformed child after birth. He said, "The infant would be delivered. The infant would be kept comfortable. The infant would be resuscitated if that's what the mother and the family desired, and then a *discussion* would ensue between the physicians and the mother" (emphasis mine).[403] This discussion did not take place in Nazi Germany. It took place in the commonwealth of Virginia in 2019. In the 2020 presidential election, the state of Colorado voted not to ban late-term abortions according to Proposition 115 results but simultaneously voted in favor of restoring gray wolf populations in Proposition 114.[404] It is difficult, at best, to substantiate a moral argument to preserve wolf populations but not unborn human beings. This is a reminder of G. K. Chesterton, who said, "Wherever there is Animal Worship there is Human Sacrifice. That is, both symbolically and literally, a real truth of historical experience."[405] With no foundation for truth, the morally confused and errors of the past that devalue human life are repeated. Abortion is murder, simply because people are created in the image and likeness of God.

The important connection to Woke religion is the fact that the people who are murdered at the highest rates are minority children. Minority black women are four to five times as likely to have abortions than non-minority white women.[406] Approximately twenty million black babies have been aborted since the *Roe v. Wade* U.S. Supreme Court decision. One of the dogmas of Woke religion is to deliver the "oppressed"; meanwhile, there is blatant disregard and hypocrisy. The most oppressed and vulnerable black babies are

403   Alexandra Desanctis, "Virginia Governor Defends Letting Infants Die," National Review.com, January 30, 2019, https://www.nationalreview.com/corner/virginia-governor-defends-letting-infants-die.

404   "Colorado," The Washington Post.com, Accessed November 5, 2020, https://www.washingtonpost.com/elections/election-results/colorado-2020.

405   G. K. Chesterton, "On Seriousness," in *The Uses of Diversity: A Book of Essays* (New York: Dodd, Mead and Company: 1920), 4.

406   "Black Abortions By The Numbers," Right to Life of Michigan online, Accessed September 22, 2020, https://rtl.org/multicultural-outreach/black-abortion-statistics.

being murdered through unjust, systemic, institutional laws at the highest level in the land. How are infanticide laws backed by the U.S. Supreme Court not the greatest example of systemic oppression of minorities?

The largest institution that carries out these atrocities is the federally funded Planned Parenthood, which was founded by Margaret Sanger. She wrote, "The most merciful thing that the large family does to one of its infant members is to kill it."[407] She was also extremely racist and likely wanted to eradicate the black population. She wrote, "We don't want the word to go out that we want to exterminate the Negro population."[408] Many have sought to defend Sanger with claims her writings have been taken out of context. Although, if Sanger wasn't really attempting to exterminate the black population, why has Planned Parenthood recently decided to remove Margaret Sanger's name from the New York City "health center"?[409]

Abortion is murder. Satan is behind the murders ultimately because he has been a murderer since the beginning. Likewise, Planned Parenthood is demonic because they systematically carry out these murders in disproportional numbers among black babies. The hypocrisy of it all is perhaps demonstrated best today by the Black Lives Matter signs outside of Planned Parenthoods—black baby slaughterhouses, founded by an ethnically genocidal, white supremacist.

---

407   Margaret Sanger, "The Wickedness of Creating Large Families," Chapter 5 in *Woman and the New Race*, (1920) http://www.bartleby.com/1013.

408   "Letter from Margaret Sanger to Dr. C. J. Gamble, December 10, 1939," Smith College Libraries online, Accessed September 22, 2020, https://libex.smith.edu/omeka/items/show/495.

409   Carrie Mumah, "Planned Parenthood of Greater New York Announces Intent to Remove Margaret Sanger's Name from NYC Health Center," Planned Parenthood of Greater New York, July 21, 2020, https://www.plannedparenthood.org/planned-parenthood-greater-new-york/about/news/planned-parenthood-of-greater-new-york-announces-intent-to-remove-margaret-sangers-name-from-nyc-health-center.

CHAPTER ELEVEN

WOKE DOGMA OF INJUSTICE VS. CHRISTIAN DOCTRINE OF SIN, LAW, AND JUSTICE

DARRELL B. HARRISON IS CORRECT: "The problem is enmity, not ethnicity."[410] Woke critical social justice is an offshoot of critical theory that maintains unbiblical, religious dogma that is incompatible with the Christian doctrine of sin as summarized in Figure 13.

---

410 Darrell B. Harrison, "The Problem is Enmity, Not Ethnicity," Sovereign Nations, November 18, 2020, YouTube video, 45:56, https://www.youtube.com/watch?v=xBNNC6y_ ojY&feature=youtu.be.

Woke Inequality Dogma	Christian Doctrine of Sin, Law, and Justice
This dogma is based upon neo-Marxist critical theory/postmodernism/identity politics/social justice.	This doctrine is based upon Scripture.
In critical social justice, everyone is complicit in inequality. It fails to realize the root of true injustice is sin in the heart of man.	"All have sinned and fall short of the glory of God" (Rom. 3:23). "None is righteous" (Rom. 3:10).
Justice is based on artificial social power structure categories.	Justice is based on the character of God and His Law.
Guilt is imputed to everyone in society on the basis of social inequalities. "Injustices" are the fabric of social structures.	All fell in Adam. The sin of Adam is imputed to man, and man commits actual sins. Sin is in the flesh and comes from the heart of man. Man is not accountable for the sins of others.
Racism is prejudice plus power structure oppression. Only whites can be racist because they're part of the oppressive hegemony.	All men and women can be ethnically prejudiced or show ethnic partiality. This is sin.
The scope of oppression is the Western world, primarily America. You can oppress people without even knowing it.	Sin transcends all nations and began at the Fall of man. Bible recognizes oppression and injustice in the fallen world as a result of sin.
It has no category of Satan or spiritual forces of evil unless it is syncritized with Christianity.	Satan tempts man to sin, has power in the world, and causes evil.

Figure 13: Woke Inequality Dogma vs.
the Christian Doctrine of Sin, Law, and Justice

The structures of society are the cause of inequality. According to DiAngelo, "Mainstream culture prevents us from understanding a central tenet of social justice education: Society is structured in ways that make us all complicit in systems of inequality; there is no neutral ground. Thus an effective critical social justice course will unsettle mainstream perspectives and institutional discourses."[411]

There is no factual evidence that proves the claim "all" are complicit in "systems of inequality." This is an overstatement. What societal structures? What systems of inequality? Critical social justice wrongly redefines the core structures of society, human moral agency, and human responsibility. In critical social justice dogma, society is unjust and oppressive but fails to recognize

---

411 Sensoy and DiAngelo, 4.

ways in which societal structures are just. In this type of unbalanced dogma, guilt is attributed to society.[412] For example, Woke objectively presupposes that racism is everywhere. Woke does not proceed upon the question, "'Did racism take place?' but rather 'how did racism manifest in that situation?'"[413] Critical social justice presupposes racism is literally everywhere. Without full recognition of the nature of sin, it is morally incoherent and unbiblical to apply guilt to everyone based on societal "injustice." This is an error because it fails to realize the true nature of injustice, namely sin.

Biblically, mankind is one corrupt race of sinful humans. Any departure from the Christian doctrine of sin will result in an error. The Bible provides the sufficient basis for how the will of man was corrupted in the Fall. Augustine says, "For when the will abandons what is above itself, and turns to what is lower, it becomes evil—not because that is evil to which it turns, but because the turning itself is wicked. Therefore it is not an inferior thing which has made the will evil, but it is itself which has become so by wickedly and inordinately desiring an inferior thing."[414]

The will of the man looking away from the Creator unto the creation was evil. Critical social justice dogma does not adequately explain the nature of evil and sin, since it is only understood in categories of societal power structures. In critical social justice dogma, the evil thing is a societal power structure. This reason alone renders critical social justice and CRT as inadequate and antithetical to the Christian doctrine of sin.

WOKE GROUP SIN VS. HUMAN SIN

According to Scripture, sin is in the heart of man (Gen. 6:5). CRT is not concerned with the heart and only understands injustice in the category of social groups, race, class, gender, sexuality, and ability. This is problematic

---

412 Bavinck, *Reformed Dogmatics*, 407.
413 Robin DiAngelo, "Anti-Racism Handout," Robin DiAngelo.com, Accessed October 2, 2020, https://robindiangelo.com/wp-content/uploads/2016/06/Anti-racism-handout-1-page-2016.pdf.
414 Augustine, 266.

because it is impossible to repent of this individually as humans because sin is effectively baked into social structures. CRT also inadequately recognizes the positive events of history that have helped to reform injustice and oppression. Some question if any reforms will be able to satisfy the demands of social justice advocates. Taunton says:

> A civil war, constitutional amendments, affirmative action, and a multitude of government programs designed to help black students, would-be homeowners, and businesses are not enough. Nothing will ever be enough. If a black man or woman fails to succeed in America, it cannot be the result of his or her own choices or limitations; it is always the fault of a racist system. And if you are white, you are part of that racist system and you must be made to pay for your sin.[415]

Taunton is right to point out the lack of emphasis on human responsibility. Critical social justice and CRT fail to recognize the important role of good or bad choices one makes in life and the consequences of our actions. The Bible reveals in Proverbs 12:28, "In the path of righteousness is life."

One of the most problematic claims of Woke dogma is that one person can oppress another without even knowing it. In CRT, since there is a lack of emphasis on individual sin and injustice is understood in the group hegemony, people are, therefore, accountable for the sins of those in their group. This includes those who committed sins in the past who are part of the oppressor group. DiAngelo follows this framework: "No individual member of the dominant group has to do anything specific to oppress a member of the minoritized group."[416] This is a staggering and unbiblical claim. Human individual responsibility is vaporized. Individuals do not have to act or express their libertarian free will to commit injustice, act immorally, or exercise their

---

415   Larry Alex Taunton, "Understanding What is Happening in America, Part II: The Pale Marxist Trojan Horse," Larry Alex Taunton.com, August 26, 2020, http://larry-alextaunton.com/2020/08/understanding-what-is-happening-in-america-part-ii-the-pale-Marxist-trojan-horse.

416   Sensoy and DiAngelo, 62.

will to oppress someone. By definition, according to Woke dogma, some people are oppressors just by their existence. Also, notice the new definition of "minoritized" group. Very often, this is taken in the context of race. The minority race is effectively oppressed by the definition of being a minority.

However, consider the fact that white Europeans would be "minorities" based on their ethnicity in most African countries. Applying critical social justice consistently would mean that the majority of ethnically African people, by their existence and without exercising their will, morally "oppress" the minority Europeans in African societies without even knowing it. Apply this anywhere in the world. Whatever race is the majority—let's say in China, Russia, Brazil, or anywhere—according to critical social justice, they oppress minorities without doing "anything specific." This, by definition, effectively creates a new moral sociological hierarchy.

Contrarily, the Bible teaches individual people cannot be held accountable for the sins of others: "The soul who sins shall die. The son shall not suffer for the iniquity of the father, nor the father suffer for the iniquity of the son. The righteousness of the righteous shall be upon himself, and the wickedness of the wicked shall be upon himself" (Ezek. 18:20). This text is in harmony with the passages that appear to show that the sons of Israel were held accountable for the sins of their fathers. Calvin explains this harmony:

> God pronounces the same thing as before, namely, that the iniquity of the fathers should fall upon the sons. (Exodus 34:7.) These passages seem opposed to each other, but it will be easy to remove the contradiction by beginning with the fall of Adam, since if we do not consider the whole race fallen in Adam, we can scarcely extricate ourselves from that difficulty which we often feel as causing pungent scruples. But the principle of one universal fall in Adam removes all doubts. For when we consider the perishing of the whole human race, it is said with truth that we perish through another's fault: but it is added at the same time, that every one perishes through his own iniquity. If then

we inquire into the cause of the curse which presses upon all the posterity of Adam, it may be said to be partly another's and partly our own: another's, through Adam's declension from God, in whose person the whole human race was spoiled of righteousness and intelligence, and all parts of the soul utterly corrupted.

According to Calvin, the passages are reconciled with the understanding that the whole human race universally fell in Adam. In this way, everyone is condemned through the fault of another, namely Adam. It also follows that we still are condemned based on our actual sins. Therefore, we are only held accountable for another's fault insofar as it is in the case of Adam, since through Adam, all sinned. In other words, we are sinners based on the guilt of Adam's sin and the actual sins we commit in our own body. Never are we held accountable for the sins of some other group. The Westminster Confession makes the distinction between the sin of Adam imputed to us and our actual sins.

> III. They being the root of all mankind, the guilt of this sin was imputed; and the same death in sin, and corrupted nature, conveyed to all their posterity descending from them by ordinary generation. VI. Every sin, both original and actual, being a transgression of the righteous law of God, and contrary thereunto, does in its own nature, bring guilt upon the sinner, whereby he is bound over to the wrath of God, and curse of the law, and so made subject to death, with all miseries spiritual, temporal and eternal.[417]

We are not accountable for the sins of others or other groups, as in Woke dogma, because we are in Adam or Christ federally. Paul writes, "Therefore, as one trespass led to condemnation for all men, so one act of righteousness leads to justification and life for all men. For as by the one man's disobedience the many were made sinners, so by the one man's obedience the many will be made righteous" (Rom. 5:18-19). We are either condemned in Adam or

---

417 "Westminster Confession of Faith," Grace and Truth RPC.org, Accessed October 2, 2020, http://graceandtruthrpc.org/wpcontent/uploads/2013/07/Westminster_Confession1647.pdf.

righteous in Christ. Adam is the representative head of all people, and all fell in Adam when he sinned, except Christ. Contrarily, "by the one man's obedience"—namely, Christ's obedience—we are made righteous.

"RACISM" VS. ETHNIC PREJUDICE

The Bible has a much different category for the sin of prejudice. "But if you show partiality, you are committing sin and are convicted by the law as transgressors" (Jas. 2:9). Contrarily, DiAngelo says:

> Racism is a system that encompasses economic, political, social, and cultural structures, actions, and beliefs that institutionalize and perpetuate an unequal distribution of privileges, resources and power between White people and people of Color. This system is historic, normalized, taken for granted, deeply embedded, and works to the benefit of whites and to the disadvantage of people of color (Hilliard, 1992).[418]

The idea that there are multiple races is a human social construct. Biblically, there are different ethnicities or nations based on the Greek word ἔθνος (ethnos). Sin is universal across all humanity because all have "fall[en] short of the glory of God" (Rom. 3:23). Therefore, everyone is a sinner and *can* be prejudiced or show partiality. Critical theory misinterprets and applies new categories to prejudice, such as institutional and systemic racism. For Woke, this is the reason why oppression and ethnic prejudice exist.

In CRT, the definition of racism changes from prejudice to prejudice-plus-power. This is especially the case for white people who have been "privileged" and are racist by their existence in the white, colonial, traditional, Western world. CRT unfairly renders all people as prejudiced, but only white people fall under the prejudice-plus-power definition of racism. In fact, for critical race theory scholars, the reason why racial disparities exist is solely due to racism, and other factors are rarely mentioned. While Kendi rightly identifies many of

---

418 DiAngelo, Ibid.

the ethnically prejudiced laws and horrific events that took place in American history, he implausibly reduces racism to the sole cause of racial disparity. He writes: "We have a hard time recognizing that racial discrimination is the *sole* cause of racial disparities in this country and in the world at large . . . When you truly believe that the racial groups are equal, then you also believe that racial disparities *must be* the result of racial discrimination."[419]

There are undeniable facts of racial discrimination in both the history and present context of America and the world. However, it is doubtful that racial discrimination is the sole cause of racial disparities in America and in the world at large, given the multitude of complex factors of human history that cause disparities such as wars, famine, genocide, disease, natural disaster, geography, cultures, tribalism, political forces, world religions, governments, laws, caste systems, economics, technology, God's providence, multitudes of sins, and spiritual forces of evil. Given the enormous variety of sins that have impacted the human race historically, it is unlikely that only one type of sin (racial discrimination) is the cause of racial disparities. Bavinck observes a host of sins that resulted in moral decay of humanity and argues this will continue until the end of the world (Matt. 24:12; 2 Thess. 2:6; Revelation). He writes:

> There is also a history, a development in the sin of the human race; of family, clan, people, humanity. Every age, clan, family, people, calling (business/agriculture, soldiers, students, fishermen, sailors), social position, era, century, environment, and climate/soil has its own sins of sensuality and pleasure, ambition, pride, vanity, weakness, cruelty, indifference, anxiety, extravagance, or miserliness, tribalism, socialism, and so forth. Eastern, western, southern, and northern nations, pagan and Christian nations all differ, as do youths and adults and the elderly, girls and women. This gives rise to sins of the family, of the clan, of the people, as well as of particularly classes and professions. Scripture speaks of a world that is in the hands of

---

419   Ibram X. Kendi, *Stamped from the Beginning: The Definitive History of Racist Ideas in America* (NY: Nation Books, 2016), 10-11.

the Evil One, with Satan as its head as the god of this age (John 14:20; Gal. 6:14; 1 John 2:14-16; 5:19). And then these sins turn into what the Bible calls "sins that cry out to heaven": murder (Gen. 4:10), sodomy (Gen. 18:20), oppression of the poor (widows and orphans, Exod. 22:22-24), and withholding wages (Exod.3:7; Lev. 19:13; Deut. 24:14; James 5:4).[420]

Since it is questionable that racial discrimination is the sole cause of racial disparity in the world, this also raises the question, "Is all racial disparity even immoral?" The answer is clearly no. Racial disparities exist in all parts of the world for numerous reasons. Nearly all countries in the world are made up of one ethic majority (otherwise they would not be the majority) which is, by definition, a racial disparity. It is implausible that racial discrimination is the only reason why even one country in the world has racial disparities, much less every country. To argue otherwise is like saying the reason why Southeast Asian countries are made up of primarily ethnically Asian people, or any other country in the world is made up of a particular ethnic majority is because they racially discriminate. This is not much different than arguing that the reason racial disparities exist in the world is because the entire world is racist. Rather, it is more likely racial discrimination is merely one factor among many for racial disparities in the world.

In fact, Sowell argues for most of human history, slavery did not even originate out of racism and was largely not the enslavement of people of different races. He writes:

> [O]nly in recent centuries has either the technology or the wealth existed to go to another continent to get slaves and transport them en masse across an ocean. People were enslaved because they were vulnerable, not because of how they looked. The peoples of the Balkans were enslaved by fellow Europeans, as well as by the peoples of the Middle East, for at least six centuries before the first African was brough to the Western Hemisphere.

---

420 Bavinck, *Reformed Ethics*, 114.

> Before the modern era, by and large Europeans enslaved other
> Europeans, Asians enslaved other Asians, Africans enslaved other
> Africans, and the indigenous peoples of the Western Hemisphere
> enslaved other indigenous peoples of the Western Hemisphere.
> Slavery was not based on race, much less on theories about race.
> Only relatively late in history did enslavement across racial lines
> occur on such a scale as to promote an ideology of racism that
> outlasted the institution of slavery itself.[421]

Only late in the history of slavery in Western civilization did racism became a dominant factor. Clearly, slavery promoted racism on a systemic scale in the American context. It is certainly plausible racial discrimination is one of the causes, even one of the most significant of racial disparity presently in America, but unlikely that it is the only one.

One of the most undeniable disparities that presently exist is within the criminal justice system. While some argue this is largely due to racial discrimination, it is unclear if that is the case. Michelle Alexander identifies alarming incarceration racial disparities among African Americans that suggests at best, the criminal justice system needs reform and at worst, is a new racial caste system meant to control the black population in ways similar to slavery and Jim Crow through legalized discrimination that is hidden to the naked eye. However, she at least grants that "old-fashioned racism" is not the main reason:

> What, then, does explain the extraordinary racial disparities in
> our criminal justice system? Old-fashioned racism seems out of
> the question. Politicians and law enforcement officials today
> rarely endorse racially biased practice, and most of them fiercely
> condemn racial discrimination of any kind. When accused of
> racial bias, police and prosecutors—like most Americans—
> express horror and outrage.[422]

---

421   Thomas Sowell, *Black Rednecks and White Liberals* (New York: Encounter Books, 2006), 113.
422   Michelle Aleander, *The New Jim Crow: Mass Incarceration in the Age of Colorblindness* (New York: The New Press, 2012), 100.

Yet, she discounts that the current political system and laws merely appear to be anti-discriminatory since she argues the criminal justice system is like Jim Crow (and slavery):

> Although this new system of racialized social control *purports to be colorblind*, it creates and maintains racial hierarchy much as earlier systems of control did. Like Jim Crow (and slavery), mass incarceration operates as a tightly networked system of laws, policies, customs, and institutions that operate collectively to ensure the subordinate status of a *group defined largely by race* [emphasis mine].[423]

In other words, the current criminal justice system, laws, and institutions seem like they are not discriminatory, but they actually are to the extent that they are a cloaked systemic and institutionalized form of Jim Crow, hence the title of the book, *The New Jim Crow: Mass Incarceration in the Age of Colorblindness*. Alexander puts her finger on perhaps the most extreme disparity that exists within society among African Americans, and she provides several ligament examples of injustice, particularly within the criminal justice system, in large part due to historically unfair legalities that were harmful to many people of color. However, the argument that disparities within the criminal justice system are in large part due to discrimination is less than convincing due to the lack of emphasis on the personal responsibility of those who broke the laws and lack of discussion of what other factors could have led to this, such as the integrity of nuclear families, marriage statistics, education, the role of the Church within the communities, and other government policies unrelated to criminal justice but associated with poverty. Instead, there is an unbalanced promotion of the idea that an ethnic group continues to be victimized slaves in America's underground vendetta and class warfare against African Americans.

---

423 Ibid, 13.

Most people agree that disparity exists, especially as it pertains to wealth and socioeconomics. However, the CRT "all-or-nothing" paradigm that all disparities can be explained by discrimination and that everyone is in one of two categories of oppressors or the oppressed is problematic. It is equally implausible that systemic and institutional racism exists nearly everywhere in America. If this was the case, it would be unlikely that Barack Obama would have been elected president of the United States for two terms; that there would be so many minorities in Congress; that the University of California would have ended the use of SAT and ACT admissions due to unfairness for minorities;[424] that the NBA would have a disparity of mostly African American players; and that laws such as the Civil Rights Act of 1964, the Voting Rights Act of 1965, and the Federal Fair Housing Act of 1968 would have been implemented.

All humans are fallen creatures, but not all humans create discriminatory "systemic" or "institutional" systems of power. It seems some are led to believe that basically every sphere of society, human rights organization, religious institution, political group, philanthropic body, non-profit, laws, man, woman, child, and virtually everything in between is racist because of "systemic" and "institutional" racism. Sure, it exists, but not everywhere in the way understood by Woke ideology. Everyone can have biases—it's human nature—but not everyone has biases all the time as if every conceivable thought and deed is purely motivated by racism. That may be a bit of an exaggeration to emphasize the point—this is a hyper pessimistic view of the world at large. There are, however, pinpointed examples of institutional injustices, such as the case in the city of Ferguson, where city officials regularly urged the chief of police to generate more revenue, which resulted in unlawful conduct within the Ferguson Police Department.[425] These examples of injustice are unacceptable, egregious, and sinful but do not substantiate the assumptions of CRT.

424   Shawn Hubler, "University of California Will End Use of SAT and ACT in Admissions," The New York Times.com, May 21, 2020, https://www.nytimes.com/2020/05/21/us/university-california-sat-act.html.

425   United States Department of Justice Civil Rights Division, "Investigation of the Ferguson Police Department," Justice.gov, March 4, 2015, https://www.justice.gov/

Furthermore, the Bible teaches prejudice, victimization, and oppression are sin. God hates unbalanced weights, partiality, and injustice. God calls Christians to liberate the oppressed, love our neighbors, and show compassion to the suffering. But that call ought not to be confused with liberation theology, critical social justice, and critical theory. Only true liberation can take place by the Gospel, "the power of God for salvation" (Rom. 1:16). God loves true justice. The psalmist recounts, "He loves righteousness and justice; the earth is full of the steadfast love of the Lord" (Psalm 33:5). "For the LORD loves justice; he will not forsake his saints. They are preserved forever, but the children of the wicked shall be cut off" (Psalm 37:28). The Bible condemns all forms of partiality, prejudice, and "unequal weights" (Prov. 20:10; Jas. 2:1-7). The horrific history of ethnic prejudice in the American context of slavery, prejudice laws, black codes, Jim Crow, Japanese internment camps, segregation, and all other forms of ethnic prejudice are sinful. The Bible sharply condemns chattel slavery: "'Whoever steals a man and sells him, and anyone found in possession of him, shall be put to death'" (Exod. 21:16).

Contrary to the critical theory dogma, the advent of oppression and ethnic prejudice transcends the context of the postmodern Western world. It was grotesque from the beginning in the East, dating back to the sin of Adam. "Sin may be called darkness," says the Puritan William Gurnall, "because the spring and common cause of sin in man is darkness. The external cause [is] Satan, who is the great promoter of it; he is a cursed spirit."[426] Critical theory dogma fails to recognize the biblical nature of sin and Satan's evil activity in the world.

Moreover, the Gospel seeks to transform structures and authorities in society that God has ordained. Bavinck rightly says:

> [Jesus] leaves the family, marriage, and the relationships between parents and children, masters and servants, and government and people intact. The gospel is not a revolutionary force but

---

sites/default/files/opa/press-releases/attachments/2015/03/04/ferguson_police_department_report.pdf.
426 Gurnall, 5918-19.

a spiritual and reforming one; it acknowledges and honors all legitimate authority rooted in creation's institutions and opposes only the sin and deception found in all areas of life."[427]

Unlike critical theory, reformation is sought through the power of the Gospel proclaimed and lived, not revolution. The Gospel "is the power of God for salvation to everyone who believes" (Rom. 1:16). It is a power that "overcomes the [temporal] world" (1 John 5:4). The Gospel proclaims that Jesus will restore creation in the new heavens and new earth (Rev. 21:1). Critical theory's influence is political. Christianity seeks reformation in society by proclaiming the Gospel and witnessing for Christ. Woke critical theory blurs the lines of injustice and oppression. Christianity makes them clear by the law of God. Critical theory seeks to deconstruct and destroy societal structures by coercion. Christianity teaches us to live peaceably and submit to God's just law.

BIBLICAL LAW AND JUSTICE

Biblical justice is founded upon the essence of God and His will (Deut. 32:4). In Scripture, the words for "righteousness" and "justice" are *tsedek* and *mishpad* and are often used together, indicating that God is both righteous and just in His character (Psalm 103:6). God is the sovereign Lawgiver Who will only do what is just and right. The measure and order of justice and righteousness in every aspect of life is ultimately found in Him. Justice and righteousness are ultimately based upon the transcendent moral standard of God, not social systems, natural law, individual will, or history. "There is only one lawgiver and judge, he who is able to save and to destroy" (Jas. 4:12). Following the Reformers, Bavinck taught three uses of the law:

1. Civil use. Here the law is used to "check all the unbridled passions of people with the reins of its own external control."

2. Pedagogic or convicting use. Here the law functions in two ways: first, it convicts us of sin (Rom. 3:19, 20; 4:15; 5:20; 7:7-20);

---

427 Bavinck, *Reformed Dogmatics*, 666.

second, it convicts us of judgment and punishment (2 Cor. 3:7; Rom. 4:15; Heb. 12:29).

3. Teaching use among believers. This use "consists in the instruction and direction of all internal and external moral actions."[428]

Transgression of God's law and the justice of God warrants eternal condemnation of which only Christ in his salvific work provides atonement. Confession of sin alone is not the means of forgiveness; we also need faith in Christ, Who is the only merit to appease God's justice and grants repentance—turning away from sin and turning to Christ as Lord. Alternatively, reconciliation from the "original sin of white guilt" falls short of recognizing the most important dimension of reconciliation, man to God. Christian theism certainly does have categories for victimhood and oppression, but they are fundamentally different from critical theory dogma. In Christianity, people are not primarily victims. The main problem is sin and being under the judgment of God. Reconciliation toward God is the main issue. Reconciliation with man can only take place once one has been reconciled to God through the cross of Christ (Eph. 2:16). It is not perpetual confession and guilt-bearing as in critical theory dogma; it is, rather, believing in Jesus Christ, Who took our sins upon Himself and paid the penalty once and for all on the cross, such that all guilt is absolved (Col. 2:14).

Biblically, the abuse of power is rooted in sin. The answer for the problem of sin and oppression is Jesus Christ and His Gospel of eternal deliverance. The Bible is concerned with caring for the sick, feeding the poor, and delivering the oppressed (Jas. 1:27). This is law. Yet the Gospel is first concerned with the eternal, ultimate deliverance from sin, appeasement of eternal suffering, and satisfaction of the Divine judgment. Paul says, "The times of ignorance God overlooked, but now he commands all people everywhere to repent, because he has fixed a day on which he will judge the world in righteousness by a man

---

428 Bavinck, *Reformed Ethics*, 226-27.

whom he has appointed; and of this he has given assurance to all by raising him from the dead" (Acts 17:30-31).

There are many moral dimensions to sin, but at the core, it is rebellion against God and lawlessness. Bavinck says, "It denotes a violation not of a human but a divine law and situates us not in relation to fellow humans, society, and the state, but to God, the heavenly Judge."[429] All power and authority is subject to God's justice. Critical social justice's futile attempt to understand justice and morality apart from God destroys justice and morality. Often, the scale of relational weight is dependent upon a new set of criteria, sometimes referred to as intersectionality. Intersectionality is "a provisional concept linking contemporary politics with postmodernism," says Crenshaw.[430] One's societal power, authority, and moral virtues are redefined according to this new power structure of critical social justice. The categories of oppressed and oppressor are based upon intersectionality of race, gender, sexual identity, and so on. This is an unbiblical error. Jesus said evil comes from within the human heart. "And he said, 'What comes out of a person is what defiles him. For from within, out of the heart of man, come evil thoughts, sexual immorality, theft, murder, adultery, coveting, wickedness, deceit, sensuality, envy, slander, pride, foolishness. All these evil things come from within, and they defile a person'" (Mark 7:20-23). If one applies this critical social justice dogma to Western civilization, then white people are oppressors because they are white. This is the definition of prejudice redefined in a flawed philosophical, sociological, political, and religious system. Critical social justice functionally dehumanizes white people or anyone in the majority and categorically redefines them as oppressive victimizers not far from being subhuman animals. One wonders how much different this is from what the Nazis did in the 1930s-40s? The Nazis dehumanized the Jews and sent them to the gas chambers. Let's hope this horrific period of history does not repeat itself.

---

429 Bavinck, *Reformed Dogmatics*, 396.
430 Kimberle Crenshaw, "Mapping the Margins: Intersectionality, Identity Politics, and Violence against Women of Color," *Stanford Law Review*, Vol. 43, No. 6 (July, 1991), 1241-99, https://www.jstor.org/stable/1229039?seq=1.

CHAPTER TWELVE

WOKE SALVATION, PRACTICE, UTOPIA, SPIRITUAL ACTIVISM VS. CHRISTIAN SOTERIOLOGY, ECCLESIOLOGY, ESCHATOLOGY, AND ETHICS

WOKE RELIGION HAS A FALSE doctrine of salvation in their cannon based on neo-Marxist critical theory, social justice, and postmodernism. This dogma is antithetical to the Gospel. Figure 14 sketches some of the discontinuities between the Christian doctrine of salvation and false teaching of Woke.

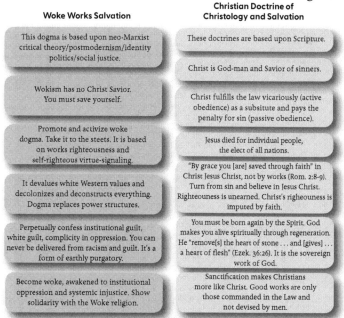

Woke Works Salvation	Christian Doctrine of Christology and Salvation
This dogma is based upon neo-Marxist critical theory/postmodernism/identity politics/social justice.	These doctrines are based upon Scripture.
Wokism has no Christ Savior. You must save yourself.	Christ is God-man and Savior of sinners.
Promote and activize woke dogma. Take it to the steets. It is based on works righteousness and self-righteous virtue-signaling.	Christ fulfills the law vicariously (active obedience) as a subsite and pays the penalty for sin (passive obedience).
It devalues white Western values and decolonizes and deconstructs everything. Dogma replaces power structures.	Jesus died for individual people, the elect of all nations.
Perpetually confess institutional guilt, white guilt, complicity in oppression. You can never be delivered from racism and guilt. It's a form of earthly purgatory.	"By grace you [are] saved through faith" in Christ Jesus Christ, not by works (Rom. 2:8-9). Turn from sin and believe in Jesus Christ. Righteouness is unearned. Christ's righeouness is imputed by faith.
Become woke, awakened to institutional oppression and systemic injustice. Show solidarity with the Woke religion.	You must be born again by the Spirit. God makes you alive spiritually through regeneration. He "remove[s] the heart of stone . . . and [gives] . . . a heart of flesh" (Ezek. 36:26). It is the sovereign work of God.
	Sanctification makes Christians more like Christ. Good works are only those commanded in the Law and not devised by men.

Figure 14: Woke Dogma of Salvation vs. Christian Soteriology

One of the most significant reasons why Woke is antithetical to the Gospel is that there is no Christ in the Woke religion. Even when Woke is combined with Christianity, Christ is reduced to a Savior Who cannot save anyone from the sin of perpetual social guilt imputed from the power structures to the oppressive group. Woke falls into the Galatian heresy. "Salvation" must be attained by works carried out through activism, continual confession of guilt that can never be absolved, and obedience to Woke dogma.

Lindsay and Pluckrose suggest that critical social justice has increasingly turned to advocacy. He cites an essay entitled, "Taking It to the Streets: The Role of Scholarship in Advocacy and Advocacy in Scholarship."[431] Postmodern theories have been fused with activism and politicized in recent history. The indoctrination in the institutions is effectively being radicalized to the degree that critical theory is no longer a theory and social justice is no longer a philosophy; they have become a religion. This is divergent from postmodern skepticism and deconstruction in the academy. The dogmas must be believed as objective truth. Submission to the dogma is religious. There is certainly a moral obligation—a call to do in the imperative. Lindsay and Pluckrose say this is "applied-postmodernism—we must now devalue white, Western ways of knowing for belonging to white Westerners and promote Eastern ones (in order to equalize the power imbalance)."[432] This is closely tied to postmodern decolonizing.

Postcolonial theory utilizes the power of language to replace individual identity with group identity.[433] Similar to deconstructionism that attacks the meaning of ideas, decolonization attacks the meaning of ideas by claiming that all ideas are colonized illusions of power. Postcolonial theory assumes all of Western society has been colonized to maintain the power dominance of Europeans or white people. Hence, the purpose of

---

431 Lindsay and Pluckrose, 64.
432 Ibid, 76.
433 Ibid, 81.

decolonization, the process of dismantling colonial power forms, whether hidden in institutions or hegemonic structures of society.[434] Decolonization has spread so far, there is even a group that wants to decolonize the planet Mars, even though it is not colonized yet.[435] Recently, Ibram Kendi equated Supreme Court Justice Amy Coney Barrett to "White colonizers" because she has two black adopted children from Haiti. "Some White colonizers 'adopted' Black children. They 'civilized' these 'savage' children in the 'superior' ways of White people, while using them as props in their lifelong pictures of denial, while cutting the biological parents of these children out of the picture of humanity," Kendi writes.[436]

Moreover, Henry van Til observed that culture is "religion externalized," meaning that your family's religious values will find their expression in a set of specific cultural choices.[437] Given that the Western world is a post-Christian context, it is not all that surprising to observe religiously charged terms in culture. Certain Protestant religious constructs of the past—such as "sin" and "salvation"—have likely carried over into the present secular, socio-political context. Bottum argues, "This demand that politics somehow solve everything is an apocalyptic, religious sense of politics. For hundreds of years American jurisprudence has worried about the impact of religion on politics. What's really extraordinary is that it is finally happening—politics is becoming religionized, but it's being done in the name of anti-religion."[438]

These traditionally Christian categories of theological knowledge are applied to alternative philosophical frameworks such as critical theory. It's

---

434 Nashrullah Mambrol, "Decolonization," Literary Theory and Criticism online, October 4, 2017, https://literariness.org/2017/10/04/decolonization.

435 "Motivation," Decolonizing Mars.org, Accessed October 2, 2020, https://www.decolonizemars.org/motivation.

436 Brian Flood, "CBS News contributor roasted for suggesting some White parents adopt Black children to use as 'props,'" Fox News.com, Accessed October 10, 2020, https://www.foxnews.com/media/cbs-news-ibram-x-kendi-white-parents-black-children-adoption.

437 Taunton, Ibid.

438 Collins, Ibid.

common to hear of racism as America's "original sin." People are woke, or awakened, to the sins of the past; and to be saved from them, a perpetual confession of them must be sought. In "Atonement as Activism," John McWhorter critiques the new religion. He explains, "White privilege is the secular white person's Original Sin, present at birth and ultimately ineradicable. One does one's penance by endlessly attesting to this privilege in hope of some kind of forgiveness."[439] Continual penance of guilt functions as soteriology. For this reason, whites must express their never-ending guilt by their inherent racism—prejudice-plus-power—so that their privilege is lowered or divested. DiAngelo makes plain that this process of penance for white guilt is perpetual.[440] Woke offers society a salvation of no deliverance. "Racism is so deeply woven into the fabric of our society that I do not see myself escaping from that continuum in my lifetime," says DiAngelo.[441] Critical race theory is a perpetual state of purgatory, where you must continually confess the guilt of the hegemony whereby atonement is impossible. Bottum agrees:

> The first idea I addressed was white guilt—that there is this inherent guiltiness that comes from being white. This notion has the same logical shape and the same psychological operation as Original Sin. The trouble is that, unlike Original Sin, there's no salvation from white guilt. But the formal structure of white guilt and Original Sin is the same. How do you come to understand that you need salvation? By deeper and deeper appreciation of your sinfulness.[442]

There are covenantal ideas, such as federal headship, wrapped up in this line of thought. Instead of Adam being the federal head of humanity of which all mankind universally receives his original sin, now, if you're a part

---

439 McWhorter, Ibid.
440 Robin DiAngelo, "White Fragility," *International Journal of Critical Pedagogy* (2011), 54-64, https://libjournal.uncg.edu/ijcp/article/viewFile/249/116.
441 Ibid, 87.
442 Collins, Ibid.

of the American hegemony—traditional power structure—the original sin of racism expressed in American slavery, Jim Crow, and injustices during the civil rights movement is imputed to you, and you bear the guilt. This is unbiblical and an error, especially when these ideas are syncretized with the Gospel.

The Bible teaches that Christ is the God-man Who is the Savior of sinners. He has indeed satisfied the wrath of God for the sins of the elect, and there is no more guilt. Salvation has been perfectly accomplished by Christ. Jesus died to bear the guilt and iniquities of His people. "Out of the anguish of his soul he shall see and be satisfied; by his knowledge shall the righteous one, my servant, make many to be accounted righteous, and he shall bear their iniquities" (Isa. 53:11). For Woke religion, there's no way to salvation from the institutional structural guilt of society. According to this new religion in America, the only solution is the confession of the guilt of someone else that has been imputed to you. This is an error, since in Woke religion, salvation functions based on works instead of grace. "But if it is by grace, it is no longer on the basis of works; otherwise grace would no longer be grace" (Rom. 11:6). Salvation is by the grace of God alone. The Father, out of an antecedent love for the elect, sent Christ to procure salvation and effectually apply His work by the power of the Holy Spirit. Owen says:

> It was because of that inexpressible love that the Son of God assumed our nature (Heb. 2:14-17). But this act of love was from his divine nature only, because it was before the human nature existed. His laying down his life for us was also an act of inexpressible love (1 John 3:16). Yet it was only the love of the human nature in which he offered himself and died. But both these acts of love were acts of his divine-human person. So it is said that God laid down his life for us, and purchased his church with his own blood.[443]

---

443 Owen, 1353.

Christian duty and motive are rooted in this love of God. There is no motive of love in Woke religion, and similar to all pagan religions, the ethics are legal and based in fear. Christian ethics is concerned with the duty toward God and man, while pagan ethics is only concerned with man (Rom. 12:1). Shedd writes, "The motive for the discharge of Christian duty is the love of God in Christ toward the forgiven sinner. There is no such motive as this in pagan ethics."[444]

Woke religion is inadequate to meet the needs of man because it fails to include the revelation of redemption. Pagan religions omit the mercy of God and only emphasize law and justice. Shedd writes:

> Natural religion is silent respecting the exercise of mercy. It reveals only law and justice *orge* not *agape* ... The distinguishing characteristic of Christianity is not the teaching of sound ethics, but the offer of mercy through a divine mediator and a radical change of human character. Christianity is gospel, not law; but Confucianism and Buddhism so far as they contain truth, are law, not gospel.[445]

While some with right intentions have claimed that social justice is a "gospel issue," it is a mistake to turn to Woke religion, since it does not secure mercy and atonement for human sin. At best, Woke religion offers a jaded version of the moral law, since "St. Paul affirms that wrath, not the compassion of God, is taught to men in the workings of conscience."[446] In the same way that no pagan religion can be syncretized with Christianity because they do not have the exclusive Gospel of Christ, Woke social justice cannot be syncretized with Christianity. Only Christianity is true religion because it is the only redemptive religion where sins are forgiven through Christ (Mark 2:7).

---

444 Shedd, *Dogmatic Theology*, 51.
445 Ibid, 88.
446 Ibid.

WOKE PRACTICE AND UTOPIA

Woke continues to diverge from Christianity in a functional form of ecclesiology and eschatology as sketched in Figure 15. In Woke, the confession of guilt is the cult-like membership requirement. Once one has confessed the imputed guilt of societal structure, you have expressed solidarity—a token of membership—with those who also confess their guilt. A false purpose and meaning are provided in the work to fight against "systemic oppression."

Woke Practice, Utopia, and Spiritual Activism	Christian Ecclesiology, Eschatology, and Ethics
This dogma is based upon neo-Marxist critical theory/postmodernism/identity politics/social justice.	This doctrine is based upon Scripture.
Confess guilt continually to join Woke social justice.	The Church is the body of Christ.
False justice is brought about by overthrowing the power structures through revolution.	Jesus will judge the just and unjust. There will be a final judgment.
One is judged by society on the basis of your group identity and what others have done.	All fell in Adam. The sin of Adam is imputed to man, and man commits actual sins. Sin is in the flesh and comes from the heart of man. Man is not accountable for the sins of others.
It causes division by design on the basis of skin color and hegemony.	It creates unity in the person of Christ who removes emnity and division.
False hope is in a temporal utopia of equal outcome. There is no final justice or judgment in Woke social justice.	Jesus will cast the wicked into Hell and consumate the new heavens and new earth.
This dogma includes activism, counterfeit spritual practices, and in some cases, riots.	This doctrine includes Christian ethics, spiritual life in Christ, loving our neighbors, seeking justice for the oppressed, and Holy Spirit-bearing fruit.

Figure 15: Woke Practice, Utopia, and Spiritual Activism vs. Christian Ecclesiology, Eschatology, and Ethics

Contrarily, in Christianity the chief end of man is determined by God, namely to glorify God and enjoy Him forever. This is primarily expressed within the covenant community of the Church. The mission of the Woke cult is carried out through organization into religious activity to express that one is righteous in the sight of the world in forms of virtue-signaling. "[T]he heartbeat of anti-racism itself is confession," says Ibram Kendi.[447] Continuous confession of guilt and public submission to Woke dogma—group confessions of racism, bowing to minorities, declaring one's positionality, disrupting white comfort (antagonizing white people dining, disturbing the peace in white suburban neighborhoods, etc.), placing one's pronouns in social media profiles, proselytizing Woke literature, engaging in public displays of Woke solidarity (kneeling for the national anthem, twerking before law enforcement, etc.), participating in organized protests—also function as levels of devotion to the Woke religion. These religious practices express solidarity with Woke, solidify membership into the religious community, and are signs of good works.

These ideas and practices are errors. By design, Woke creates an artificial division based on skin color and hegemony. Christianity contrarily creates unity in the person of Christ (Gal. 3:28). The Westminster Confession states:

> The catholic or universal Church, which is invisible, consists of the whole number of the elect, that have been, are, or shall be gathered into one, under Christ the Head thereof; and is the spouse, the body, the fullness of Him that fills all in all. The visible Church, which is also catholic or universal under the Gospel (not confined to one nation, as before under the law), consists of all those throughout the world that profess the true religion; and of their children: and is the kingdom of the Lord Jesus Christ, the house and family of God, out of which there is no ordinary possibility of salvation.[448]

---

447 Kendi, 286.
448 Westminster Confession of Faith, Ibid.

The true Church consists of the elect, who are the family of God. The true Church professes true religion. The true Church teaches and embraces the Doctrines of the Gospel, not the doctrines of demons. According to the Westminster Confession, even some of the purest churches have degenerated into errors and become apostate.

> This catholic Church has been sometimes more, sometimes less visible. And particular Churches, which are members thereof, are more or less pure, according as the doctrine of the Gospel is taught and embraced, ordinances administered, and public worship performed more or less purely in them. The purest Churches under heaven are subject both to mixture and error; and some have so degenerated, as to become no Churches of Christ, but synagogues of Satan. Nevertheless, there shall be always a Church on earth to worship God according to His will.[449]

Degenerate churches are called "synagogues of Satan" in the Confession. If the Church today mixes teaching with Woke religion, they will be subjected to errors and risk apostasy. The practices and works of Woke religion are also not compatible with the Christian good works commanded in the law. The Puritan divines wrote:

> Good works are only such as God hath commanded in His holy Word, and not such as, without the warrant thereof, are devised by men, out of blind zeal, or upon any pretence of good intention. These good works, done in obedience to God's commandments, are the fruits and evidences of a true and lively faith: and by them believers manifest their thankfulness, strengthen their assurance, edify their brethren, adorn the profession of the Gospel, stop the mouths of the adversaries, and glorify God, whose workmanship they are, created in Christ Jesus thereunto; that, having their fruit unto holiness, they may have the end, eternal life.[450]

---

449 Ibid.
450 Ibid.

The practices and works of Woke social justice are devised by men, out of blind zeal, and are unwarranted biblically, even if they are of good intention since they are not commanded in God's Word or done in obedience to God's commands. Instead of feasting on the ordinary means of grace of preaching, prayer, and the sacraments of the Lord's Supper and baptism on the Lord's day, Woke religion emphasizes the neo-Marxist social justice, "white guilt," "white privilege," systemic racism, injustice according to the oppressor/oppressed paradigm, and identity politics. There is no way to accommodate to the doctrines of Woke and maintain the purity of the Church. Would a Reformed Church start incorporating the Book of Mormon in their preaching? It is no different to teach Woke doctrine in the Church today. It is not love to teach God's people errors or mix Christianity with counterfeit religion. Addressing sin with the philosophy of man in the Church is a rejection of the Gospel; it is a false gospel. This is why the true Church can never be woke.

Woke also has a false view of the future that is focused only on the temporal world. Linsday says, "A 'liberated' Utopia in which the systems of oppressive power don't exist is precisely the objective of the Critical Social Justice project. They are quite explicit that they seek a revolution that will unmake the current system and thereby end racism, sexism, homophobia, misogyny, and all of the other systemic oppressions."[451] It promises an eschatological destiny of equities, a utopia of equal outcome for the victims of oppression. The way to achieve this is by revolution. The revolution of critical social justice is to be applied in every sphere of society, including early childhood education. This includes the application of postcolonial theory in children's education. "We believe that the construction of the child and the subsequent treatment of those who are younger in years should be considered through the lens of postcolonial critique. For a variety

---

451 James Linsday, "A First-Amendment Case for Freedom from the Woke Religion," New Discourses.com, September 9, 2020, https://newdiscourses.com/2020/09/first-amendment-case-freedom-from-woke-religion.

of reasons the labels, forms of representation, and positions imposed on those who are younger can be categorized as oppressive, controlling, and even colonizing."[452]

Woke is designed to indoctrinate an alternative worldview to achieve the critical social justice utopian revolution, starting with your children. If you're thinking about sending your kids to public school or public universities that are influenced by Woke dogma, you might want to reconsider, unless you want them to come home woke. Kendi was paid twenty thousand dollars by a Virginia public school district for a one-hour virtual event.[453] Sensoy and DiAngelo make clear the ambitions of Woke critical social justice: "This action requires a commitment to an ongoing and lifelong process . . . Critical social justice recognizes inequality as deeply embedded in the fabric of society (i.e., as structural), and actively seeks to change this."[454] Woke religion deems the structural essence of society unjust and seeks a social revolution to dismantle it and replace it with a world of critical social justice wokeness.

In Woke, there is no God of justice; there is no final judgment. There is only temporal Woke social justice by works. These ideologies and methods of Woke are in error because they are categorically antithetical to Scripture. The Westminster Confession states:

> God has appointed a day, wherein He will judge the world, in righteousness, by Jesus Christ, to whom all power and judgment is given of the Father. In which day, not only the apostate angels shall be judged, but likewise all persons that have lived upon earth shall appear before the tribunal of Christ, to give an account of their thoughts, words, and deeds;

---

452 Gaile Sloan Cannella and Radhika Viruru, *Childhood and Postcolonization: Power, Education, and Contemporary Practice* (New York: Routledge, 2004), 83.

453 Eric Quintanar, "Virginia Public School District Spent $20,000 To Host Anti-Racism Author Ibram Kendi For An Hour," The Daily Wire.com, September 24, 2020, https://www.dailywire.com/news/virginia-public-school-district-spent-20000-to-host-anti-racism-author-ibram-kendi-for-an-hour.

454 Sensoy and DiAngelo, xviii-xx.

and to receive according to what they have done in the body, whether good or evil.

The confession makes it clear that we will be given an account for our thoughts, words, and deeds. Nowhere are we required to give an account for the words or actions of other people. This is one of the most problematic claims of Woke and one of the most common errors coming into the Church today. The Bible says we will be judged based on what we have done in the body, not according to "identity" within groups. "For we must all appear before the judgment seat of Christ, so that each one may receive what is due for what he has done in the body, whether good or evil" (2 Cor. 5:10). Scripture teaches that when we appear before Christ in judgment, we are judged according to what we have done, not what other people have done or groups have done or nations have done or what our parents have done or what our spouse has done—but what we have done in our own body.

"So then each of us will give an account of himself to God" (Rom. 14:12). In the original, Paul, inspired by the Holy Spirit, uses the genitive masculine third person singular ἑαυτοῦ (heautou) "himself." The account given to God is not in the plural. Paul writes "himself." The preposition περὶ (peri) "of" makes it clear that the account given is "of himself." Not of another. Not of a group. Not of a nation. Not of a friend. Not of an ethnic group. Not of anything or anyone but HIMSELF. From exegesis, as surely as God is God, we do not give account for the sins of others, only our own in the final judgment.

The Bible also says Christians ought to pray for our leaders that we may live in peace, not revolt against them. Paul writes, "First of all, then, I urge that supplications, prayers, intercessions, and thanksgivings be made for all people—for kings and all who are in high positions, that we may lead a peaceful and quiet life, godly and dignified in every way" (1 Tim. 2:1-2). Christians have the sure hope of Heaven, where there will be no sin or suffering. Bavinck says:

God's honor consists precisely in the fact that he redeems and renews humanity, the same world, the same heaven, and the same earth that have been corrupted and polluted by sin. Just as anyone in Christ is a new creation in whom the old has passed away and everything has become new (2 Cor. 5:17), so also this world passes away in its present form, in order out of its womb, at God's word of power, to give birth and being to a new world.[455]

The Bible reveals our hope is not in a neo-Marxist utopia but in Christ, Who will return visibly and renew Heaven and Earth, whereby "the creation itself will be set free from its bondage to corruption and obtain the freedom of the glory of the children of God" (Rom. 8:21). Outside of the heavenly city will be "the dogs and sorcerers and the sexually immoral and murderers and idolaters, and everyone who loves and practices falsehood" (Rev. 22:15). In the final judgment, the Lord Jesus Christ executes perfect, Divine justice. Those who are not in Christ will be cast into eternal Hell. Woke social justice is problematic because there is no doctrine of Hell, and therefore, it fails to achieve true biblical justice. According to Shedd, "The strongest support of the doctrine of endless punishment is the teaching of Christ."[456] Jesus said, "And he shall set the sheep on his right hand, but the goats on the left. Then shall he say unto them on the left hand, Depart from me, you cursed, into everlasting fire prepared for the devil and his angels. And these shall go away into everlasting punishment (Matt. 25:33-34, 41, 46).

WOKE PROSELYTIZATION: BLACK LIVES MATTER

Woke proselytizes their religion through social media, popular culture, government, corporate training based on CRT, and organizations such as Black Lives Matter. BLM follows the critical theory and critical social justice dogma. Patrisse Cullors, one of the co-founders of the Black Lives Matter

---

455 Bavinck, 16549.
456 Shedd, 888.

movement, who describes herself as a "trained Marxist," unabashedly admits, "We're not just having a social justice movement, this is a *spiritual movement*" (emphasis mine).[457] It is clear that the BLM movement is not merely a movement; it is a religion. Their beliefs include being against the traditional marriage, traditional family unit, new forms of sexuality, confusion of gender, and abortion. Some of the BLM belief statements as of September 15, 2020 (some of these have since been scrubbed from their website) include (emphasis mine):

- "We disrupt the Western-prescribed *nuclear family* structure."[458]
- "We make space for *transgender* brothers and sisters to participate and lead."[459]
- "We foster a *queer*-affirming network."[460]

More recently, this group has also been associated with the destruction of property and looting. While Christians believe in the value, dignity, and worth of all people, the BLM platform is antithetical to Christianity and should be abhorrent to Christians as a demonstration of depravity (Rom. 12:9). To affirm queerness and transgender is to deny Christ. This is wicked, and it is a part of Woke. Jesus said, "'Have you not read that he who created them from the beginning made them male and female" (Matt. 19:4). It is an attack upon the creative ordinance of God to create humans male and female, which is an attack upon God Himself. It is an attack upon the God-ordained marriage that marriage is between a man and a woman. Jesus quoted the Old Testament when He said, "'Therefore a man shall leave his father and his mother and hold fast to his wife, and the two shall become one flesh'" (Matt. 19:4-5).

---

457   Ryan Foley, "BLM leaders practice 'witchcraft' and summon dead spirits, black activist claims," September 1, 2020, https://www.christianpost.com/news/blm-leaders-practice-witchcraft-and-summon-dead-spirits-black-activist-warns.html

458   "What We Believe," Black Lives Matter.com, Accessed September 12, 2020, https://blacklivesmatter.com/what-we-believe.

459   Ibid.

460   Ibid.

Some troubling facts emerged from a conversation between Cullors and Melina Abdullah, a professor of African studies at California State University Los Angeles, who founded the BLM group's L.A. chapter. Abdulla said, "You know, I laugh a lot with Wakiesha . . . I didn't meet her in her body, right? I met her through this work." Abdullah is referring to Wakiesha Wilson, an African-American woman who was found dead in Los Angeles in 2016. Abraham Hamilton III argues that this conversation between Cullors and Abdullah proved that Black Lives Matter leaders were "summoning the spirits of the dead [and] using the power of the spirits of the dead in order to give them the ability to do what they're calling the so-called justice work." According to Hamilton, the BLM leaders summon the spirits of the dead in adherence to "the Yoruba religion of Ifa." Hamilton stated, "One of the touchstones of this religious practice is ancestral worship. Guess what the Bible calls that, folks? Witchcraft."[461] Hamilton's assessment is accurate, especially given Cullors statement:

> I started to feel personally connected and responsible and accountable to them, both from a deeply political place but also from a deeply spiritual place . . . In my tradition, you offer things that your loved one who passed away would want, whether it's like honey or tobacco, things like that . . . It's so important, not just for us, to be in direct relationship to our people who have passed, but also for them to know we've remembered them . . . I believe so many of them work through us.[462]

Abdullah states, "And it took almost a year for me to realize that this movement is much more than a racial and social justice movement . . . At its core, it's a spiritual movement because we're literally standing on spilled blood."[463] This religion has created a form of liturgy, including the application of changes to invoke spirits. For example, the Black Lives Matter movement

---

461 Foley, Ibid.
462 Ibid.
463 Ibid.

evokes the repetitive chant, "Say her name." Abdulla explains that "when we say the names, right, so we speak their names, we say her name, say their names, we do that all the time, *that you kind of invoke that spirit. And then those spirits actually become present with you*" (emphasis mine).[464] Hamilton argues that Abdullah and Cullors "really believe that the names of the folks that they are saying have become ancestral gods."[465]

The religious practice of invoking dead spirits as practiced by members of BLM and viewed as a core spiritual tenant is strictly condemned by Scripture as wicked. More specifically, Deuteronomy 18:10-12 states, "There shall not be found among you anyone who burns his son or his daughter as an offering, anyone who *practices divination* or tells fortunes or interprets omens, or a sorcerer or a charmer or a medium or a necromancer or one *who inquires of the dead,* for whoever does these things is an abomination to the LORD" (emphasis mine). This passage of Scripture defines those who practice divination and inquire of the dead to be an abomination of the Lord. Therefore, the actions of Black Lives Matters participants, based on their description of practices, are partaking in a religion. The LORD says, "They sacrificed to demons that were no gods, to gods they had never known, to new gods that had come recently, whom your fathers had never dreaded" (Deut. 32:17).

Cullors states, "*Spirituality is at the center* of Black Lives Matter . . . I think that's not just for us . . . I feel like so many leaders and so many organizers are deeply engaged in . . . a pretty important spiritual practice" (emphasis mine). These excerpts make it clear that Cullors and other Black Lives Matter leaders embrace the spiritual nature of their work as a fundamental element of the movement. Moreover, Cullors argues, "I don't think . . . I could do this work without that. I don't think I could do it as long as I've done it and as consistently. It feels like if I didn't do that, it

464 Ibid.
465 Ibid.

would be antithetical to this work."[466] The work that Cullors is referring to is a spiritual work, a religious work, whereby she and others associated with BLM invoke the dead.

Another antibiblical practice promoted by Black Lives Matter is violence and civil unrest. During the summer of 2020 in response to an incident involving inexcusable police brutality, marchers under the Black Lives Matter flag and in concert with extremist groups took over portions of cities,[467] destroyed property,[468] attacked counter-protestors, and were associated with murder.[469] America watched as cities burned for weeks with very little government response, resulting in billions of dollars in damages, communities destroyed, and lives lost.[470] For many in the Woke religion, this was a sign of "justice" and progress to destroy the structures of injustice. Jesus said, "You will recognize them by their fruits" (Matt. 7:16). It is apparent that Woke religion and activist organizations associated with the Woke religion, such as BLM, have bad fruit marked by division, hostility, and spiritual darkness.

The fundamental reason why Woke functions in American society as an alternative religion to Christianity is that people were created by nature to worship and are, therefore, religious. People are no less religious or spiritual than they were in the pre-modern "enchanted" world. Scripture declares everyone is created with a spirit (Gen. 2:7), and God desires man to worship Him in Spirit and truth (John 4:24). God has designed man to be spiritual;

---

466 Ibid.
467 Konstantin Toropin, "Another shooting in Seattle's police-free autonomous zone kills man and critically injures boy," CNN.com, June 29, 2020, https://www.cnn.com/2020/06/29/us/chop-seattle-shooting/index.html.
468 Joe Kelly, "Wisconsin Governor Declares State of Emergency Over Kenosha Protests," Courthouse News Service online, August 25, 2020, https://www.courthousenews.com/wisconsin-governor-declares-state-of-emergency-over-kenosha-protests.
469 Jordan Lancaster, "Woman Shot And Killed After Group Says 'All Lives Matter,'" Daily Caller.com, July 12, 2020, https://dailycaller.com/2020/07/12/woman-shot-indianapolis-all-lives-matter/?utm_source=.
470 David Aaro, "St. Louis police officer dies after being shot in head; family writes heartfelt letter," Fox News.com, August 30, 2020, https://www.foxnews.com/us/st-louis-police-officer-shot-in-head-after-responding-to-call-dies.

thus, man is inherently religious. The problem is that since the Fall of man, sin and the devil have inclined men to form alternative religions and worship false gods. These false gods are demons: "They sacrificed to demons that were no gods, to gods they had never known, to new gods that had come recently, whom your fathers had never dreaded" (Deut. 32:17). The apostle Paul warns, "Now the Spirit expressly says that in later times some will depart from the faith by devoting themselves to deceitful spirits and teachings of demons" (1 Tim. 4:1).

PROCLAMATION OF THE GOSPEL OF GRACE AND CHRISTIAN ETHICS

The road to reconciliation, healing, and justice in society is not the perpetuation of other forms of injustice, law-breaking, and immorality but rather the Gospel of grace, mercy, and forgiveness. In the greatest act of wickedness in the history of redemption, the Lord cried out from the cross at Golgotha, "Father, forgive them, for they know not what they do" (Luke 23:34). Only the Gospel of Jesus Christ has the power to transform, restore, and bring justice to the fallen, sin-laden, wicked world by giving man what he truly needs—a new heart. The resurrected Lord, Who has conquered the last enemy—death itself—says, "Come to me, all who labor and are heavy laden, and I will give you rest. Take my yoke upon you, and learn from me, for I am gentle and lowly in heart, and you will find rest for your souls. For my yoke is easy, and my burden is light" (Matt. 11:28-30).

Empty philosophy and false religion are not the answers to sin and evil in this world. Jesus Christ is the answer. Jesus did not command the disciples to do social justice activism as in Woke religion. Jesus commanded the disciples to preach the Gospel of grace into all the Earth: "And Jesus came and said to them, 'All authority in heaven and on earth has been given to me. Go therefore and make disciples of all nations, baptizing them in the name of the Father and of the Son and of the Holy Spirit, teaching them to observe all that I have commanded you. And behold, I am with you always, to the end of the age" (Matt. 28:18-20).

As Christians make disciples, we also follow Him as our example by His grace. John Bolt points out Bavinck's view: "Christ is not only a king, a priest, and a prophet, but also a model, an example, and an ideal. This implies that we must follow Christ . . . imitating Christ consists in 'the recognition of Christ as Mediator.'"[471] Since Christ is our Mediator, we ought to recognize that He is the One Who transforms us inwardly, while we are conformed to Him outwardly in love, joy, peace, and patience. The mediation and intercession of Christ is profoundly described by Thomas Goodwin, who wrote, "And when you pray, it is the Spirit that indites your prayers, that 'makes intercession for you' in your own hearts (Romans 8:26), which intercession of his is but evidence and echo of Christ's intercession in heaven. The Spirit prays in you, because Christ prays for you. He is an intercessor on earth, because Christ is an intercessor in heaven."[472]

The spiritual fellowship of the Christian with God, while distinct, cannot be separated from our moral and ethical life. How we ought to live ethically proceeds from God, through God, and to God. For Bavinck, "Ethics concerns itself with how we use our natural, created gifts, how we receive the gospel of grace and are regenerated, and how our lives, remaining subject to sickness, temptation, and struggle, can be directed to God's law."[473] This is why dependence upon the Scriptures is absolutely fundamental to the Christian life.

Part of the motivation for social justice within evangelicalism is a desire for morality and ethics. However, ethics and morality alone cannot usher us into the Kingdom of Heaven. To gain Heaven, first we must crucify our earthly morals and trust in Christ's righteousness because even our best works are filthy rags (Isa. 64:6). Nevertheless, ethics are still essential to the

---

471 Bavinck, *Reformed Ethics*, xxxi.
472 Thomas Goodwin, *The Heart of Christ* (UK: The Banner of Truth Trust, 2011), 37.
473 Bavinck, *Reformed Ethics*, 2.

Christian life. Christian ethics was practiced in all periods of Church history, and there is much to learn from it for the Church today in how we ought to think about social justice ideology. Bavinck reminds us:

> The West remained more practical and reserved as its morality became more tied to the church . . . With Constantine the world pushed in the church, and monasticism along with asceticism rose in opposition. Representatives of this ascetic spirit include Athanasius, Basil the Great's Ascetica, Gregory of Nyssa, and others . . . The Western church was more practical, but morality became more legalistic.[474]

There is a danger in our efforts to combat the false ideologies of social justice to respond like the monastics in a functional legalism. We have to be careful in our opposition of false teaching that we do not forsake the desire to care for the poor, seek justice for the oppressed in society, and stay true to our duty to the law in Christian ethics. It is an error not to acknowledge the earthly realm.

In the Middle Ages, the scholastics began to systematize ethics (faith, hope, love, justice, courage, prudence, and temperance), and mysticism reacted against the scholastic method. The Reformers separated works from grace, and Scripture was understood as the sole source of moral knowledge.[475] The Reformed churches produced edifying ethical works but also made some errors. Bavinck writes, "Above all, he [Zwingli] sought ethical reformation, a renewal of life and morality in accordance with Holy Scripture. His fundamental error was in his understanding of the relation between civil and divine justice, between nature and grace."[476] The Reformers were right to derive their ethics solely from the Scriptures and duties from the Lord's Prayer and moral law, particularly, the Ten Commandments. The Heidelberg Catechism states:

---

474 Ibid, 4.
475 Ibid, 6-9.
476 Ibid, 7.

Since we have been delivered from our misery by grace through Christ without any merit of our own, why then should we do good works? A. Because Christ, having redeemed us by his blood, is also restoring us by his Spirit into his image, so that with our whole lives we may show that we are thankful to God for his benefits, so that he may be praised through us, so that we may be assured of our faith by its fruits, and so that by our godly living our neighbors may be won over to Christ.[477]

Christian ethics flows out of a spiritually regenerated life in Christ. Since we have saving fellowship with Him, our example of Christ's life is essential. Bavinck says, "This is a necessary task. We need to know the nature, character, and fruit of the spiritual life, because we need to unmask hypocrites, lift up the downtrodden, comfort the sorrowful, heal the sick, and guide the strong . . . Dogmatics proceeds from God; ethics returns to God. In dogmatics, God loves us; in ethics, therefore, we love."[478]

The spiritual life of the Christian affects the moral life. As Paul said, "Christ . . . lives in me. And the life I now live in the flesh I live by faith in the Son of God" (Gal. 2:20). Bavinck summarizes, "The purpose and task of ethics . . . is therefore to describe how regenerate people are to manifest their eternal heavenly life in the form of the temporal earthly life."[479]

This section has shown that Woke religion is false, since it maintains a doctrine that is antithetical to Christianity theologically. It is clear Woke religion is making further inroads into American society as a whole and alarmingly into American evangelicalism. We grieve that this false religion has begun to influence the evangelical church and turn to this discussion in the following chapters.

---

477 "Heidelberg Catechism," Christian Reformed Church.org, Accessed January 28, 2021, https://www.crcna.org/welcome/beliefs/confessions/heidelberg-catechism#toc-part-iii-gratitude.

478 Bavinck, *Reformed Ethics*, 20.

479 Ibid, 235.

PART FIVE
WOKE CHURCH

CHAPTER THIRTEEN

WOKE EVANGELICALISM: HOW WOKE RELIGION SYNCRETIZED WITH EVANGELICAL CHRISTIANITY

"You played the whore also with the Assyrians, because you were not satisfied; yes, you played the whore with them, and still you were not satisfied."

—Ezekiel 16:28

THIS FINAL SECTION PROVIDES AN overview of how Woke religion syncretized with evangelicalism, is presently being taught within the evangelical church, and provides a response by Christians against Woke evangelicalism. This is the most difficult section to write because I grieve for Christians who have accommodated to Woke dogma and how it has been united with Christian teaching. It is my understanding that the syncretism of Woke religion is primarily happening because of the ignorance of the danger and rapid increase of Woke ideology within secular culture. Nevertheless, whether knowingly or unintentionally, the embrace of a false religion and propagation of false gospel is inexcusable and cannot be tolerated biblically within the Church. The passage from Ezekiel 16 is a helpful, biblical comparison of what is happening in evangelical churches in America. Insofar as evangelicalism has combined Woke dogma with Christianity, as Ezekiel said of Israel, they "played the whore."

This chapter demonstrates that many pastors, professors, and evangelical leaders have mixed their teaching with the Woke religion. Many examples of this had to be excluded for the sake of chapter length. There are two basic categories of the influence of Woke religion in evangelicalism. Some evangelical leaders actively promote Woke religion, and others merely use bits and pieces of the Woke teaching in their ministry. It is harder to identify the latter because the language used in these cases sounds Christian, but the ideas behind it are not. At best, evangelical leaders have been influenced by Woke dogma, and at worst, some are teaching a false gospel. No evangelical church or institution is immune from the danger of false teaching. I hope that this chapter will serve to warn the flock as Peter has said, "But false prophets also arose among the people, just as there will be false teachers among you, who will secretly bring in destructive heresies, even denying the Master who bought them, bringing upon themselves swift destruction" (2 Peter 2:1). Readers can discern for themselves how the claims and statements below measure up with the authority of Scripture.

In the twentieth century, theological liberalism, liberation theology, the New Left social justice movement, and postmodernism reaped havoc on the Church. Each of these systems led to the combining of the Woke religion with evangelicalism. They functioned like stepping stones to bring Woke social justice in the Church. Theological liberalism left a graveyard of churches because of the abandonment of the orthodox doctrine of the Word of God. One of the largest denominations to survive the tug of war between theological conservative and liberal evangelicals was the Southern Baptist Convention, although sadly, they have since been in decline.[480]

Liberation theology was a significant part of this unity. Liberation theology overemphasizes the political and social implications of Jesus' ministry. One of the problems with liberation theology is:

---

480 Chuck Lawless and Adam W. Greenway, eds., *The Great Commission Resurgence: Fulfilling God's Mandate in Our Time* (Nashville: B&H Publishing, 2010), 35-49.

The uniqueness of Jesus' cross lies not in the fact that God, at a particular point in space and time, experienced the suffering intrinsic to humankind's sinfulness in order to provide a way of redemption. Jesus' death is not a vicarious offering on behalf of humankind who deserve God's wrath. Jesus' death is unique because he historicizes in exemplary fashion the suffering experienced by God in all the crosses of the oppressed.[481]

The liberation theology "socialized gospel" reduces Christianity down to merely relieving the oppressed from temporal needs and omits the eternal redemption of Christ. Weber is right: "Liberation Theology threatens to politicize the gospel to the point that the poor are offered a solution that could be provided without Jesus Christ."[482] Woke evangelicals tend to combine these aspects of liberation theology into Christianity; thus, it functions as one part of the Woke religion. Liberation theology uses words and ideas that sound Christian but are foreign to the Bible. They are simply bathed in Christian language, so it sounds true. This is most common in the use of the phrase "social justice." It sounds biblical because justice is a Christian word, but it means something completely different from the way it is defined in Scripture and understood historically in Western culture.[483]

The "Christian" social justice movement has also played a significant role that led to the emergence of Woke evangelicalism. In a sense, the social justice movement, in combination with liberation theology, was like gateway drugs to Woke religion, which is a dangerous form of merging with Christianity. Jon Harris insightfully chronicles the 1970s era New Left social justice movement within evangelicalism sewing progressive seeds through the 2000s.[484] This historical work rightly identifies the Left evangelical movement through men such as Jim Wallis, Richard Mouw, and Ron Sider and concludes with an appendix

---

481   Walter Elwell, *Evangelical Dictionary of Theology* (Grand Rapids: Baker Academic, 2001), 688.
482   Ibid.
483   Scott David Allen, *Why Social Justice is Not Biblical Justice: An Urgent Appeal to Fellow Christians in a Time of Social Crisis* (Grand Rapids: Credo House Publishers, 2020), 2.
484   Jon Harris, *Social Justice Goes to Church: The New Left in Modern American Evangelicalism* (Greenville, SC: Ambassador International, 2020).

on Tim Keller. The evangelical radical Left movement was, in part, a reaction to the fundamentalism of the mid-twentieth century and overshadowed by the religious Right movement of the 1980s-90s. Nevertheless, the Left ideology within evangelicalism and their critical reaction to a conservative evangelical background is a very important piece of the story leading to Woke evangelicalism.

Furthermore, by the late 1990s and early 2000s, postmodernism was on the rise and flooded into churches through the emergent church movement within evangelicalism. This movement functioned to mainstream postmodernist ideologies within the Church through books like *The Church on the Other Side: Doing Ministry in the Postmodern Matrix* by Brian McLaren. Evangelical postmodernist deconstruction and decolonization studies were in print by the early 2010s, such as *Evangelical Postcolonial Conversations*. This is significant because postmodern deconstruction began to be combined with postcolonial theory to undermine the meaning of power structures and destabilize them. Deconstruction was used to dismantle the ideas of Christian history in America, not merely for the sake of new meaning but for the establishment of new power structures. By the mid-2010s, postmodernism was impacting large Christian denominations, and then came the final piece. Critical theory.

What critical theory did was marry postmodernist deconstruction into the oppressor-oppressed neo-Marxist paradigm. Critical theory, combined with postmodern deconstruction, teaches that traditional gender, sexuality, beliefs, norms, and institutions—including Christianity—are interdependent structures of injustice and discrimination.

As Woke ideology was boiling over in the secular spheres of society, large, evangelical institutions were increasingly being troubled by and offering public lament for the horrific history of slavery and racism among Christian establishments.[485] This was when the imperfect storm happened within evangelicalism, and all the pieces came together: Woke religion was

---

485 "Report on Slavery and Racism in the History of the Southern Baptist Theological Seminary," Ibid.

born within evangelicalism. Liberation theology, the New Left social justice, emergent church postmodernism, and neo-Marxist critical theory had fully matured into the merger of Woke religion with evangelicalism, as sketched in Figure 16. In effect, large parts of the evangelical church became Woke.

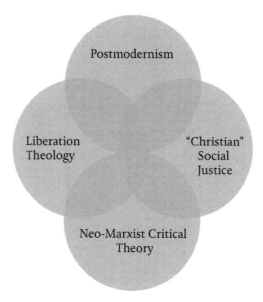

Figure 16: The Imperfect Storm, Woke Evangelicalism

The postmodern deconstruction applied to the Church is designed to redefine the meaning of Christianity, and the postmodern decolonization is designed to dismantle the historical power structures of Christianity. As it all came to a head, tools were needed to identify and destroy the systemic and institutional racism of Christianity and rebuild it from the ground up. What would be the primary "tools" of choice? Critical race theory and intersectionality. Critical race theory, combined with deconstructionism, was the mechanism for tearing down the power structures within the Church, especially institutional and systemic racism. Intersectionality is the tool to rebuild the power structures according to the neo-Marxist postmodern categories. Woke religion is a poisonous well that has the potential to tear down traditional Christianity and replace it with Woke Christianity. In other words, replace Christianity with counterfeit religion.

WOKE EVANGELICALISM

In 2019, the Southern Baptist Convention voted to adopt Resolution 9, which deceptively supports critical race theory as an "analytical tool." The most alarming portion of the resolution states, "WHEREAS, Critical race theory is a set of *analytical tools* that explain how race has and continues to function in society, and intersectionality is the study of how different personal characteristics overlap and inform one's experience" (emphasis mine).[486] Resolution 9 passed after being touted as useful, similar to how Paul engaged philosophies on the Areopagus and used the tool of being subservient to the authority of Scripture. In response, Pastor Tom Ascol, one of the leaders in the Founders organization of the SBC, asked for the resolution to be amended but was denied. According to Ascol, the committee "altogether rewrote" the resolution submittal that had previously denounced critical race theory and intersectionality and warned the Church against them.[487]

"Obviously, I think the resolution is problematic—not so much because it says too much but because it says too little," said Ascol, "and thereby gives a wrong impression about what Critical Race Theory and Intersectionality are."[488] According to Ascol and many others who rightly opposed Resolution 9, it failed to recognize the fact that critical race theory and intersectionality are entirely incompatible with Christian categories and that not enough language is provided to explain the major errors of the worldview. The passing of Resolution 9 may have been inevitable, since critical theory is already being taught in SBC seminaries and being preached in the churches.[489]

---

486 "On Critical Race Theory and Intersectionality," SBC.net, June 1, 2019, https://www.sbc.net/resource-library/resolutions/on-critical-race-theory-and-intersectionality.
487 Tom Ascol, "Resolution 9 and the Southern Baptist Convention 2019," Accessed October 3, 2020, https://founders.org/2019/06/15/resolution-9-and-the-southern-baptist-convention-2019.
488 Ibid.
489 Bob Allen, "Speaker at Baptist college warns that Marxist thought is creeping into SBC seminaries," Baptist News Global online, March 13, 2020, https://baptistnews.com/article/speaker-at-baptist-college-warns-that-Marxist-thought-is-creeping-into-sbc-seminaries/#.X2bL1WdKhsM.

Curtis Woods, a graduate of Southern Baptist Theological Seminary, was the chairman for the resolutions committee that duplicitously passed Resolution 9. In a defense of the resolution, Woods said, "What we are saying is that this can be utilized simply as an analytical tool, not a transcendent worldview above the authority of Scripture. And we stand by the strength of this resolution."[490] Anyone who has studied CRT understands the issue of this claim. CRT cannot function as a mere tool because it is dominated by an entire neo-Marxist and postmodernist worldview that is antithetical to the Gospel. Moreover, Woods has a biased view, since he is clearly a proponent of critical race theory, based upon the fact that his Ph.D. dissertation utilizes critical race theory.[491] Woods writes in his dissertation, "I will, therefore, employ principles of critical race theory to guide the conversation."[492] Woods says, "Nevertheless, Kendi's work is *phenomenal because he deftly incorporates critical race theory*, theology, anthropology, sociology, and philosophy in narrating the history of racist ideas in America" (emphasis mine).[493] One must wonder why and how a Ph.D. dissertation that contains and is, at some level, sympathetic toward critical race theory would be supported by the seminary and overseeing advisors.[494] Is it possible that the leading flagship SBC seminary is more influenced by critical theory than otherwise thought? Does the seminary not hold to the conservative theological convictions laid out in the Abstract of Principles? They state:

> Every professor of the institution shall be a member of a regular Baptist church; and all persons accepting professorships in this seminary shall be considered, by such acceptance, as engaging

490 "Word Foundations INSIGHTS AND COMMENTARY FROM A BIBLICAL PERSPECTIVE," Accessed October 3, 2020, https://www.wordfoundations.com/pastor-tom-ascol-seeks-to-amend-resolution-9.

491 Ibid, 207.

492 Curtis Woods, "The Literary Reception of the Spirituality of Phillis Wheatley (1753-1784): An Afrosensitive Reading, Ph.D. Dissertation, Southern Baptist Theological Seminary, 2018, https://repository.sbts.edu/bitstream/handle/10392/5714/Woods_sbts_0207D_10471.pdf?sequence=1&isAllowed=y.

493 Ibid.

494 Ibid.

to teach in accordance with, and not contrary to, the Abstract of Principles hereinafter laid down, a departure from which principles on his part shall be considered grounds for his resignation or removal by the Trustees, to wit:

I. The Scriptures

The Scriptures of the Old and New Testaments were given by inspiration of God, and are the only sufficient, certain and authoritative rule of all saving knowledge, faith and obedience.

If critical race theory is a worldview that is entirely incompatible with Scripture teaching, was utilized and supported in the Ph.D. dissertation, and was approved by the faculty, then is this not a violation of the Abstract of Principles?

Moreover, Dr. Jarvis Williams, a professor at Southern Baptist Seminary, and Dr. Kevin Jones write in their book *Removing the Stain of Racism from the Southern Baptist Convention*:

The Southern Baptist Convention has a big, dark, historical stain on it: racism. Evident by the SBC's affirmation of slavery, its failure to repudiate this sin until 1995, and the numerous segregated Southern Baptist churches, this stain continues to hinder Southern Baptist churches from embracing the one new man in Christ outlined in Ephesians 2:11-22 and from participating in the new song of those saints from every tongue, tribe, people, and nation referenced in Revelation 5:9. The gospel of Jesus Christ requires and demands all Southern Baptists to do their parts to erase this stain from the SBC—or at least to make the stain less apparent.[495]

I respect Williams, Jones, and others for their work to address issues of racism within the SBC but have concerns that the distinctions between the Gospel and the Law in their work is, at times, unclear. They are right in their

---

495 Jarvis Williams and Kevin Jones, *Removing the Stain of Racism from the Southern Baptist Convention: Diverse African American and White Perspectives* (Nashville: B&H, 2017), xxv.

assessment of the grievous history and lack of ethnic diversity among SBC churches; there is much to be done for the sake of the Gospel. However, it is important to clarify that despite sin, including the sin of ethnic prejudice, the power of the Gospel by grace alone enables all Christians to become one with Jesus Christ without hindrance and to inherit the Kingdom of Heaven. This good news and work of sovereign grace are fundamentally distinct from what we do as Christians in keeping the Law of God. Yes, as Christians, we ought to do all we can to remove hindrances of people from coming to Christ and all we can to keep our brothers and sisters from stumbling because this is the fulfillment of the Law to love our neighbor as ourselves. Yet, it is equally important to emphasize by the power of the Gospel, the work of Christ alone makes Christians one in Him, such that all sins, hindrances, stains, and enmity are nailed to the cross of Christ. The apostle Paul addresses this point in his letter to the church of Colossi: "And you, who were dead in your trespasses and the uncircumcision of your flesh, God made alive together with him, having forgiven us all our trespasses, by canceling the record of debt that stood against us with its legal demands. This he set aside, nailing it to the cross" (Col. 2:13-14).

As Christians, we ought to be fair in our treatment of the history of Christianity, particularly within America, grieving the wicked portions and offering thanksgiving for the providential graces of God during reformation. We ought to be balanced in the faithful exhortation to love our neighbors, proclaim salvation is fully accomplished through the vicarious work of Christ, and be biblically clear lest Christians conflate the moral law of God with the Gospel of God.

Moreover, in a roundtable discussion about the book *Removing the Stain of Racism*, Dr. Albert Mohler, the president of Southern Baptist Seminary who for decades has respectably championed the Gospel in the Augustinian tradition, makes some puzzling statements in regards to the "stain of racism." He says, "Stain is exactly the right word,[sic] it's a stain that we're going to carry as a denomination forever until Jesus comes."[496] Although the SBC was historically slow to publicly denounce the sins of ethnic prejudice within the denomination, according to Mohler, that is not enough to erase the stain. In fact, according to Mohler, nothing will ever be enough. To be fair, Mohler has spoken against CRT, particularly in response to Resolution 9. However, it is clear he merely critiques the origins and consequences of the theory and not the theory itself.[497] Nevertheless, the descriptions of institutional stains of racism never going away may still have some alignment with CRT ideology. Critical race theory teaches racism is systemic and so embedded into the fabric of society, it is essentially impossible to get rid of. Contrarily, Scripture teaches the blood of Christ washed away sin so that the Church is no longer "stained" (1 John 1:7). So, if the stain is racism, and racism is a sin, and this sin is going to have to be carried in the SBC until Jesus returns, has this sin really been forgiven by Christ? Or is racism functioning like the unforgivable sin in the SBC?

It is more evident CRT is taught at Southern since it has been reported former faculty were fired for whistleblowing against it. Several professors, including Dr. Russell Fuller, claim they were dismissed from Southern for speaking out against critical theory. "Nobody likes to be fired," said Dr. Fuller in an interview. "But I have a clear conscience about the stuff I did there. *I stood up against Critical Race Theory that is being taught there and Social Justice.* And not only that. There are other things being taught there like *postmodernism.* I stood up against that and I think there was a price to be paid for that" (emphasis mine).[498] Dr. Fuller went on to state, "We are living

---

496 "Stain of Mohler 3," The New Calvinist, November 25, 2019, YouTube video, 1:04:36, https://www.youtube.com/watch?v=MIlnLU-vt_g.

497 Rudy Gray, "SBC Resolution 9: Statement on Critical Race Theory & Intersectionality Point of Controversy and Disagreement," The Courier.com, June 26, 2019, https://baptistcourier.com/2019/06/sbc-resolution-9-statement-on-critical-race-theory-intersectionality-point-of-controversy-and-disagreement.

498 "Whistleblower: 'Dangerous' theology taught at Al Mohler's SBTS seminary," Capstone Report.com, May 18, 2020, https://capstonereport.com/2020/05/18/whistleblower-dangerous-theology-taught-at-al-mohlers-sbts-seminary/34410.

a lie when we say Critical Race Theory—Social Justice—has never been taught on this campus. We are living a lie." Also in the interview, Dr. Fuller stated he could not criticize Southern Seminary for the rest of his life if he signed a non-disparagement agreement that offered extended monetary benefits to not say anything negative against the seminary.[499] Dr. Fuller was one of the last remaining professors at Southern willing to take a stand against Woke social justice.

Southern Baptist Theological Seminary board member Pastor Tom Rush confirms several issues surrounding the influence of Woke social justice. He points out that Sam Allberry's problematic positions concerning same-sex attraction were being supported in a podcast put out by Southern Seminary.[500] In a conversation with Dr. Mohler, Rush claims the video was going to be taken down from the seminary's website, but to Rush's knowledge, it never was removed. Rush also discussed with Dr. Mohler the concerns of the Woke social justice movement and the teachings of critical race theory at Southern Seminary. Rush obtained class notes from Dr. Jarvis Williams, a professor at Southern Seminary, that clearly reveals Dr. Williams was teaching critical race theory and intersectionality. In a trustee meeting, Rush questioned Dr. Mohler about this. Rush states, "His response was we are not teaching Critical Race Theory, we are teaching about it."[501] Furthermore, according to Rush, Dr. Mohler is against signing the Dallas Statement of Social Justice (this statement critiques some of the Woke social justice positions), and a professor told Rush that Dr. Mohler forbids any professor from signing it. Rush assumes that perhaps the faculty have also been told they cannot speak negatively against social justice. He states, "It's a downgrade if you will. And the slide is happening almost right under our noses. So that's why we have got to sound

---

499 Ibid.
500 Hershael York, "Episode 7: Singleness, same-sex attraction, and preaching with Sam Allberry," Southern Seminary.edu, July 12, 2019, https://equip.sbts.edu/podcast/episode-7-singleness-sex-attraction-preaching-sam-allberry.
501 Tom Rush's Facebook page, Accessed July 21, 2020, https://www.facebook.com/tom.rush33/videos/10224630958901031.

the warning . . . it's an inability to tell the whole truth . . . if the truth gets out that we really are teaching CRT but we have said that we are not, that's not going to look good."[502]

Concerning the terminations of several of the professors at Southern Seminary, Rush believes that they are directly related to the professor's position against social justice. This is clearly the case since the reason given for the terminations by the seminary were financial concerns; however, a short time later, more professors were hired. Rush states he did everything he could to keep Dr. Mohler from using the non-disparagement agreement. Rush states:

> I can't call that severance pay. I call that earned pay. If they would sign this separation and release agreement then they would receive that pay and of course their retirement benefits and insurance benefits and so forth. *I don't know any other way to look at that other than hush money.* In other words, we are going to ask you to sign an agreement that you're not going to say anything bad. There's no reason to do that unless you suspect that they might have something bad to say [emphasis mine].[503]

Rush submitted a motion to the board of trustees that Dr. Mohler require the administration pay Dr. Fuller and Dr. Jim Orrick to receive the full payment and benefits if they did sign the separation agreement. The motion failed because it never received a second. Another motion was submitted to the board by Rush; the non-disparagement agreement would be illuminated until approval by the board of trustees, but it also failed to receive a second.

Moreover, Dr. Matthew Hall, provost at Southern Baptist Theological Seminary, openly confessed, *"I am a racist* . . . I am going to struggle with racism and white supremacy until the day I die and get my glorified body and a completely renewed and sanctified mind because I am immersed in a

---

502 Ibid.
503 Ibid.

culture where I benefit from racism all the time" (emphasis mine).[504] Trustee Rush spoke with Dr. Mohler about the Provost Dr. Matt Hall's statements. To Rush's knowledge, Dr. Hall said he probably should have chosen his words more wisely, but there was not any indication that he would change his words or back down from them.

Dr. Hall's statements are similar to what CRT scholars teach. For example, DiAngelo writes, "When I say that only whites can be racist, I mean that in the United States, only whites have the collective social and institutional power and privilege over people of color. People of color do not have this power and privilege over white people."[505] Even though Hall has rejected a commitment to CRT, he is clearly influenced by the CRT ideology. In particular, Dr. Hall agrees with the CRT claim that if one is white, then one cannot be rid of ethnic prejudice. Also notice, Hall admits that he benefits from ethnic prejudice all the time. Again, this is very similar to CRT ideology that teaches that whites benefit from the oppressive power structures at the cost of the minorities. DiAngelo explains this CRT idea:

> Individual whites may be "against" racism, but they still benefit from a system that privileges whites as a group. David Wellman succinctly summarizes racism as "a system of advantage based on race." These advantages are referred to as white privilege, a sociological concept referring to advantages that are taken for granted by whites and that cannot be similarly enjoyed by people of color in the same context (government, community, workplace, schools, etc.).[506]

Critical race theory, white privilege, and systemic racism are clearly ideologies of Woke religion. It is evident this Woke dogma is taught at evangelical seminaries and is clearly gaining influence among other evangelical leaders.

---

504 Tom Ascol, "Matthew Hall's Rejection of Critical Race Theory," Founders.org, Accessed October 3, 2020, https://founders.org/2019/12/03/matthew-halls-rejection-of-critical-race-theory.
505 DiAngelo, 22.
506 DiAngelo, 24.

Pastor Matt Chandler seems to have been influenced by critical race theory concepts of white privilege. Chandler says, "What is so deceptive about white privilege is that it is different from blatant racism or bias. A privileged person's heart may be free from racist thoughts or biased attitudes, but may still fail to see how the very privilege afforded to him or her shapes how he or she interprets and understands the situations and circumstances of people without privilege."[507] This concept of privilege is foreign to the Bible but important teaching in CRT. DiAngelo says, "Race science was driven by these social and economic interests, which came to establish cultural norms and legal rulings that legitimized racism and the privileged status of those defined as white."[508]

Furthermore, in an emotionally charged sermon, Chandler preached to his congregation:

> We must grow in the hope that *God will heal the wounds of racism*, and what we're watching on our TV unfold again will one day cease. Look at me—*this is our inheritance*. This is mine. This is yours. What you're seeing play out right now in violent riot and in murder . . . that is a robbing of our inheritance. *I'm talking to the church*. I'm talking to followers of Jesus Christ—it's mine! Bought by the blood of Jesus Christ we are to grow and hope that this is possible [emphasis mine].[509]

What Chandler seems to imply is that the Church has inherited the wounds of ethnic prejudice. This also is clearly similar to statements made by Pastor David Platt, who blamed the Church for some of the historical racism in America. He says, "I trust we know in every era of American racism white

---

507 Samuel Smith, "Matt Chandler: Church has mostly 'refused to participate' on race, 'turned over' inheritance," Christian Post.com, June 10, 2020, https://www.christian-post.com/news/matt-chandler-church-has-mostly-refused-to-participate-on-race-turned-over-inheritance.html.

508 DiAngelo, 16.

509 "Matt Chandler Rips Christian Church, Says It Has Mostly 'Refused to Participate; on Race Issues," CBN News.com, June 14, 2020, https://www1.cbn.com/cbnnews/us/2020/june/matt-chandler-rips-christian-church-says-it-has-mostly-refused-to-participate-on-race-issues.

Christians have often been found complicit, if not contributing . . . I would include many of the pastors and theologians I quote from . . . I think we need to at least ask the question will history see a stain in us?"[510] To be fair, all Christians ought to recognize that sin has impacted the history of the world, including America. Church history reveals Christians were men and women of clay feet that were flawed. There were glorious times of triumph, and there were dark points. The context of American slavery was undoubtedly a very dark point for the Church, but not all white Christians were contributing to slavery; many stood against it and praised God that it was abolished. It is also perplexing how the "wounds of racism" are the inheritance of the Church today. According to the apostle Peter, the inheritance of the Church is in Heaven:

> Blessed be the God and Father of our Lord Jesus Christ! According to his great mercy, he has caused us to be born again to a living hope through the resurrection of Jesus Christ from the dead, to an inheritance that is imperishable, undefiled, and unfading, kept in heaven for you, who by God's power are being guarded through faith for a salvation ready to be revealed in the last time (1 Peter 1:3-5).

According to Platt, the historical stain of ethnic prejudice may have been credited to the Church today. Otherwise, why would the question need to be asked, "Will history see a stain in us?" What is more important to emphasize, despite all the sins and stains of sinners, is what God has done for the Bride of Christ. The apostle Paul tells us precisely what Jesus has done: "Christ loved the church and gave himself up for her, that he might sanctify her, having cleansed her by the washing of water with the word, so that he might present the church to himself in splendor, without spot or wrinkle or any such thing, that she might be holy and without blemish" (Eph. 5:25b-27). By the mercy of

---

510 "Praying and Working for Justice: Racialization," McLean Bible Church, May 27, 2020, YouTube Video, 45:38, https://m.youtube.com/watch?v=UUs5mQoWBP8.

Jesus Christ, the wretched, rebellious worms stained with a legion of sins have been covered with His precious blood so that there are no more stains!

On another occasion, Chandler stated, "A lot of times the systemic racism can't even be seen by the people that are in the system, like priests that were given terrible sacrifices at the temple in the Old Testament."[511] This statement sounds somewhat similar to John Piper, who said, "The more dominant the culture is the more invisible it seems to us. And I think it is true that there is more cultural captivity in our churches and in our lives than most of us realize. So that's the first thing I wanted to say to us who are white."[512] No one would argue that Christians are not blind to sin. Surely, all ethnicities of people can be blind to sins or exercise partiality, but that is not what is said. Rather, these statements seem to be rooted less in Scripture and more in standpoint epistemology and Woke CRT dogma, since they emphasize white people, dominant culture, invisibility, and unseen racism. For example, according to the *Encyclopedia of Diversity and Social Justice*, "CRT emphasizes that overt expressions of racism have gone underground and are now expressed through insidious and covert methods."[513] It is astonishing how similar these statements are with Piper's above. Piper also uses Justin Brierley as an example to encourage Christians to be cautious against slanderous, pejorative labels such as CRT. Brierley complains, "The church is being brought ethical concerns and is responding with epistemological critique."[514] To be fair, there are ethical concerns with ethnic prejudice that Christians ought to address. However, the larger problem is when those ethical concerns are understood

---

511 "Matt Chandler on Privilege: What It Is, Why It's White, and Who It Affects," Exponential, September 18, 2020, YouTube video, 1:05:28, https://m.youtube.com/watch?v=QgSK63ZaHI4.

512 John Piper, "Together for Good? My Burden for Our Racial Brokenness – John Piper," Desiring God, November 30, 2017, YouTube video, 49:55, https://youtu.be/6Bsdy_IGEZQ.

513 Sherwood Thompson, ed., *Encyclopedia of Diversity and Social Justice* (London: Rowman & Littlefield, 2015), 65.

514 Neil Shenvi and Rasool Berry, "Is Critical Race Theory compatible with Christianity? Neil Shenvi & Rasool Berry," Unbelievable?, October 16, 2020, YouTube video, 1:18:51, https://www.youtube.com/watch?v=KbzPDoEgO_s.

through and addressed with CRT. The critique of CRT is largely warranted because it not only has epistemological issues but also ethical implications that are incompatible with Scripture as I have addressed in previous chapters. Ironically, Piper cautions Christians against using CRT as a pejorative label to slander, when he clearly sympathizes with elements of it.[515] He says:

> So, critical race theory (add race to critical theory) tries to understand and challenge (deal critically with) the power and oppression relationships that have marked racial groups historically, and still do to this day. Now, it's true that the focus on groups, while minimizing the individual, and the focus on power, while minimizing other relational dynamics (like love and humility and graciousness), can skew our understanding and yield unhelpful strategies. Nevertheless, those very focuses, misleading as they might be in some ways, can also reveal insights that may be strategically helpful in moving toward greater justice.[516]

It is problematic that Piper believes critical race theory's focus on groups can be helpful in achieving justice. It is clearly warranted to charge evangelicals of sympathizing with CRT, including Piper, and this is not slander; this is a matter of fact by their own words.

In his book *Woke Church*, Eric Mason says being woke is to be "socially aware of issues that have systemic impact . . . seeing all of the issues and being able to connect the cultural, socio-economic, philosophical, historical, and ethical dots."[517] Wokeness is dominated by looking at social issues through the lens of systemic causes or impacts while denying the root cause of sin in the heart of man. Perhaps more problematic is the statement by Mason: "Justification is a huge greenhouse of truth that extends beyond 'being declared

---

515   John Piper, "Critical Race Theory, Part 1," Desiring God.org, November 23, 2020, desiringgod.org/interviews/critical-race-theory-part-1.

516   John Piper, "Critical Race Theory, Part 2," Desiring God.org, November 24, 2020, https://www.desiringgod.org/interviews/critical-race-theory-part-2.

517   Eric Mason, *Woke Church: An Urgent Call for Christians in America to Confront Racism and Injustice* (Chicago: Moody Publishers, 2018), 25.

righteous'! Justified isn't merely a position, but a practice."[518] It is clear Mason has confused or misunderstood the cardinal doctrine of justification by faith here. At times, he sounds Roman Catholic.

It is also clear that D.A Horton's "thebonics" from Eric Mason's *Woke Church* are impacting evangelism and the methodology of community outreach.[519] Seth Richardson recounts that as a result of being influenced at a conference hosted by Mason, an elder at his church caused evangelism to change in their church and community. As a result, Richardson was told by this elder, "[W] e should approach men, especially young black men . . . differently than we would approach white men on the street . . . We had to come to them more in a posture of humility with our head down . . . I think he was feeling guilt and he lumped us all into his guilt."[520]

Richardson expressed his concerns with his leadership and was introduced to "white privilege," which he was wrongly led to believe blinded him to the reality of true issues. "It seemed to be more building the ethnic dynamic of the church . . . That seemed to be the goal. I think it is pressure from the Southern Baptist Convention."[521]

I can relate to this statement by Richardson because when I attended the 2013 Southern Baptist Convention in Houston, Texas, I experienced something similar. During the meeting, a group of students, alumni from an SBC seminary, and I were effectively shamed by Danny Akin, the president of Southeastern Baptist Theological Seminary, that the room was filled with mostly white people and lacked ethnic minorities. The repeated claim was our churches ought to ethnically look like our communities. The push to bring about ethnic diversity in churches and institutions may have had good intentions, since the text often cited to enact this is Revelation chapters four

---

518   Ibid, 45.
519   Seth Richardson, "How Woke Evangelism Corrupts the Gospel with Seth Rich-ardson," Conversations That Matter, June 25, 2020, YouTube video, 22:28, https://www.youtube.com/watch?v=ou9Vsds9Wh8&list=PLqA7HoggRbpy5id8A3_Dbod5slS1Jrgbk&index=21.
520   Ibid.
521   Ibid.

and five. The idea is that since Heaven is made up of people from all different ethnic groups, our churches must do the same. However, this is a category error because it confuses the eternal kingdom of God in the new heavens and new earth with the temporal, ethnic demographic of the local church today. Yes, churches ought to be multiethnic insofar as their local demographic is multiethnic. However, this rule can lead to unbalanced applications and unintended consequences. Churches can fall into error by only presenting the Gospel in minority communities and, in effect, being prejudiced or partial in evangelism. It can lead to the primary goal that the Church needs to be an "ethnically diverse church," instead of making disciples of all nations for God's glory. It can lead to designing evangelicalism methods that hyper-emphasize ethnic identity. Worst of all, it can lead to the embrace of secular ideology, such as critical race theory and syncretization of Woke dogma within the Church, which is happening in American evangelism.

In a *New York Times* interview with Dr. Walter Strickland, professor at Southeastern Baptist Theological Seminary, the journalist writes, "When he speaks to conservative white congregations, he is careful."[522] Strickland said, "While Cone's ideas are in play, I don't mention him by name, because I don't want to put unnecessary stumbling blocks in their way." Scripture's authority comes first. "If I'm able to demonstrate that this black man in front of them has read the Bible, I gain credit with them."[523] In a discussion called "Remembering James Cone," Strickland says:

> Dr. Cone opened my eyes to the idea that Christ is trying to restore brokenness, you know, and he really had a focus on that brokenness manifesting as oppression racially speaking. He showed me that you know God is after redeeming the brokenness in society through the work of Christ. So as Dr. Cone almost sees the implications of the gospel as the totality of the gospel

---

522   Molly Worthen, "Can Black Evangelicals Save the Whole Movement?," New York Times.com, April 20, 2019, https://www.nytimes.com/2019/04/20/opinion/sunday/black-evangelicals-diversity.html.

523   Ibid.

it would seem; at times I sort of am looking at you know this big umbrella of God's redemption and seeing it both as individual and social because Christ said it himself to his disciples, that a summary of the gospel is not to bifurcate (split) loving God and loving neighbor but it is to love God and neighbor . . . Dr. Cone allowed me to see a new vista, a new space, a new avenue to allow the gospel to be made manifest. So I sort of look at what the gospel is doing as a more broad reality now. Not that I've switched the spiritual for the physical or the social but both.

It is clear among other issues here, Dr. Cone's influence upon Strickland appears to cause him to conflate the Law with the Gospel. Strickland says above that a summary of the Gospel is loving God and loving neighbor. However, that is Law—the first and second greatest commandments. Law is not the Gospel—good news. In all charity, Strickland may have misspoke, or that may have not been what he meant. To be clear, the Gospel is the finished work of Christ, which included Jesus keeping the Law on behalf of His people as a substitute Sacrifice.

It is somewhat troubling that Cone, who is a heretic, had such an influence on the theological formation of a professor at Southeastern Baptist Theological Seminary. Cone's heretical views are widely known. Cone writes, "God transformed lynched black bodies into the recrucified body of Christ."[524] Cone's theology is embedded in Martin Luther King and Malcom X's ideologies. He writes, "For me, the burning theological question was, how can I reconcile Christianity with Black Power, Martin Luther King, Jr.'s idea of nonviolence and Malcolm X's 'by any means necessary' philosophy?"[525] In James Cone's theology, black liberation from white oppression is the gospel.

Liberation theology can be categorized into black, feminist, and third-world theologies. A common theme of these various forms of liberation theology is that the power classes of society have oppressed the less powerful or powerless

---

524 James Cone, *The Cross and the Lynching Tree* (New York: Orbis Books, 2011), 158.
525 James Cone, *Black Theology and Black Power* (New York: Orbis Books, 1997), viii.

classes. Theologically, salvation consists in the liberation of the less powerful classes, which is an error. This is demonstrated by the statement by Cone: "Black theology cannot accept a view of God which does not represent him as being for blacks and thus against whites. Living in a world of white oppressors, black people have no time for a neutral God."[526] This system advocates that God's main goal is to deliver black people from the oppression of white people through political effort and revolution. Clearly committed to liberation theology, Cone writes, "What else can the crucifixion mean except that God, the Holy One of Israel, became identified with the victims of oppression? What else can the resurrection mean except that God's victory in Christ is the poor person's victory over poverty?"[527] Liberation theologians argue that the Marxist analytical system divides society between oppressors and oppressed to engage in transformation. According to Webster, one of the problems with liberation theology is it "threatens to politicize the gospel to the point that the poor are offered a solution that could be provided without Jesus."[528]

Finally, in a video discussion, Strickland says of Cone, "He's prolific, he's written monograph after monograph . . . you may agree with more or less of what he says. But either way you will be blessed by that."[529] One wonders how Christians can be blessed by heresy. In this same book, *The Cross and His Lynching Tree*, Cone writes, "The gospel is found wherever poor people struggle for justice, fighting for the right to life, liberty, and the pursuit of happiness."[530] This statement evidences liberation theology. Biblically, the Gospel is found wherever Christians proclaim Christ's life, death, burial, and resurrection. Sey connects Cone's theology with Woke Christianity. He says, "Woke Christianity embraces several concerning elements of Black Liberation Theology. For instance, woke Christianity does not entirely reject James

---

526 Cone, *Black Theology*, 131-32.
527 James Cone, *Speaking the Truth: Ecumenism, Liberation, and Black Theology* (New York: Orbis Books, 1999), 6.
528 Elwell, 687.
529 "By What Standard? God's World . . . God's Rules (CINEDOC)," Founders Ministries, June 8, 2020, YouTube video, 1:50:29, https://www.youtube.com/watch?v=pFHfaos1XLM.
530 Cone, *The Cross and the Lynching Tree*, 155.

Cone's position that Black people are in some ways, morally superior to White people. Woke Christianity subscribes to the 'prejudice plus power' definition of racism, suggesting that Black people cannot be racists."[531]

The prejudice-plus-power definition of ethnic prejudice overlaps with critical race theory. Sey writes, "[Woke Christianity] makes liberation from perceived racial injustice a central message of the gospel."[532] The evident relationship between Woke Christianity and Cone's liberation theology renders the influence of Cone more questionable. Yet in the "Remembering James Cone" discussion, Strickland says, "For me, I can follow James Cone into this new theological space but still there's room enough in that space to do it with my own theological convictions, my own theological presuppositions, and then there's lots of diversity in that mix."[533] It is evident from Strickland's words that he was influenced by Cone, admires him, and unites his theology with Cone. This is one example that demonstrates the syncretization of the liberation theology component of Woke religion into evangelicalism.

Tim Keller also appears to be influenced by liberation theology and critical theory. In his best-selling book *The Reason for God*, Keller explains his first exposure to critical theory in college. He writes, "The history and philosophy departments were socially radicalized and were heavily influenced by the neo-Marxist critical theory of the Frankfurt School. In 1968, this was heady stuff. The social activism was particularly attractive, and the critique of American bourgeoisie society was compelling."[534]

---

531 Samuel Sey, "Black Liberation Theology and Woke Christianity," SlowtoWrite. com, May 5, 2018, https://slowtowrite.com/black-liberation-theology-and-woke-christianity.

532 Ibid.

533 "Christian Voices on the Cultural Moment: A Collection of Essays by Southeastern Women on Issues Facing Christians Today," The Pulpit and the Pen.org, Accessed September 14, 2020, https://pulpitandpen.org/wp-content/uploads/2019/05/WOKE-SEBTS_watermark-2.pdf.

534 Timothy Keller, *The Reason for God: Belief in an Age of Skepticism* (New York: Penguin Books, 2009), xi-xii.

Keller admits early on to being "emotionally drawn" to neo-Marxist social justice.[535] Of course, that was several decades ago, but notice in the book, he also writes, "The story of the gospel makes sense of moral obligation and our belief in the reality of justice, so Christians do restorative and redistributive justice wherever they can. The story of the gospel makes sense of our indelible religiousness, so Christians do evangelism, pointing the way to forgiveness and reconciliation with God through Jesus."[536]

The Gospel story affects a moral obligation to do redistributive justice? Other evangelicals appear to agree. Thabiti Anyabwile, pastor of Anacostia River Church in Washington, D.C., suggests reparations ought to be given to African Americans and that opposing them comes from the devil.[537] In a discussion on acknowledging the evil that took place in America's past, particularly among native Americans and African Americans, he explains, "You realize that there is a root of pride there that is resistant to repentance, is resistant to culpability, is resistant to any form of redress or reparation. This strong cold of sort of whiteness and white identity and pristineness is really part of what keeps us from making any progress on this because if for Christians in particular it should not be a threat to be wrong."[538]

He is right that it is prideful to not acknowledge the sins of American's past insofar as history reveals. However, it is clear he wants Christians to do more than acknowledge history. He inaccurately implies that it is prideful to resist culpability, redress, or reparation and that "whiteness" limits progress. It is unclear if reparations would right the wrongs of the past or if this is biblical. What is more troubling is the claim that pride is the cause for why

---

535 Ibid, xii.
536 Ibid, 233.
537 Jeff Maples, "Thabiti Anyabwile Says Opposing Reparations for Blacks Comes From the Devil," Reformation Charlotte.org, March 16, 2019, https://reformationcharlotte.org/2019/03/16/thabiti-anyabwile-says-opposing-reparations-for-blacks-comes-from-the-devil.
538 Thabiti Anyabwile and Soong Chan Rah, "Repenting of American Exceptionalism and Whiteness - Thabiti Anyabwile & Soong Chan Rah," VergeNetwork, August 21, 2020, YouTube video, 5:34, https://youtu.be/y7oxoTiCh34.

white Christians resist culpability for the evil that took place in America's history. This is one of the mistakes of Woke social justice, since it is biblically impossible to be held culpable for the sins of others, particularly white people who lived in the 1800s. Anyabwile is clearly influenced by CRT in his understanding of the doctrine of sin, given that CRT teaches group identity and white guilt ideology.

Moreover, in a question and answer session at Redeemer Presbyterian Church, Keller said, "If you have white skin, it's worth $1,000,000 over a lifetime . . . you have to say . . . 'I am the product of and standing on the shoulders of other people who got that through injustice' . . . the *Bible says you are involved in injustice, and even if you didn't actually do it*" (emphasis mine).[539]

These staggering claims suggest that all white people have wealth because they received it unjustly. This ideology has been widely taught in critical theory because white people are part of the oppressive class and are involved in injustices they did not commit, since they are part of the oppressor group, functioning like avatars or ambassadors of their group, which incorporates people who are dead. In this way, the injustices of the past can functionally be charged to you if you are representative of that particular group. According to critical race theory, one has committed injustice and is racist simply by being white, identifying them with the oppressor group.

Moreover, Keller writes in *Generous Justice*, "Jesus, in his incarnation, 'moved in' with the poor . . . In Proverbs we see God identifying with the poor symbolically. But in the incarnation and death of Jesus, we see God identifying with the poor and marginal literally."[540] This concept comes from liberation theology and social justice. Naylor critiques Keller when he says, "The Bible does not present the incarnation as moving in with the poor. Christ came into the world to save sinners . . . When Keller focuses on poverty

---

539 "Grace, Justice, & Mercy: An Evening with Bryan Stevenson & Rev. Tim Keller Q&A," RedeemerCFW, June 3, 2016, YouTube video, 51:32, https://youtu.be/32CHZiVFmB4.

540 Timothy Keller, *Generous Justice: How God's Grace Makes Us Just* (New York: Penguin Books, 2012), 185-86.

and injustice, he distorts the incarnation and crucifixion, and takes us away from the purpose of both—which was to save sinners—and leads us into the byway of social transformation. He is leading us to concentrate on the wrong goal."[541] Apparently, "He agreed with Liberation theologian James Cone that slaves, because of their 'experience of oppression,' were able 'to see things in the Bible' like a 'God who comes down from heaven and becomes a poor human being,' which 'many of their masters were blind to.' This difference in experience was so great it nurtured a 'real Christianity' as opposed to the oppressive 'Master's religion.'"[542] Keller is also critiqued for failing to omit the true mission of the church, to "make disciples of all nations" (Matt. 28:19).[543] It is clear that at best, Keller places an unbalanced emphasis on social justice rather than preaching the eternal salvation of Christ to lost sinners, who are in rebellion against God, under condemnation. Does one wonder if the Gospel for Keller is Christ alone or Christ plus social justice?

While Keller sometimes seems to embrace critical theory, on other occasions, he rightly critiques it. Perhaps the most significant criticism of critical theory is:

> Finally, it [postmodern—power] is prone to domination. This theory sees liberal values such as freedom of speech and freedom of religion—as mere ways to oppress people. Often this view puts these "freedoms" in scare quotes. As a result, adherents of this theory resort to constant expressions of anger and outrage to silence critics, as well as to censorship and other kinds of social, economic, and legal pressure to marginalize opposing views. The postmodern view sees all injustice as happening on a human level and so demonizes human beings rather than recognizing the evil forces–"the world, the flesh, and the devil"–at work

541 Iain Campbell and William Schweitzer, eds., *Engaging with Keller: Thinking Through the Theology of an Influential Evangelical* (Darlington: Evangelical Press, 2013), 158-59.

542 "Tim Keller and Progress Evangelicalism," Enemies Within the Church.com, August 22, 2020, https://enemieswithinthechurch.com/2020/08/22/tim-keller-and-progressive-evangelicalism.

543 "Keller's Political Motivation," The New Calvinists.com, Accessed September 8, 2020, http://www.newcalvinist.com/kellers-political-motivation.

through all human life, including your own. Adherents of this view also end up being utopian—they see themselves as saviors rather than recognizing that only a true, divine Savior will be able to finally bring in justice. When dealing with injustice we do confront human sin, but in addition "we wrestle not [merely] with flesh and blood (Ephesians 6:12).[544]

In the same article, he inconsistently uses critical theory language of privilege in his Gospel presentation. He writes, "So in Jesus we see God laying aside his privilege and power—his 'glory'—in order to identify with the weak and helpless" (Phil. 2:5-8).[545] This creates confusion and leads to error. We live in a time that needs clear biblical exegesis, not the combination of ideas from a counterfeit secular ideology and false religion. Furthermore, in this same phrase, "identify with the weak and helpless," Keller is using liberation theology similar to Cone's. Weber is correct to critique this same use of liberation theology in the *Evangelical Dictionary of Theology*: "[Liberation Theology] claims [Jesus] is different from us by degree, not by kind, and that his cross is the climax of his vicarious identification with suffering humankind rather than a substitutionary death offered on our behalf to turn away the wrath of God and triumph over sin, death, and the devil."[546]

Keller is inserting alien teaching from Woke dogma into the text. Also, notice that the words *privilege* or *identify* do not appear in the verses he cites from Philippians: "Have this mind among yourselves, which is yours in Christ Jesus, who, though he was in the form of God, did not count equality with God a thing to be grasped, but emptied himself, by taking the form of a servant, being born in the likeness of men. And being found in human form, he humbled himself by becoming obedient to the point of death, even death on a cross" (Phil. 2:5-8).

---

544 Timothy Keller, "A Biblical Critique of Secular Justice and Critical Theory," Life in the Gospel online, Accessed October 1, 2020, https://quarterly.gospelinlife.com/a-biblical-critique-of-secular-justice-and-critical-theory.
545 Ibid.
546 Weber, 688.

James White also points out these same errors in Keller's teaching. White comments on Keller's claims:

> You will not find weak and helpless anywhere in Philippians 2:5-8. What you will find is the Son taking on human nature. And by the way, God in his grace has saved rich men, powerful men. Believe it or not, God has even saved White men. And he never ever says that decision is based upon ethnicity and race . . . No where . . . are we told that He laid aside His glory to identify with the weak and helpless. He took on a perfect human nature so that He might die upon the cross. And when you place dying upon the cross of Calvary with some kind of Social Justice theory you are this close to walking right out of the Faith.[547]

Keller then claims, "And yet, through the endurance of violence and human injustice he paid the rightful penalty of humanity's sin to divine justice (Isaiah 53:5)."[548] To which White responds, "God used violence and human injustice but to make them the primary category is to miss the whole point of the submission of the Son to the Father in the perfect provision of salvation itself."[549] As I discussed Keller's teaching as charitably as possible, I agree in principle with Keller that the Church ought to do more to love our neighbors, relieve the poor, seek justice for the oppressed. This is undeniably biblical, good, and right. However, given the influence that Keller has among evangelicals, it is important to examine his teaching for balance, potential syncretism with non-biblical philosophies, and the influence of Woke religion.

Given that many evangelical leaders sympathize or embrace Woke social justice, it follows that churches have been influenced by the ideologies, and the fruit has been destructive. One of the most disturbing examples of dangerous impacts has been exposed in First Baptist Church Naples, Florida.

547 James White, "Woke Religion with Tim Keller, Fulgentius of Ruspe on the Hypostatic Union," Alpha and Omega Ministries, August 4, 2020, 01:17:43, https://www.aomin.org/aoblog/exegesis/woke-religion-with-tim-keller-fulgentius-of-ruspe-on-the-hypostatic-union.
548 Keller, Ibid.
549 White, Ibid.

After a series of controversial circumstances that led to the resignation of their senior pastor, leaders within the SBC strongly advocated that they vote in another pastor, Marcus Hayes. Hayes clearly sympathized with Woke ideology, including his endorsement of the book, *Woke Church*.[550] Within forty-eight hours after the majority of the members did not vote in Marcus Hayes, seventeen members were excommunicated without following the Matthew 18 model for church discipline.[551] In an open letter to the SBC, the executive pastor charged, "19% that voted against Marcus Hayes did so based on racial prejudices."[552] These unfounded allegations continued to spread by J.D. Greear and other leaders of the SBC on Twitter. Greear wrote, "Sin has to be taken seriously in the church, and racial bias belies our gospel."[553] These smears of racism are deeply troubling and demonstrate the fruit of the Woke social justice influence upon the Church. Woke social justice continues to harm countless Christians, scatter believers, and divide evangelical churches across America.

I am saddened that these selected sources reveal Woke religion, at best, has influenced evangelical leaders and at worst, in some cases, been embraced. The marriage of Woke religion with evangelicalism has not gone unnoticed by Christians, and an increasing number of evangelicals are responding to this phenomenon. We will turn to this Christian response now in the next chapter.

---

550 "Enemies Within The Church: The Story of First Baptist Church Naples," Enemies Within, November 25, 2020, YouTube video, 38:21, https://www.youtube.com/watch?v=3zoe6tNmRyk&feature=youtu.be.

551 Ibid.

552 John D. Edie to Southern Baptist Convention, October 31, 2019, Letter, https://documentcloud.adobe.com/link/track?uri=urn%3Aaaid%3Ascds%3AUS%3A7a882a55-9dfd-4ba0-9d12-2eb675b1bc4d#pageNum=1.

553 Julie Roys and Josh Shepherd, "Excommunicated Baptists Say Megachurch Smeared Them as Racists—and so did SBC Leaders," The Roys Report online, March 17, 2020, https://julieroys.com/excommunicated-baptists-say-megachurch-smeared-them-as-racists-and-so-did-sbc-leaders.

CHAPTER FOURTEEN

AN EVANGELICAL RESPONSE TO WOKE

IN RECENT YEARS, THERE HAS been a growing coalition of evangelicals standing firm against Woke. Conferences, books, statements of faith, sermons, and other materials have been produced in opposition to the counterfeit Woke religion. There are too many to name here, so only a few important points of response will be mentioned. One indication evangelicals are organizing in opposition to this false teaching is that at least 14,484 people have signed the Statement on Social Justice that rejects critical theory. The section on Race/Ethnicity states:

> WE DENY that Christians should segregate themselves into racial groups or regard racial identity above, or even equal to, their identity in Christ. We deny that any divisions between people groups (from an unstated attitude of superiority to an overt spirit of resentment) have any legitimate place in the fellowship of the redeemed. We reject any teaching that encourages racial groups to view themselves as privileged oppressors or entitled victims of oppression. While we are to weep with those who weep, we deny that a person's feelings of offense or oppression necessarily prove that someone else is guilty of sinful behaviors, oppression, or prejudice.[554]

---

554 "The Statement on Social Justice & the Gospel," Statement on Social Justice.com, Accessed September 20, 2020, https://statementonsocialjustice.com/wp-content/uploads/2018/09/SSJG-FINAL.pdf.

Supporters of the statement of social justice have called on progressive evangelical leaders who promote the social justice movement and grievance gospel (Woke religion) to resign. Dr. Josh Buice, founder of G3 Ministries, "called out two prominent Southern Baptist promoters of Neo-Marxist ideology—Russell Moore, president of the Ethics and Religious Liberty Commission (ERLC) of the Southern Baptist Convention (SBC), and Ed Stetzer, former LifeWay VP and SBC Resolutions Committee Chairman."[555] Dr. Buice has stated, "If your church is hitched to the woke movement and the woke message (CRT/I) it's time to find a new church. The grievance gospel is a false gospel."[556]

One of the main deceptions of Woke religion is to mask Christian ideas into neo-Marxist ideology. Allen provides a powerful testimony that exposes the counterfeit nature of Woke religion. He writes in his book *Why Social Justice is Not Biblical Justice*:

> Over time I came to see that the Marxist worldview assumptions do far more to harm the poor than to help them. I did not see the poor as fully human, created in the image of God, with dignity, responsibility, and the capacity to create new wealth and new opportunities. My former Marxist-influenced worldview saw them largely as helpless victims, dependent upon the beneficent Westerners to overcome poverty.[557]

This is a helpful critique, since much of the influence of social justice upon the Church has been as a result of a genuine concern for the poor, oppressed, and justice. Evidently, evangelical churches have abandoned biblical justice for the false teachings of Woke religion and the worldview of what Allen coins, "ideological social justice." Christians rightly express

---

555 "Josh Buice: Russell Moore, Ed Stetzer should resign," Capstone Report.com, October 10, 2020, https://capstonereport.com/2020/10/10/josh-buice-russell-moore-ed-stetzer-should-resign/35026.

556 Josh Buice, Twitter Post, October 13, 2020, 8:31 AM, https://twitter.com/JoshBuice/status/1315993622068813824.

557 Allen, 6.

biblical commitment to the justice of the moral law, loving our neighbor, and loving God. Christians also understand that there is an important distinction between the Law and the Gospel. The Gospel "is the power of God for salvation to everyone who believes" (Rom. 1:16). The Gospel saves sinners from Hell, gives them a new heart, and gives them the desire and ability to keep the Law by the Holy Spirit.

The Puritan divines write, "The Spirit of Christ subduing and enabling the will of man to do that freely, and cheerfully, which the will of God, revealed in the law requires to be done."[558] The reformation of churches, communities, government, and all levels of society can take place by God's sovereign grace and mercy as a result of lives transformed by the Gospel of Christ. Alternatively, it is an error to adopt extra-biblical systems of philosophy for this end, especially those maintained by Woke dogmas that are antithetical to Christianity. Would Christians accept the utilization of Islamic, Buddhist, or other false religious teachings to address moral and social issues? If not, then why ought Christians to integrate the neo-Marxist teachings of Woke religion into the Christian teachings to address problems in the Church and society? Is not the Scripture sufficient? Christians are right to not reduce the effect of sin within society and injustices that have manifested in the world since the Fall. However, Christians should not embrace the empty philosophy of the world to address sin.

Voddie Baucham is one of the prominent evangelical leaders who have stood against Woke religion. He coined the phrase "ethnic Gnostism" from the Greek word *gnosis*—secret knowledge—similar to perspectivism.[559] Gnostism was a cult in the first century of the Church, whereby the material world was thought to be evil—deliverance from it only came through *gnosis*—and salvation was a heretical form of philosophical dualism—from it came secret knowledge or gnosis. Ethnic gnostism is very similar to CRT and rooted in

---

558 The Westminster Confession of Faith, Ibid.

559 *Merriam Webster Dictionary*, s.v. "perspectivism," accessed November 5, 2020, https://www.merriam-webster.com/dictionary/perspectivism.

neo-Marxism in that only the minority group can know ethnic prejudice or "gnosis" or true knowledge. Voddie points this out: "[In] cultural Marxism you divide the world between those who establish and benefit from the cultural hegemony and everyone else who is oppressed by it because for one reason or another they are not part of the dominate group. This idea [Ethnic Gnostism] is rooted in that."[560]

Many Woke evangelicals call people to "listen" to the minorities in society. The Bible teaches that Christians ought to do more than listen; we ought to obey God and care for orphans and widows because this is pure religion (Jas. 1:26-27). The context of oppression and injustice in the Bible is not the same as the categories of Woke religion. In Scripture, the oppressed are those in a foreign land that may not speak the same language, orphans who do not have fathers to protect them, or widows without husbands. Furthermore, the Scripture says, "Beloved, do not believe every spirit, but test the spirits to see whether they are from God, for many false prophets have gone out into the world" (1 John 4:1). Christians ought to exercise biblical discernment and wisdom in these matters to determine what is just, right, and good.

African American Anglican pastor Sam Murrell no longer will participate in "racial reconciliation" church worship services. He says:

> Too often, the premise of the worship service is that Whites are guilty because they are White. This is evident in the fact that the white people present at such events are expected, even pressured, to confess the sin of racism even if they cannot recall any specific instances of racist action that they have perpetrated. The assumption is that because you are white then you must have knowingly, or unknowingly, cause[d] offense towards Blacks (and maybe other ethnic minorities too).[561]

---

560 Voddie Baucham, "Ethnic Gnosticism," Founders.org, Accessed September 15, 2020, https://founders.org/sermons/ethnic-gnosticism.

561 Sam Murrell, "Why I No Longer Participate in Racial Reconciliation Services," The Pulpit and Pen.org, January 27, 2018, https://pulpitandpen.org/2018/01/27/no-longer-participate-racial-reconciliation-services.

This teaching creates division based on skin color and neo-Marxist categories. The Gospel, on the other hand, creates unity among Christians. In a sermon on Ephesians 2, Voddie quotes Ephesians 2:14-16:

> "But now in Christ Jesus you who once were far off have been brought near by the blood of Christ. For he himself is our peace, who has made us both one and has broken down in his flesh the dividing wall of hostility by abolishing the law of commandments expressed in ordinances, that he might create in himself one new man in place of the two, so making peace, and might reconcile us both to God in one body through the cross, thereby killing the hostility."[562]

Voddie says, "That is reconciliation. And it is not something you and I have to achieve. It is something you and I have to believe because Christ has already achieved it. It is done. It is real. We are one in Christ. And the rest of it is just walking in that reality."[563]

John MacArthur has been one of the chief evangelical proponents against CRT, social justice, and Woke. In an article published by *The Daily Wire*, he writes, "We all acknowledge that racism exists and that it is a manifestation of sin of partiality which the Bible directly condemns (James 2:9). In case you are not familiar with CRT, it is vicious, pernicious, and virulent brand of identity politics that results when neo-Marxist social philosophy is blended with postmodern theory."[564] Interestingly, he connects the same stain language to CRT by stating, "'Racism' is unconquerable and ubiquitous; it is the singular evil that underlies virtually everything wrong with our culture. It is 'the stain that will never be removed.'"[565] One reason John MacArthur has been perhaps the most outspoken critic of wokeness among evangelicals is that

---

562 Voddie Baucham, "Racial Reconciliation - Ephesians 2:10-11," Founders Ministries, March 27, 2019, YouTube video, 54:03, https://www.youtube.com/watch?v=FoJGYCc7EUg.
563 Ibid.
564 MacArthur, Ibid.
565 Ibid.

he has a strong understanding of the major doctrines. He provides a concise summary of them as follows:

- "Systemic racism" and "unconscious bias" are built into the current structure of western society. This cannot be remedied apart from the wholesale dismantling and restructuring of political mechanisms, economic, policies, moral standards, and other social norms.

- White people are members of the world's most privileged ethnic group. "White privilege" is not only one of the main proofs of systematic racism; it is also a subtle but sinister injustice to other people groups.

- The term *racism* describes a uniquely white pathology. Members of less privileged ethnic groups are victims, not perpetrators, of social injustice—and it is therefore legitimate for them to retaliate with retributive violence or expressions of ethnic contempt. This is not "racism," but an appropriate response to the oppression they suffer . . .

- "White supremacy so permeates out institutions, policies, practices, and ways of knowing that it is nearly impossible to think outside it." It is full-on "racial terrorism."

- All White people are racists, whether they want to be or not.

- "Whiteness" is therefore an evil that must be confessed and repudiated, but without any guarantee of forgiveness.

- Members of privileged ethnic groups who deny being racists are guilty of perpetuating racism.[566]

MacArthur goes on to explain that it is no wonder after a decade of indoctrination of this toxic ideology, the consequence has been an "explosion of animosity and civic unrest."[567] This worldview has been designed and

---

566 Ibid.
567 Ibid.

strategically built to create destruction. MacArthur says it "deliberately ferments and feeds on resentment, strife, hatred, and division."[568]

MacArthur believes critical race theory is a "ruthlessly cynical, divisive, pessimistic, misanthropic, sociological cancer."[569] Then he makes an extraordinary statement that should not go unnoticed: "It is the greatest danger our nation currently faces, but no national leader has stood up to half its spread until now."[570] Throughout the article, MacArthur makes clear the CRT has no scriptural basis and that the president may even get pushback from the pastors and church leaders "who are already too heavily invested in sociological theories that have no basis in Scripture." The most important part of MacArthur's stand against CRT here is that CRT fails to identify the real problem of the human race—sin and being under Divine judgment. It also focuses on the temporal and substitutes the centrality of Jesus Christ and the cross with vain, earthly things. CRT twists reconciliation, hope, and forgiveness for sinners with the lie that people are victims of other's sins. MacArthur argues that today's evangelicals like many pragmatists in the last century by the changing of the wind will buy into the latest cultural movement, fad, theory, or ideology to maintain being "relevant." By the beginning of the twenty-first century, this is precisely what happened when postmodernism was "repacked and aggressively promoting itself as the Emerging Church Movement."[571]

He rightly identifies the multi-headed dragon of postmodern critical theory married to identity politics. "Today," says MacArthur, "critical race theory, feminism, 'toxic masculinity,' intersectional theory, LBGT advocacy . . . and other left-wing political causes are all actively vying for evangelical acceptance under the rubric of 'social justice.'"[572] Most significantly, as I have shown examples of above, MacArthur agrees that evangelical leaders are employing the same language and philosophy of victimhood versus

---

568 Ibid.
569 Ibid.
570 Ibid.
571 Ibid.
572 Ibid.

oppression that is utilized by the secular critical theorists. "Indeed, as social justice rhetoric has gained currency among evangelicals," says MacArthur, "just about every cause that is deemed politically correct in the secular world has found a foothold among evangelicals. CRT is one of those causes. It would be folly to pretend CRT and the social justice movement pose no thread whatsoever to evangelical conviction."

Moreover, MacArthur points out that Baptist seminaries now feature "courses and seminars indoctrinating students with CRT principles."[573] He agrees that key evangelical leaders are preaching using the language and ideas from CRT literature. MacArthur says:

> Over nearly the past decade evangelical Christian conferences have been solely devoted to race and social justice, and the message being sent is heavily influenced by the ideology of CRT. Viewpoints and vocabulary like "white privilege" and "systemic racism" have liberally been added to the liturgy or adopted as articles of faith in some evangelical organizations.[574]

MacArthur agrees with Lindsay, "CRT is a Trojan horse that will undermine and eventually eliminate core biblical values and doctrines."[575] One wonders how Trump and Lindsay (a professed atheist) could have a more spiritual backbone than evangelical pastors. Concerning evangelical pastors, MacArthur questions, "Don't they have more discernment than Trump? Apparently not."[576]

Pastors are drawing strong parallels to the Old Testament prophets to point out the errors and false shepherds within Woke. Israel forsook God and prostituted herself to false gods, according to the prophet Ezekiel. In Ezekiel 16:31-32, the Lord says, "Yet you were not like a prostitute, because you scorned payment. Adulterous wife, who receives strangers instead of her husband! Men

---

573 Ibid.
574 Ibid.
575 Ibid.
576 Ibid.

give gifts to all prostitutes, but you gave your gifts to all your lovers, bribing them to come to you from every side with your whorings." Jeff Durbin uses this passage to confront the harlotry of Woke. According to Durbin, Woke pastors, in effect, have prostituted the evangelical church in spiritual adultery against God. He says, "Woke pastors . . . You shallow the member of the Marxist denying what God says about our unity and identity in the Messiah, and you teach people our identity is in our color. Shame on you. You deny God's own word accusing people of guilt for the sinful color of their ancestors."[577]

Other evangelical teachers have given strong biblical rebukes to Woke evangelical pastors. According to Dr. Owen Strachan, *Woke* must not be tolerated in the Church. Where people have embraced Woke, Strachan states:

> We want unity in the truth of Jesus Christ, but where people have embraced Wokeness we must follow the steps of discipline per Matthew 18:15-20. We need to treat them as if they are being taken captive by ungodly ideology because they are . . . Even as we also publicly confront those teaching unbiblical ideas in a broader sense . . . excommunication must be enacted for those who after going through the Matthew 18 steps. We pray we do not have to go all the way to the end, but if we do, excommunication must happen for those who do not repent of teaching CRT, Wokeness, and intersectionality. At the institutional level the same principle applies, trustees, voting members, organizational heads, educational boards, and so on, must not tolerate the spread of Wokeness any longer. Not one day more. Not one hour more. It is time. It is time for a line in the sand.[578]

Dr. Strachan's approach demonstrates the serious nature of the false gospel of Woke religion by calling for church discipline for those who practice it.

---

577 "Jeff Durbin Confronts The Woke Church," Apologia Studios, October 5, 2020, YouTube video, 6:43, https://www.youtube.com/watch?v=QzWZtqYxl4Y.

578 Dr. Owen Strachan, "Session 3: Christianity & Wokeness | Dr. Owen Strachan | Why is Wokeness an Ungodly System?," Redeemer Bible Church, October 5, 2020, YouTube video, 1:06:59, https://www.youtube.com/watch?v=vvWbf_9WAoY&list=PLO3HHien ooFWA733Fms4nKNvO5jG52h8N&index=3.

2020 PRESIDENTIAL ELECTION

MacArthur cites the forty-fifth president of the United States, Donald Trump, who said CRT is a "sickness." Leading up to the election, President Trump called for an end of critical race theory in the Federal government and education. CRT appears in government as "racial sensitivity training and inclusion," but it is not that at all. A memo to Federal agencies reads:

> All agencies are directed to begin to identify all contracts or other agency spending related to any training on "critical race theory," "white privilege," or any other training or propaganda effort that teaches or suggests either (1) that the United States is an inherently racist or evil country or (2) that any race or ethnicity is inherently racist or evil . . . should begin to identify all available avenues within the law to cancel any such contracts and/or to divert Federal dollars away from these un-American propaganda training sessions.[579]

It is likely that the Biden administration will roll back Trump's executive order against critical race theory.[580] Given President Biden's position in support of critical race theory and other elements of Woke social justice, a significant question to ask is did evangelical leaders help influence evangelicals not to vote for Trump? There are many examples where evangelical leaders have taken a stance politically against Trump, especially leading up to the election. There were seminary professors in roundtable discussions,[581] recent books

579 Matthew Schwartz, "Trump Tells Agencies To End Trainings On 'White Privilege' And 'Critical Race Theory,'" NPR.org, September 5, 2020, https://www.npr.org/2020/09/05/910053496/trump-tells-agencies-to-end-trainings-on-white-privilege-and-critical-race-theory.

580 Jessica Guynn, "Joe Biden administration likely to overturn controversial Donald Trump diversity training executive order," USA Today.com, November 8, 2020, https://www.usatoday.com/story/money/2020/11/08/donald-trump-diversity-executive-order-joe-biden/6180668002.

581 William Willimon, Donald Matthews, Colin Adams, and James White, "The Lingering Effects of Lynching: A Reflection," Library talk, The Library at Southeastern, Wake Forest, NC, April 12, 2019, https://intersectproject.org/faith-and-culture/the-lingering-effects-of-lynching-a-reflection.

published,[582] and blogs published[583] from prominent evangelical leaders—in some cases, just prior to the election—that cast Trump in a negative light or presented arguments that would suggest not to vote for Trump. It is clear some evangelicals may have had interest in President Trump not being reelected. On Friday, November 6, 2020, a date when many allegations of voting irregularities and investigations of fraud were taking place across many states, the Ethics Religious Liberty Commission (ERLC) headed by Russell Moore posted on their website:

> Currently, there has been no evidence that voter fraud has been occurring . . . There are numerous reasons why widespread election fraud is difficult, if not impossible, to pull off at the presidential level. Political parties appoint partisan poll watchers to monitor polling places and election offices. For instance, an election office in the Democratic stronghold of Detroit had 134 Republicans, 134 Independents, and 134 Democrats as poll watchers. Extensive research has shown that voter fraud is exceeding[ly] rare, that voter impersonation is virtually nonexistent, and that many instances of alleged fraud are merely mistakes by voters or election administrators.[584]

This is no surprise to some who argue that Russell Moore and the ERLC have worked to influence voters leading up to the presidential election. A commentator for the Capstone Report wrote, "It is difficult not to assume that the ERLC (Ethics and Religious Leadership Commission) is purposefully seeking to influence the election outcome . . . Dr. Russell Moore, the president of the ERLC, has consistently and publicly opposed Donald Trump and actively sought

---

582 David Platt, *Before You Vote: Seven Questions Every Christian Should Ask* (Birmingham: Radical Inc., 2020), 30, 61-62.

583 John Piper, "Policies, Persons, and Paths to Ruin: Pondering the Implications of the 2020 Election," Desiring God.org, October 22, 2020, https://www.desiringgod.org/articles/policies-persons-and-paths-to-ruin.

584 "Explainer: What's going on with the presidential election?," Ethics and Religious Liberty Commission online, November 6, 2020, https://erlc.com/resource-library/articles/explainer-whats-going-on-with-the-presidential-election.

to undermine his evangelical reach."[585] The political direction of the ERLC has come under controversy in recent years, perhaps most significantly for the MLK50 conference because of the emphasis on social justice. It has even been reported, according to Jeff Maples, the ERLC MLK50 event allegedly received one hundred thousand dollars[586] from the Islamic billionaire Pierre Omidyar.[587]

There are indications that the Woke social justice language used by evangelicals is also being used by those who influenced the election for President Joe Biden. According to John Solomon, "The elections board in Wayne County, Michigan's largest metropolis and home to the city of Detroit, initially refused Tuesday night to certify the results of its Nov. 3 election before an angry outcry led two Republican members to compromise and approve results showing Joe Biden won."[588] What was the angry outcry that compelled Republicans to change their decision? During comments, one Michigan business owner decried both Republicans as racist. He ranted:

> The Trump stain, the stain of racism that you . . . have covered yourself in, is going to follow you throughout history. Your grand children [sic] are going to think of you . . . you will forever be known in southeastern Michigan as two racists who did something so unprecedented that they disenfranchised hundreds of thousands of black voters in the city of Detroit.[589]

585 Henry Anderson, "Documents link Democrat billionaires to Southern Baptist ERLC & Russell Moore," Capstone Report.com, November 12, 2020, https://capstonereport.com/2020/11/12/documents-link-democrat-billionaires-to-southern-baptist-erlc-russell-moore/35181.
586 "Ideas Grants Database," Democracy Fund online, Accessed November 12, 2020, https://democracyfund.nclud.com/for-partners/grants-database.
587 Jeff Maples, "ERLC Received $100K From Muslim Billionaire for MLK50 Conference," Reformation Charlotte.org, July 11, 2020, https://reformationcharlotte.org/2020/07/11/erlc-received-100k-from-muslim-billionaire-for-mlk50-conference/#.X62GBQ6rprs.twitter.
588 John Solomon, "Michigan's largest county fails to certify election results, then reverses course as GOP bends," Just the News.com, November 17, 2020, https://justthenews.com/politics-policy/elections/breaking-michigans-largest-county-fails-certify-election-results.
589 Ariel Zilber and Andrew Court, DailyMail.com, November 19, 2020, https://www.dailymail.co.uk/news/article-8964937/Two-Michigan-Republicans-demand-RESCIND-votes-certifying-Wayne-County-election-results.html.

Notice the "stain of racism" language that is used is the same language used, albeit in softened forms, by leading evangelicals. Though the Republican canvassers rescinded their vote, this is the Woke social justice authoritarian dogma and identity politics in action, directly impacting the presidential election. It is reasonable to conclude many evangelical leaders, especially those sympathetic toward Woke social justice, were not sympathetic to Trump.

The influence of evangelical leaders to politically sway Christians away from Trump is somewhat controversial but worth probing to understand the impact of Woke social justice. Trump supporters argue that Trump's executive order against CRT/I and stance against abortion were among the many reasons to endorse Trump. Perhaps one of the biggest reasons is his strong advocacy for religious liberty and appointment of three conservative Supreme Court justices. As the tyrannical Covid-19 lockdowns[590] have prohibited many religious groups, including Christians from meeting, the SCOTUS, in a historic five-to-four decision, ruled against closing churches on the basis of the first amendment. Honorable Judge Gorsuch wrote in the decision:

> As almost everyone on the Court today recognizes, squaring the Governor's edicts with our traditional First Amendment rules is no easy task. People may gather inside for extended periods in bus stations and airports, in laundromats and banks, in hardware stores and liquor shops. No apparent reason exists why people may not gather, subject to identical restrictions, in churches or synagogues, especially when religious institutions have made plain that they stand ready, able, and willing to follow all the safety precautions required of "essential" businesses and perhaps more besides. The only explanation for treating religious places differently seems to be a judgment that what happens there just isn't as "essential" as what happens in secular spaces. Indeed, the Governor is remarkably frank about this: In his judgment

---

590 Douglas Axe, William M. Briggs, Jay W. Richards. *The Price of Panic* (Washington, D.C.: Regnery Publishing, 2020), 51.

laundry and liquor, travel and tools, are all "essential" while traditional religious exercises are not. That is exactly the kind of discrimination the First Amendment forbids.[591]

This ruling relaxes the restrictions that were previously imposed in a similar suit in May of 2020, also a five-to-four decision made in part by the late Justice Ruth Bader Ginsburg. Many are citing the drastic change in the November twenty-fifth ruling happened because of the rapid appointment of Amy Coney Barrett.[592] The morning after the decision, MacArthur wrote on Twitter, "It's divine providence at work as the Lord uses the death of Ruth Bader Ginsberg, the hubris of @NYGovCuomo, the determination of @realDonaldTrump, and the convictions of Justice Barrett to protect the freedom of His church."[593] This shift in the court majority because of Trump's appointments has already had an important impact on religious liberty. Clearly, this victory directly combats the deconstructionist ideology of Woke social justice to remove traditional beliefs, norms, and values, including the free exercise of religion guaranteed in the Constitution—the right for churches to assemble in the United States of America.[594]

Echoing Dr. Strachan, Dr. MacArthur, and an increasing number of evangelicals, the syncretization of Woke teaching with Christianity must be repented of and condemned as a false gospel. The biggest problem with the merger of Woke religion with Christianity is the false gospel that is proclaimed, and the consequences are far-reaching. This is a false gospel that proclaims Jesus died for your sins but not the "plus structural injustice" and

---

591 Roman Catholic Diocese Of Brooklyn, New York v. Andrew M. Cuomo, Governor Of New York, 592 U.S. 20A87 (2020), https://www.supremecourt.gov/opinions/20pdf/20a87_4g15.pdf.

592 Mark Wingfield, "What does the Supreme Court's midnight COVID ruling really mean for religious liberty?," Baptist News Global online, November 27, 2020, https://baptistnews.com/article/what-does-the-supreme-courts-midnight-covid-ruling-really-mean-for-religious-liberty/#.X8Elv6pKhsM.

593 John MacArthur, Twitter Post, November 26, 2020, 11:22 AM, https://twitter.com/johnmacarthur/status/1331996773217431557.

594 "United States of America 1789 (rev. 1992)," Constitute Project.org, Accessed November 27, 2020, https://www.constituteproject.org/constitution/United_States_of_America_1992.

"not the white privilege." This is a false gospel that the Church will always have the stain of racism and always bear the guilt. The Woke gospel is a false gospel of Jesus plus postmodernism, critical theory, social justice, and liberation theology. The Woke gospel is a false gospel.

CONCLUSION

CHRISTIANS IN AMERICA RIGHTLY RECOGNIZE those who have been treated unfairly, acknowledge the horrific history of sin—including slavery and ethnic prejudice—have compassion on the oppressed, and seek justice in the world. We "rejoice with those who rejoice, weep with those who weep" (Rom. 12:15), and empathize with those who have been hurt by the devastating effects of sin in our world. We also read in Scripture that Jesus said, "You will recognize them by their fruits" (Matt. 7:16). The fruit of Woke religion is rotten. Americans have been bombarded with constant conditioning that white people are racists, nearly all societal power structures are oppressive, only the minorities have true knowledge, the transsexual curriculum for fifth graders ought to be normalized, unimaginable sexual perversion ought to be celebrated, the police ought to be defunded, the Church is "non-essential," technocratic media censorship is needed,[595] infanticide is moral, and ever-emerging forms of Woke dogma are acceptable.

Woke ideology manifests division, chaos, and destruction. It fuels racial upheaval that threatens the civility of the Western world. This creates oppression and suffering and often takes place in impoverished communities. The ideology of this religion facilitates false teaching, revolution, riots, and violence. The fundamental reason why the fruit is rotten is because the root is grounded in poison. Woke social justice ideology is antithetical to the Bible because it is not based on the Bible. It is based on the empty philosophy of

---

595 Axe, 43.

the world. Even worse, the teaching of Woke social justice is currently being combined with Christianity in America, thus forming a counterfeit religion. Contrarily, Christianity is based upon the Scriptures as the source of truth. The Bible teaches the Gospel of salvation in Jesus Christ from eternal judgment, love for our neighbors, justice for the oppressed, and hope of eternal life.

This book demonstrates the fact that this is not a battle merely over ideology, politics, and diametrically opposed worldviews; this is a deeply spiritual battle because Woke social justice is a religion in American evangelicalism. The false gospel of Woke is a spiritual attack against the Church and Christ. One of the chief devices Satan uses in spiritual warfare is false teaching. The history of redemption testifies to the raging spiritual war and the preservation of God's people from Satan's attacks. The philosophy of nearly the last five hundred years prepared the seedbed for Woke religion as the Scriptures were replaced by empty philosophies of carnal men.

The categories of Woke dogma are unbiblical, false, and demonstrate the reality of spiritual warfare. The nature of this counterfeit religion has been made apparent. Many evangelical leaders who have genuine concerns about racism, injustice, oppression, and lack of diversity in churches—however, in varying degrees—have grievously united this counterfeit religion with the Gospel. Addressing sin within the Church with empty philosophy and the doctrines of Woke teaching is not acceptable. The apostle Paul warns, "But even if we or an angel from heaven should preach to you a gospel contrary to the one we preached to you, let him be accursed" (Gal. 1:8). Christians ought to take heed. Errors and false teaching in the Church are dangerous. Paul warned, "For if someone comes and proclaims another Jesus than the one we proclaimed, or if you receive a different spirit from the one you received, or if you accept a different gospel from the one you accepted, you put up with it readily enough"(2 Cor. 11:4).

In the Church of Corinth, there were opponents to Christ who rejected the Gospel to satisfy the desire to proclaim the philosophical wisdom of the first-century world. Some self-proclaimed false apostles pretended to be Christian but were servants of Satan. False teachers will use Christian words; but underneath the surface, there are errors, and the truth is twisted. Paul wrote, "For such men are false apostles, deceitful workmen, disguising themselves as apostles of Christ. And no wonder, for even Satan disguises himself as an angel of light" (2 Cor. 11:13-14). To join the false apostles was spiritual suicide because it would destroy the life and ministry of the Church.

The device of Satan to afflict the Church with false teaching and the rejection of the Scriptures as the source of truth has increasingly led to the adoption of this counterfeit religion. No one who claims to be a Christian can entertain this religion and must reject it as Scripture commands. "Jesus spoke to them, saying, 'I am the light of the world. Whoever follows me will not walk in darkness, but will have the light of life'" (John 8:12). In America, the Church must not turn a blind eye to this counterfeit religion. Christians must take heed to the warnings of Scripture. "See to it that no one takes you captive," says Paul, "through philosophy and empty deceit, according to human tradition, according to the elemental spirits of the world, and not according to Christ" (Col. 2:8). It is not biblical to tolerate portions of false religion in the Church. This is like claiming portions of Islam, Buddhism, or any other counterfeit religion ought to be tolerated, can be used as tools, taught, and believed within the Church.

Instead, the Church ought to hope in God and return to the eternal counsel of His Word, since, "The counsel of the Lord stands forever, the plans of his heart to all generations" (Psalm 33:11). Do not hope in the false gospel of Woke; hope in God like the psalmist sings: "Let your steadfast love, O LORD, be upon us, even as we hope in you" (Psalm 33:22). Luke reminds us of Peter's sermon that Jesus was raised to turn us from wickedness. He writes, "God, having raised up his servant, sent him to you first, to bless you by turning every one of you from your wickedness" (Acts 3:26). The Church ought to return to the Scripture and to Jesus Christ—the whole person of Christ and the whole work of Christ. All truth is found in Christ. Owen says, "Let it be evinced that all true and solid knowledge is laid up in, and is only to be attained from and by, the Lord Jesus Christ, and the hearts of men, if they are but true to themselves, and their most predominate principles, must needs be engaged to him."[596]

AN ADMONISHMENT TO CHRISTIANS

I wrote this book to carefully explain the emergence of a counterfeit religion called Woke social justice. My goal is to demonstrate the teachings of this counterfeit religion are based upon toxic, empty philosophy, antithetical to Christianity, and are being syncretized with Christianity in a spiritual battle that is spreading in churches all over America. This work is also an admonishment for Christians to embrace the true Gospel of Christ and reject the false gospel of Woke social justice. The following are ten practical applications of admonishment that Christians can consider in their spiritual battle against the counterfeit Woke gospel:

1. BELIEVE THE TRUE GOSPEL.

There is good news for Christians that "there is therefore now no condemnation for those who are in Christ Jesus" (Rom. 8:1). If you have been influenced by Woke religion and deceived by the false-guilt narratives of critical theory, turn from it, and believe the true Gospel of Jesus Christ. Though damage may have been done to you spiritually, the apostle Paul says, "The one who sows to the Spirit will from the Spirit reap eternal life" (Gal. 6:8). Jesus vicariously fulfilled all righteousness in the place of His people, including fulfillment of the entire Law of God to do justice, have mercy on the oppressed, serve the poor, love our neighbors, and love God. This is Jesus' active obedience that is ours by faith (Rom. 5:18-21). Jesus also paid the penalty for the sins of His people on the cross and satisfied the wrath of God as a Substitute (Rom. 3:24-25). There is no more guilt (Heb. 8:12). Jesus has paid it all.

---

596 Owen, 1526-27.

Believe the many wonderful truths of Scriptures (2 Tim. 3:16) and the promise of Christ that "it is finished" (John 19:30). You do not have to do good works to earn your salvation. Salvation is an unmerited gift from God, "for by grace you have been saved through faith" (Eph. 2:7-8). The Holy Spirit regenerates God's people; the "heart of stone" is removed; and Christians have been given the power and desire to keep the Law of God (Ezek. 36:26; John 3:7; 1 John 5:1). Nothing "will be able to separate us from the love of God in Christ Jesus our Lord" (Rom. 8:39).

2. FIND A CHURCH THAT PREACHES THE TRUE GOSPEL OF CHRIST.

Christians ought to take heed from the danger this false religion exposes to the Church. Paul wrote to Timothy, "But understand this, that in the last days there will come times of difficulty. For people . . . having the appearance of godliness, but denying its power. Avoid such people" (2 Tim. 3:1:5). "For the time is coming when people will not endure sound teaching," says Paul, "but having itching ears they will accumulate for themselves teachers to suit their own passions" (2 Tim. 4:3). In thousands of years of Church history, the answer to addressing sin, even ethnic prejudice, was not Woke social justice grievance gospel. The only way to address sin in the fallen world is the Gospel of Jesus Christ. Never is it right to turn to alternative religions, secular ideology, or empty philosophy. The Scriptures are sufficient.

"We must love the truth of the Bible. Truth is the food of the soul," the Puritan divine Spurstowe said.[597] Those who actively teach and embrace the false Woke social justice gospel are wolves in sheep's clothing, and Christians must depart from their midst. Paul warns we are not to yoke together with unbelievers, who may gain a stronghold over the influence of our lives. Paul wrote:

> Do not be unequally yoked with unbelievers. For what partnership has righteousness with lawlessness? Or what fellowship has light with darkness? What accord has Christ

---

597 Beeke and Jones, 7761-66.

with Belial? Or what portion does a believer share with an unbeliever? What agreement has the temple of God with idols? For we are the temple of the living God; as God said, "I will make my dwelling among them and walk among them, and I will be their God, and they shall be my people. Therefore go out from their midst, and be separate from them, says the Lord, and touch no unclean thing; then I will welcome you (2 Cor. 6:14-17).

Christians must not dwell in the midst of unbelievers lest they be led astray into error.

Christians have no fellowship with darkness (2 Cor. 6:14), and Christians must separate from it (2 Cor. 6:17). Pray and find a true Church that preaches the true Gospel of Jesus Christ (Gal. 1:8-9; 1 Tim. 4:1; 2 Peter 2:20-22; Heb. 3:12). It is encouraging that many Christian leaders are increasingly standing against the counterfeit Woke social justice religion. However, I am saddened that some evangelical leaders sympathize with and are influenced by tenants of this counterfeit religion. Christians will need to pray, search the Scriptures for wisdom, use careful discernment, and test the Spirits to determine if their Church has embraced this false gospel and teaches it (1 John 4:1).

In many cases, the reason why counterfeit religion is embraced is because the sufficiency of Scripture is denied. If the Church does not affirm the sufficiency of Scripture, it is likely in one generation that the Church will lose the Gospel. Christians ought to never be ashamed of the greatest privilege of knowing the Gospel of Jesus Christ. Christians are heirs of a kingdom that cannot be shaken and sinners saved by grace. Never accept feeling shame for the Gospel of Jesus Christ and the privileges of God's goodness to us, His children.

3. SUPPORT CHRISTIANS WHO PREACH THE TRUE, UNADULTERATED GOSPEL OF JESUS CHRIST.

It is important for Christians to support their local Gospel-proclaiming churches by assembly, service, prayer, and giving (Eph. 6:18; 2 Cor. 9:6-7; Heb. 10:25). Christians ought to also pray for pastors, educational institutions, and organizations that perpetuate Woke social justice ideology that they would turn from this counterfeit religion. Christians should wisely reconsider their participation and support of evangelical ministries that have combined elements of Woke religion and ideology into their teachings (Matt. 10:16; Rom. 12:2). Participating in conferences, buying books, subscribing to content on digital platforms, partnering on social media, receiving email distributions, and associating in other ways with those who teach, promote, and proactively advocate Woke social justice is, at best, biblically unwise (Matt. 7:15-20; 2 Cor. 6:17; 2 Peter 2:1; Jude 4). John writes, "If anyone comes to you and does not bring this teaching, do not receive him into your house or give him any greeting" (2 John 10). To not welcome someone into their house in the context of John's letter was to not support their ministry.

4. KEEP A CLOSE WATCH ON YOUR SOUL AND FAMILY MEMBERS' SOULS.

Christians ought to keep a close watch on their souls and doctrine. The apostle Paul charges Timothy, "Keep a close watch on yourself and on the teaching. Persist in this, for by so doing you will save both yourself and your hearers" (1 Tim. 4:16). Christians ought to "examine [themselves], to see whether you are in the faith" (2 Cor. 13:5). This must include affirming the sufficiency of Scripture and continue believing the Holy Scriptures (2 Tim. 3:14). As this book has discussed, the denial of Scripture has resulted in the dangerous secular ideologies, teachings that are antithetical to Christianity, and the philosophical foundation for Woke social justice. Christians ought to be careful not to repeat the same errors of Church history in this regard. The battle for the Gospel in every generation is first a battle for the sufficiency of Scripture.

Practically, consider refraining from listening to sermons and teachings that have been poisoned with Woke ideology because it is toxic to your soul. It is important to be aware of Satan's devices, but Christians ought to be careful not to immerse in them (1 Cor. 10:13; 1 Thess. 5:22; 1 Peter 3:15). Instead, listen to sound teaching, immerse yourself in the Word of God, read sound, Christian materials that will edify your soul, and be built up in the most holy faith (2 Tim. 2:15; Jude 20).

Christians ought to keep a close watch on their family members, especially parents with their children, so that they are not indoctrinated with the Woke religion. Woke ideology is infiltrating large swaths of society, public institutions, education, churches, government, social media, television, internet, and surrounding secular culture. Society is being increasingly conditioned, indoctrinated, and desensitized to Woke ideology so that it becomes normative by design. Parents, especially fathers—since they are the head of the family—are exhorted to "train up [their children] in the way [they] should go" (Prov. 22:6) and nurture them in the instruction and admonition of the Lord (Eph. 6:4). God says, "And these words that I command you today shall be on your heart. You shall teach them diligently to your children, and shall talk of them when you sit in your house, and when you walk by the way, and when you lie down, and when you rise" (Deut. 6:6-7).

5. STAND FIRM AGAINST WOKE SOCIAL JUSTICE
IN GOVERNMENT AND TYRANNY.

Instead of sympathizing with political platforms that promote Woke social justice, the Church must stand and speak out against government leaders and policies that contradict the moral law. Glenn Sunshine provides helpful ways American evangelicals can preserve their liberties in America. This is applicable to evangelical Christians who exercise their constitutional right to stand firm against Woke social justice:

> Our first step in response to attacks on our liberty is to use the legal means at our disposal to preserve our rights and the rights of others. We vote; we write letters to government officials; we educate; we seek to sway public opinion . . . Working through the lesser magistrate is also a possibility: there have been

instances of sheriffs refusing to enforce laws they believed to be unconstitutional.[598]

The rule of law is crumbling in America because the moral law has been disregarded in the government, the public square, and even the Church. Christians should not obey unjust or immoral policies that contradict the moral Law of God, since we are to obey Christ, not the state. Trewhella points out, "Christianity acts as a check to tyranny. The whole of society should be thankful for the preservation of liberty that Christianity engenders. Christians are the best of citizens."[599] Christians ought to be most aware of the governments who slowly enslave citizens by the moral approval of their own system. C.S. Lewis wrote, "Of all tyrannies, a tyranny sincerely exercised for the good of its victims may be the most oppressive."[600] It is worth mentioning, what we are witnessing in America, as I write this, is the stepping-stone to soft totalitarianism, where the government is infringing upon the most basic religious rights, determining when, where, and how worship takes place. Despite the first amendment to the Constitution, religious groups are being regulated with restrictions that have closed many churches and hindered the free exercise of religion. Hypocritically, secular groups are not being held to the same restrictions by the government. This is all the more reason for the doctrine of the lesser magistrate to be taught and exercised, particularly among Christians. Trewhella rightly states, "[T] he lesser magistrates have the right and duty to interpose against law and policy that violates the Constitution (regardless of how the U.S. Supreme Court defines violations), and/or that attacks the person, property, or liberty of those within their jurisdiction of authority, and/or that impugns the law of God.[601]

---

598 Sunshine, 175.
599 Trewhella, 28.
600 C.S. Lewis, *God in the Dock: Essays on Theology and Ethics* (Grand Rapids: Eerdmans Publishing Company, 1970), 292.
601 Trewhella, 62.

Perhaps now more than ever in our nation's history, Christians must make every effort to stand firm against social justice in government and tyrannical attacks against the Church. Dreher contends we are living in the West under pre-totalitarian conditions. He rightly argues, "Social atomization, widespread loneliness, the rise of ideology, widespread loss of faith in institutions, and other factors leave society vulnerable to the totalitarian temptation to which both Russia and Germany succumbed in the previous century." Lest we are conditioned to surrender our freedom, this generation should be mindful of the evils of the prior generations, soviet communism, the gulags, and tyranny. If we are drifting toward even a hint of totalitarianism, we would do well to take heed to these words: "The Marxist Mordor was real, but the faith of those who resisted outlasted it, because totalitarianism met something harder: the truth."[602]

6. PRAY FOR THOSE IN AUTHORITY.

Christians ought to pray for those in positions of authority so that we may live peacefully. Scripture teaches, "First of all, then, I urge that supplications, prayers, intercessions, and thanksgivings be made for all people, for kings and all who are in high positions, that we may lead a peaceful and quiet life, godly and dignified in every way" (1 Tim. 2:1-2). As we pray for our leaders, we can also be subject to our local and national governments while voting for policies that stop Woke social justice ideology (Deut. 1:13; Rom. 13:1-14). In principle, it is important to engage with our local governing leaders, city councils, and communities for the sake of righteousness in society (Prov. 14:34). Christians ought to consider signing statements of faith and petitions that affirm the Gospel of Jesus Christ and biblical justice and reject Woke ideology (Matt. 10:33; John 12:42; Acts 20:21; 1 Thess. 5:21-22; 1 John 1:6).

---

602 Dreher, 213.

7. LOVE GOD AND LOVE YOUR NEIGHBOR.

The greatest commandment is to love God, and the second is to love our neighbor (Matt. 22:36-40). The apostle John wrote, "And this is love, that we walk according to his commandments; this is the commandment, just as you have heard from the beginning, so that you should walk in it" (2 John 1:6). To love our neighbor is to keep God's commandments. However, Woke teaching tends to function as a form of antinomianism that forsakes the whole duty of man for empty philosophy. It says we don't need to keep God's law for the sake of holiness. As God said, "Be holy, for I am holy" (1 Peter 1:16).

Instead, Woke teaching hyper-emphasizes the justice of the law and our relationship to our neighbor but says little-to-nothing about the first commandment to love God. In effect, Woke teaching says we can live how we want so long as we keep the law of justice toward man. Christians ought to keep the whole law, and that includes loving God and loving your neighbor. If we love God, we will keep his commands, which includes doing justice, loving mercy, and living humbly (Micah 6:8). In parallel to antinomianism, Woke teaching can also tend to be legalistic because of the unbalanced emphasis to keep the justice of the law of God with little-to-no mention of Christ, Who ultimately kept the just law of God vicariously on behalf of sinners and satisfied the justice of God as a Substitute for sinners on the cross. Therefore, Christians ought to love God and love their neighbor according to Scripture and reject the antithetical secular ideologies of Woke teaching and unbalanced emphasis Woke places upon one aspect of the law of God.

8. PREACH CHRIST CRUCIFIED.

The apostle Paul wrote, "For I decided to know nothing among you except Jesus Christ and him crucified" (1 Cor. 2:2). In the midst of Woke influences within society and the Church, Christians ought to learn from Paul and preach Christ crucified. The first-century church certainly faced many afflictions and errors, and they stood against them. There is a danger for the Church to go silent in a functional form of monasticism that lacks engagement of the world with the Gospel and defending the faith that was once for all delivered to the saints. As Christians, we ought to be unashamed "of the gospel, for it is the power of God for salvation to everyone who believes" (Rom. 1:16). This means Christians ought to be prepared to defend the faith against Woke social justice and must not be silent. The Woke influence within evangelicalism will tend to center the message of teaching upon ethnic prejudice, social justice, and social issues. Christians ought to not ignore these issues but must not address them with secular ideologies. Christians ought to keep the central focus of Christianity on Christ and Him crucified. The Christ-centered Gospel is the only true Gospel that can redeem lost sinners, bring reconciliation to man and God, and reform the Church.

9. TRUST IN THE SOVEREIGN GOD IN SPIRITUAL BATTLE.

The Church ought to trust in the sovereign God, Who orchestrates all things according to the counsel of His will, including spiritual warfare. Christians ought to take heed and be alert because we are not merely in political, social, and ideological dialogue, we are in a spiritual battle. According to Gurnall, in the midst of our current spiritual warfare, the Christian ought to do the following:

> Take heart therefore, O ye saints, and be strong; your cause is good, God himself espouseth your quarrel, who hath appointed you his own Son, General of the field, called "the Captain of our salvation," Heb. 2:10. He shall lead you on with courage, and bring you off with honour. He lived and died for you; he will live and die with you; for mercy and tenderness to his soldiers, none like him.[603]

We ought not to fear in this life because our God is the sovereign Ruler of all natural and supernatural things. Not one hair can be touched upon

---

603 Gurnall, 5918-19.

our head without His command. "Satan cannot so much as untie our shoes without God's commission," says Beeke. Caryl adds, "If the devils could not go into the swine, much less can they meddle with a man, made after God's image, till God gives them leave."[604] Christians must be strong in the Lord and stand firm in this spiritual battle and defend the faith with the true Gospel of Jesus Christ (Eph. 6:1). Nevertheless, our battle against the forces of darkness is real, and we must take up the mind of Christ—even the mind of the Spirit. "They [demons] can act upon the 'fancies' or imaginations of men," says Beeke, "injecting thoughts or bringing up sensual memories in the human mind, thereby stirring the affections toward 'wrath, pride, covetousness, lusts.'"[605]

The Larger Catechism says people, by nature, are "wholly inclined to do the will of the flesh and of the devil" (Q. 192). The wicked are unhindered from the harassments of the devil, so we ought to pray for God's mercy and destruction of the spiritual enemy, namely Satan. Thomas Brooks (1608–1680) said, "Christ, the Scripture, your own hearts, and Satan's devices, are the four prime things that should be first and most studied and searched."[606] Particular sins ought to be resisted with utmost strength and frequency, especially in keeping the mind from the deceptions of the devil (1 Kings 22:21; Matt. 4:9). One of the chief devices of the devil is to seduce men into false teaching and doctrinal error (2 Thess. 2:1-2; 2 Peter 2:1). All false doctrine is ultimately from Satan, since he is a liar (Gal. 3:1; John 8:44). In our spiritual combat, we ought to learn from Spurstowe, who wrote, "In resisting temptations, make use of Christ as a pattern . . . Observe the weapon Christ chose to foil him by, and to resist all the temptations of Satan with. He could as easily, by His power, have rebuked and silenced him as he did the wind and waves, but He did it by the Word."[607]

---

604 Beeke and Jones 6788-90.
605 Ibid, 7651-52.
606 Thomas Brooks, *Precious Remedies Against Satan's Devices, Apples of God for Young Men and Women, the Mute Christian . . . Rod, a String of Pearls*, in *The Complete Works of Thomas Brooks, Vol.1.*
607 Beeke and Jones, 7763-66.

As Christians, we must take up the Word of Almighty God as our sword in our spiritual battle. May God grant that army of Christians full of the Holy Spirit might storm the gates of Hell, proclaiming the unadulterated TRUE GOSPEL OF JESUS CHRIST with the zeal of Jeremiah, who said, "If I say, 'I will not mention him, or speak any more in his name,' there is in my heart as it were a burning fire shut up in my bones, and I am weary with holding it in, and I cannot" (Jer. 20:9). Those who say the Church needs true revival are right, but this will only come after the proclamation of the true Gospel.

10. HOPE IN CHRIST FOR ETERNAL GLORY.

Woke religion has become a new religion in America, but true Christianity will never be Woke. Yet Woke may not be that new of a religion after all, when one considers who is behind it—the old serpent, the devil. The counterfeit Woke social justice gospel will never bring justice, reconciliation, and salvation to sinners because it is not from God. Instead, it will result in more injustice, division, and, ultimately, destruction because it is based on lies from Satan. The Puritans remind us that Christ has "bruised" Satan's head (Gen. 3:15) by His finished work on the cross (Heb. 2:14), resurrection from the dead (Psalm 68:18), and ultimately, final judgment (Rev. 20). Jesus will make all His enemies a footstool under His feet. Christ will seize the dragon and cast him eternally into Hell, and the ancient enemy of the Church will be done away with forever. The Church militant will be glorified into the Church triumphant in the new heavens and new earth.

As eternal glory draws near in our Christian sojourning toward the celestial city, we long for Jesus Christ, not power; we await the vindication of perfect justice in the final judgment, not equity; our identity is in Christ, not social groups; we are imputed with Christ's righteousness, not our nation's past; our citizenship is in Heaven, not a utopian society; we are at the mercy of God's providence, not privilege; we are covered with the righteous robes of the Son of God, not guilt; we are washed with the precious blood of the Lamb of God, not stained; we believe the Word of God, not wokeness; we herald the true Gospel of the Lord Jesus Christ, not the false gospel of Woke social justice; we preach Christ crucified, not Woke religion. We are not yoked to Woke evangelicalism; we are unworthy slaves of Jesus Christ. We will never be woke because we are already awakened by the power of God. We will never confess the creeds of Woke social justice because we will not deny our Master. We will never join a counterfeit religion because we already have the truth. Our God is not Woke. Our God is raised from the dead. We will not bow to Woke religion because we bow to the King of kings and Lord of lords—Jesus Christ. "Now to him who is able to keep you from stumbling and to present you blameless before the presence of his glory with great joy, to the only God, our Savior, through Jesus Christ our Lord, be glory, majesty, dominion, and authority before all time and now and forever. Amen" (Jude 24-25).

A LETTER FROM UNCLE LEGION

MY DEAR YOUNGER BROTHER IN THE FAITH,

I note what you mentioned about leading our victim's studies and doing well to be sure he is influenced by his Woke pastor. I gather his emotions are primed to be driven away from the Enemy's errors. This would not have been the case if we were dealing with him several centuries ago. The Enemy was more equipped to show there is truth, absolutes, and objectivity as categories of knowledge. Keep our victim thinking along with the ways of skepticism, deconstruction, and most of all, the social power structures of oppressor and oppressed. We need him to embrace his new identity as an oppressor, remind him of his skin color, and emphasize how critical race theory must be true since it is taught by his pastors. Do not waste time making him think postmodernism will lead to despair, but instead awaken him to his oppression. Keep him fixated on his relation to everyone in society in our oppressor system. Let him realize the hegemonic power structures are the real enemy, and at all costs, never let him encounter a true—we are forbidden to say the word—you know, those who follow after our greatest Enemy. Suggest to his doubts that those followers are false and make it a habit that some false followers of the way become his acquaintance to solidify his suspicions. This will lead to his full embrace of our clever system that I am so proud of you for helping build. Our father will be very pleased.

Remember he is not like you, a pure spirit, but needs more time out in the streets to believe what he has read these years in our schooling. We have many friends in schools and are making many more, who are supporting our new religion. Yes, compel him that he, too, is a part of our religion but don't tip him off that it is the religion of our father; and never use this name—religion—in reference to our movement. It's your job to emphasize religion ended long ago—is to be blamed by the things we really did through the centuries and because of words that have gained traction with victims, like secularization. Our victim has learned very quickly that in the beginning were the oppressed and oppressors, the victimizers and the victims, the majority and the minority. Push him further in your next opportunity to see that the victimizers, especially the ones who they call white, are deemed in all places as racists. If you sense that he is doubting this, remember our father had made this a part of our plans for a long time now. Better to make him think he is an oppressor for his whiteness and because he came from a "well-to-do family," as they like to say.

He remembers his childhood religion, so you can confuse him with these ideas into our new religion. One of our great allies currently are Christians anyway. We have many like us working hard in the Church adopting our religion. Those who have not awakened to our cause we have deceived into silence. We have a great advantage over the Enemy when their soldiers surrender their sword to our cause. Little do they know the true power of their little book they carry. The father has forbidden us to speak of that book.

Focus your efforts on your victim's sense of guilt—it will drive him mad. Once you have him in a state of guilt, there will be no power stronger within our victim's soul but the weight of guilt that we have so cleverly set upon him and our victims. Convince him that the oppressed have really been victims and guilt him into joining our cause in solidarity. The more guilt our victims feel, the more they will believe in our cause, looking for appeasement. Our father will grant them no lasting satisfaction but will continually lead them into believing if they are members of our cause, then they are saved.

This is playing out all so well. Already, our guilty victims are congregating regularly—all according to our father's cause. Some of their best works are the fires, destruction of their property, and plots against what they call "law enforcement." Some of our friends convince their leaders they are what they call "peaceful," like our Enemy's nature, but we use that as a guise for one of our father's ultimate ends—murder. Our father loves this because it is his very nature.

See if you can probe our victim to confess his guilt to his new critical race theory friends at church. We are always nearby and always like to hear our victims blaspheme our Enemy. He must awaken to everything I have written to you about and begin to worship in our newly formed activist groups. Especially since these groups will subtly destroy the family—one of our greatest enemies—and help confuse our victims about their gender and sexuality. The more they can act upon this the better—it is our secret that our victims have lust within them already. The more you can exploit this weakness, the easier it will be for you to lead our victims to the father.

Their colorful rags remind us of our Enemy's permission to flood the ancient world, but it suits our cause of rebellion against the Enemy, so the father allows it. It would be good for your victim to take small steps until he is given over; suggest things like placing our cause's signs around one or two of our temples. We have temples everywhere, and they are heavily protected by our friends in their government—so any will do. Although, never let your victim know what is happening inside. If you sense he is curious, find a way for one of our slogans to come across his mind like, "my body, my choice" *or* "it's only a fetus." *Any will do. Our friends inside would be delighted to see our causes unite. Anything that is against our enemy is best.*

If they use our old technique of science, remind them that science is of the traditional oppressive group and cannot be trusted, especially since the havoc we caused in the world wars led by our clever father.

Next time, I will fully unveil our plan to have the activists convince the governing leaders to rid the West of the filthy church. We can use our canceling techniques, and if we have to enlist more help by those who are afflicting and confusing the virus efforts, I will make that request to father.

A few pointers before I have to attend to other students, our victim must embrace our creed that systems oppress people of color, are complicit with the oppressors, and must do the works of our religion to be anti-racist. This will result in everyone's equal outcome. And remember to tempt our victim's pride—that he can do the work himself.

It will be received well as a badge of virtue and self-righteousness. Many are doing so already and are very pleased with themselves. To our surprise, their hatred of their civilization and our Enemy naturally builds once they have awakened to our cause.

One of our strongest supporters reused an old tactic we've used in the past that many victims gradually joined—you'll see their fists in the air if you haven't already. I'm sure you already know this is to provoke fear in the Enemy followers and keep all our victims enslaved to fear and our incredibly great power. As you grow in your powers, you will also learn the ability to confuse their language with our truths. This is for our good cause—especially in the name of our Enemy's character of justice. We know our victims have a grasp of justice because many were almost subdued by our Enemy in their earlier years. One of our deceptive friends, who has now climbed up the ranks close to the father, has convinced nearly all victims that justice is overthrowing the values like our Enemy's practice, traditions, norms, and power structures of their awful democracy. This work began long ago in our liberation and social justice schools. We have many clergy members of our cause entrenched deep within them all over. We found that social justice has been one of our best ways to attract victims because our victims are mostly oblivious to what our true social justice actually is.

If anyone is allowed to question your victim, have him come across our standard arguments to defuse the Enemy—you know . . . if the oppressors question us, that will prove they are the oppressors or that only the minority has true knowledge. I am glad our victims are so inconsistent in logic. Our clergy are working very hard to deceive with confusing language and word games to keep even the more intelligent of the victims from realizing they are activists on behalf of an objective orthodoxy while simultaneously selling their soul to skeptic postmodernist theory.

If all else fails, guilt and anger will help you. Provoke him on his social media with allies from our cause and remind him of the vision—it's about overturning the oppressive power in the revolution. If there is any chatter of what will replace the current system, only speak in vague generalities and, at all costs, avoid any appeals to our foiled plots of the twentieth century. Our father was very angry about this but not as angry as those who are speaking about the powers of our Enemy. I must warn you, our victims must never begin to believe in our Enemy's message, especially that their only hope is in our Enemy and our Enemy's work on that unspeakable Roman device for murder. The temporal utopia is what matters.

Make him think the oppressed groups need deliverance by running his mind across all our slogans. Use his pastors to promote political inclusion and diversity within the church that will really serve our cause of division. Never allow anyone to mention our Enemy's eternal kingdom; we will rage against them, so do not be discouraged. Our father is not permitted to do all he desires by nature because of our Enemy, but there is much good we can do for our cause with what we've been allowed. We have much better plans as of late that have greater potential for our father's kingdom in the world. Hold your victim in this state of mind as long as it takes to keep him in the fold as one of us.

I am very pleased to note the original stain of what they call racism has resonated well with the churches we've been working in. Remember, there is no way for them to find atonement, but convince him he will find it by identifying with our religious cause. Never let him hear of our Enemy's power to satisfy for all his sins. Never even mention that he has committed individual sin. We are forbidden to speak of individual sins, lest they actually seek salvation in our Enemy. Our aim is to confuse racism as a group system of oppression—never an individual sin—so reconciliation can never be found between our victims and the Enemy. If Enemy soldiers come near him, wreak havoc on them and send word for me immediately, lest they unveil our system of guilt inherited from the oppressive power structures.

For now, the Enemy's meeting places are mostly not habitable because of our friends confusing the governments. There are many more plots I cannot tell you now. Beware of the enemy's outposts; they are heavily guarded with men who know the truth but we can circumvent them with our religion. Our time is short, but there is still much to be done for our cause.[608]

Your Affectionate Uncle,
Legion

---

608 Lewis, Ibid.

BIBLIOGRAPHY

"1619 Project." New Discourses.com. Accessed October 2, 2020. https://newdiscourses.com/tftw-1619-project.

"About." Black Lives Matter.com. Accessed October 3, 2020. https://blacklivesmatter.com/about.

Adams, Maurianne and Lee Anne Bell, and Pat Griffin. *Teaching for Diversity and Social Justice: A Sourcebook.* New York: Routledge, 1997.

Allen, Bob. "Speaker at Baptist college warns that Marxist thought is creeping into SBC seminaries." Baptist News Global online. Accessed October 3, 2020. https://baptistnews.com/article/speaker-at-baptist-college-warns-that-Marxist-thought-is-creeping-into-sbc-seminaries/#.X2bL1WdKhsM.

Allen, Scott David. *Why Social Justice is Not Biblical Justice: An Urgent Appeal to Fellow Christians in a Time of Social Crisis.* Grand Rapids: Credo House Publishers, 2020.

Andersen, Margaret. *Race, Class, and Gender: An Anthology. 7th Edition.* Belmont: Wadsworth, 2009.

Ascol, Tom, Voddie Baucham, and Timon Cline, et al. *By What Standard? God's Rules . . . God's World.* Cape Coral: Founders Press, 2020.

Ascol, Tom. "Matthew Hall's Rejection of Critical Race Theory." Founders Ministries.org. Accessed October 3, 2020. https://founders.org/2019/12/03/matthew-halls-rejection-of-critical-race-theory.

Ascol, Tom. "Resolution 9 and the Southern Baptist Convention 2019." Founders Ministries.org. Accessed October 3, 2020." https://founders. org/2019/06/15/resolution-9-and-the-southern-baptist-convention-2019.

Augustine, St. *The City of God*. New York: Random House Publishing Group, 1999.

Axe, Douglas, William M. Briggs, and Jay W. Richards. *The Price of Panic: How the Tyranny of Experts Turned A Pandemic into a Catastrophe*. Washington, D.C.: Regnery Publishing, 2020.

Barnett, Joshua Trey and Corey Johnson. *Encyclopedia of Diversity and Social Justice s.v.* "Queer." Sherwood Thomson (ed.). London: Rowman & Littlefield, 2015.

Bastiat, Frederic. *The Law*. Hudson: Foundation for Economic Education, 1847/2007.

Baucham, Voddie. "Ethnic Gnosticism." Founders Ministries.org. Accessed September 15, 2020. https://founders.org/sermons/ethnic-gnosticism.

Baucham, Voddie. "Racial Reconciliation - Ephesians 2:10-11." Founders Ministries. March 27, 2019. YouTube video. 54:03. https://www.youtube. com/watch?v=FoJGYCc7EUg.

Bavinck, Herman. *Reformed Dogmatics: Abridged in One Volume*. Ed. John Bolt. Grand Rapids: Baker Academic, 2011.

Bavinck, Herman. *Reformed Ethics: Created, Fallen, and Converted Humanity*. Ed. John   Bolt. Grand Rapids: Baker Academic, 2019.

"Becoming Teachers for Social Justice: Raising Critical Consciousness." *The Clearing House: A Journal of Educational Strategies, Issues and Ideas*. 92, No. 1-2 (2019): 9-14. Accessed October 8, 2020.

Beeke, Joel R. and Mark Jones. *A Puritan Theology: Doctrine for Life*. Grand Rapids: Reformation Heritage Books, 2012.

Beeke, Joel R. and Paul Smalley. *Reformed Systematic Theology Volume 2: Man and Christ*. Wheaton: Crossway, 2020.

Berkhof, Louis. *Systematic Theology*. Grand Rapids: Eerdmans, 2011.

Bhambra, Gurminder, Kerem Nisancioglu, and Delia Gebrial. *Decolonizing the University*. London: Pluto Press, 2018.

"Black Abortions By The Numbers." Right to Life of Michigan online. Accessed September 22, 2020. https://rtl.org/multicultural-outreach/black-abortion-statistics.

Buttom, Joseph. *An Anxious Age*. New York: Crown Publishing Group, 2014.

"By What Standard? God's World . . . God's Rules (CINEDOC)." Founders Ministries. June 8, 2020. YouTube video. 1:50:29. https://www.youtube.com/watch?v=pFHfa0s1XLM.

Calvin, John. *The Institutes of the Christian Religion*. Edinburgh: Printed for The Calvin Translation Society, 1845.

Campbell, Iain and William Schweitzer. *Engaging with Keller: Thinking Through the Theology of an Influential Evangelical*. Darlington: Evangelical Press, 2013.

Carson, D.A. *The Intolerance of Tolerance*. Grand Rapids: Eerdmans, 2012.

"Christian Voices on the Cultural Moment: A Collection of Essays by Southeastern Women on Issues Facing Christians Today." The Pulpit and the Pen.org. Accessed September 14, 2020. https://pulpitandpen.org/wp-content/uploads/2019/05/WOKE-SEBTS_watermark-2.pdf.

Chumley, Cheryl. "Netflix: Pandering to pedophiles everywhere." The Washington Times.com. August 20, 2020. https://www.washingtontimes.com/news/2020/aug/20/netflix-pandering-pedophiles-everywhere.

Cline, Timon. "Identity Politics and the Bondage of the Will." Founders Ministries.org. Fall 2019. https://founders.org/2020/02/10/identity-politics-and-the-bondage-of-the-will.

Collins, Patricia Hill and Sirma Bilge. *Intersectionality*. Cambridge: Polity Press, 2016.

Collins, Sean. "Wokeness: old religion in a new bottle." Spiked-online.com. August 14, 2020. https://www.spiked-online.com/2020/08/14/wokeness-old-religion-in-new-bottle.

Cone, James. *Black Theology and Black Power*. New York: Orbis Books, 1997.

Cone, James. *Cross and the Lynching Tree, The*. New York: Orbis Books, 2011.

Cone, James. *Speaking the Truth: Ecumenism, Liberation, and Black Theology*. New York: Orbis Books, 1999.

Crenshaw, Kimberle, Neil Gotanda, Gary Peller, and Kendall Thomas, eds. "Critical Race Theory, Archie Shepp, and Fire Music: Securing an Authentic Intellectual Life in a Multicultural World." In *Critical Race Theory: The Key Writings that Formed the Movement*. New York: New York Press, 1995.

Crenshaw, Kimberle. "Mapping the Margins: Intersectionality, Identity Politics, and Violence against Women of Color." Stanford Law Review, Vol. 43, No. 6 (July 1991). https://www.jstor.org/stable/1229039?seq=1.

Delgado, Richard and Jean Stefancic. *Critical Race Theory: An Introduction*, Second Edition. New York: NYU Press, 2012.

Desanctis, Alexandra. "Virginia Governor Defends Letting Infants Die." National Review.com. January 30, 2019. https://www.nationalreview.com/corner/virginia-governor-defends-letting-infants-die.

Devine, Mark. "Princeton's Woke Letter on Systemic Racism Backfires." The American Spectator.org. September 26, 2020. https://spectator.org/princeton-racism-letter.

DiAngelo, Robin. "Anti-Racism Handout," Robin DiAngelo.com, Accessed October 2, 2020. https://robindiangelo.com/wp-content/up-loads/2016/06/Anti-racism-handout-1-page-2016.pdf.

DiAngelo, Robin. *White Fragility: Why It's So Hard for White People to Talk About Racism.* Boston: Beacon Press, 2018.

Dreher, Rod. *Live Not by Lies: A Manuel for Christian Dissidents.* New York: Penguin Random House, 2020.

Edwards, Jonathan. *A History of the Work of Redemption.* Ontario: Devoted Publishing, 2020.

Elwell, Walter. *Evangelical Dictionary of Theology.* Grand Rapids: Baker Academic, 2001.

Encyclopedia Britannica. s.v. "critical theory." Accessed October 3, 2020. https://www.britannica.com/topic/critical-theory.

Engelbrecht, Edward, Laura Lane, Robert Clouse, et al. *The Church from Age to Age: A History from Galilee to Global Christianity.* St. Louis: Concordia Publishing House, 2011.

Felluga, Dino Franco. *Critical Theory: The Key Concepts.* Abingdon: Routledge, 2015.

Foley, Ryan. "BLM leaders practice 'witchcraft' and summon dead spirits, black activist claims." Christian Post.com. September 1, 2020. https://www.christianpost.com/news/blm-leaders-practice-witchcraft-and-summon-dead-spirits-black-activist-warns.html.

Frame, John. *The Doctrine of the Christian Life (A Theology of Lordship).* Phillipsburg: P&R Publishing, 2008.

Garris, Zachary M. *Masculine Christianity.* Santa Clara: Zion Press, 2020.

"Girl Scouts of Northern California Volunteer Policy for Building Equitable Community for All, The" Girl Scouts Northern California.org. Board Approved July 18, 2020. https://www.gsnorcal.org/content/dam/

girlscouts-gsnorcal/documents/volunteer_resources/volunteer-essen-tials/volunteering-volunteer-policy.pdf.

"Grace, Justice, & Mercy: An Evening with Bryan Stevenson & Rev. Tim Keller Q&A." RedeemerCFW. June 3, 2016. YouTube video. 51:32. https://youtu.be/32CHZiVFmB4.

Gurnall, William. *The Christian in Complete Armour, or, A Treatise on the Saints' War With the Devil.* London: Andesite Press, 1862.

Harris, Jon. *Social Justice Goes to Church: The New Left in Modern American Evangelicalism.* Greenville, SC: Ambassador International, 2020.

Keller, Timothy. "A Biblical Critique of Secular Justice and Critical Theory." Life in the Gospel online. Accessed October 1, 2020. https://quarterly.gospel-inlife.com/a-biblical-critique-of-secular-justice-and-critical-theory.

Keller, Timothy. *Generous Justice: How God's Grace Makes Us Just.* New York: Penguin Books, 2012.

Keller, Timothy. *Reason for God: Belief in an Age of Skepticism, The.* New York: Penguin Books, 2009.

"Keller's Political Motivation." The New Calvinists.com. Accessed September 8, 2020. http://www.newcalvinist.com/kellers-political-motivation.

Kendi, Ibram X. *How to Be an Antiracist.* New York: One World, 2019.

Kern, Soeren. "Black Lives Matter: 'We Are Trained Marxists' - Part I." GatestoneInstitute.org. Accessed October 2, 2020. https://www.gatestoneinstitute.org/16181/black-lives-matter.

Kirk, Marshal and Hunter Madsen. *After the Ball: How America Will Conquer Its Fear & Hatred of Gays in the 90's.* New York: Penguin Group, 1989.

Kuyper, Abraham. *Lectures on Calvinism: Six Lectures from the Stone Foundation Lectures Delivered at Princeton University.* Grand Rapids: Eerdmans Publishing Company, 1943.

"Letter from Margaret Sanger to Dr. C. J. Gamble, December 10, 1939." Smith College Libraries online. Accessed September 22, 2020. https://libex. smith.edu/omeka/items/show/495.

Lewis, C.S. *God in the Dock*. Grand Rapids: Eerdmans Publishing Company, 1970.

Lewis, C.S. *The Screwtape Letters*. San Francisco: HarperOne, 2015.

Lindsay, James and Helen Pluckrose. *Cynical Theories: How Activist Scholarship Made Everything about Race, Gender, and Identity—And Why This Harms Everybody*. Durham: Pitchstone Publishing, 2020.

Lindsay, James and Mike Nayna. "Postmodern Religion and the Faith of Social Justice." Areomagazine.com. December 18, 2018. https://areomagazine. com/2018/12/18/postmodern-religion-and-the-faith-of-social-justice.

Lindsay, James. "First-Amendment Case for Freedom from the Woke Religion, A." New Discourses.com. September 9, 2020. https://newdiscourses. com/2020/09/first-amendment-case-freedom-from-woke-religion.

Lindsay, James. "Bodies." New Discourses.com. September 17, 2020. https:// newdiscourses.com/tftw-bodies.

Lindsay, James. "Derridean." New Discourses.com. July 13, 2020. https:// newdiscourses.com/tftw-derridean.

Luther, Martin. *The Bondage of the Will*. Peabody: Hendrickson Publishers, 2008.

MacArthur, John. "MACARTHUR: Critical Race Theory, A Sickness That Cannot Be Allowed To Continue." The Daily Wire.com. Accessed October 2, 2020. https://www.dailywire.com/news/ macarthur-a-sickness-that-cannot-be-allowed-to-continue.

MacArthur, John. "MACARTHUR: Losing Our Religion." The Daily Wire. com. Accessed October 2, 2020. https://www.dailywire.com/news/ macarthur-losing-our-religion.

Machen, Gresham. "Christianity and Liberalism." Grand Rapids: Eerdmans Publishing Company, 2009.

Mambrol, Nasrullah. "Decolonization." Literary Theory and Criticism online. October 4, 2017. https://literariness.org/2017/10/04/decolonization.

Mason, Eric. *Woke Church: An Urgent Call for Christians in America to Confront Racism and Injustice*. Chicago: Moody, 2018.

"Matt Chandler Rips Christian Church, Says It Has Mostly 'Refused to Participate; on Race Issues." CBN News.com. June 14, 2020. https://www1.cbn.com/cbnnews/us/2020/june/matt-chandler-rips-christian-church-says-it-has-mostly-refused-to-participate-on-race-issues.

McGrath, Alister E. *Historical Theology: An Introduction to the History of Christian Thought*. Hoboken: Blackwell, 2013.

McWhorter, John. "Atonement as Activism." The American Interest.com. Accessed October 2, 2020. https://www.the-american-interest.com/2018/05/24/atonement-as-activism.

Mocombe, Paul. "Against Critical Race Theory." *Ethnic Studies Review*. 37/38. No. 1, (2017).

"Motivation." Decolonizing Mars.org. Accessed October 2, 2020. https://www.decolonizemars.org/motivation.

Mouw, Richard. *Political Evangelism*. Grand Rapids: Eerdmans Publishing Company, 1973.

Muller, Richard A. *Post-Reformation Reformed Dogmatics Prolegomena to Theology*. Ada: Baker Academic, 2003.

Mumah, Carrie. "Planned Parenthood of Greater New York Announces Intent to Remove Margaret Sanger's Name from NYC Health Center." Planned Parenthood.org. July 21, 2020. https://www.plannedparenthood.org/planned-parenthood-greater-new-york/about/news/

planned-parenthood-of-greater-new-york-announces-intent-to-remove-margaret-sangers-name-from-nyc-health-center.

Murrell, Sam. "Why I No Longer Participate in Racial Reconciliation Services." The Pulpit and Pen.org. January 27, 2018. https://pulpitandpen.org/2018/01/27/no-longer-participate-racial-reconciliation-services.

Newbigin, Lesslie. *The Gospel in a Pluralist Society.* Grand Rapids: Eerdmans, 1989.

Norris, Pippa. *Sacred and Secular: Religion and Politics Worldwide.* Cambridge: Cambridge University Press, 2004.

"On Critical Race Theory and Intersectionality." SBC.net. June 1, 2019. https://www.sbc.net/resource-library/resolutions/on-critical-race-theory-and-intersectionality.

Owen, John. *Glory of Christ, The.* Edingurgh: Banner of Truth, 2012.

Owen, John. *Indwelling Sin in Believers.* Edinburgh: Banner of Truth, 2012.

Owen, John. *Of Temptation.* Edinburgh: Banner of Truth, 2012.

Ozment, Steven. *Protestants: The Birth of a Revolution.* New York: Doubleday, 1992.

Packer, J.I. *An Anglican to Remember—William Perkins: Puritan Popularizer.* London: St. Anthonlin's Lectureship Charity Lecture, 1996.

Platt, David. "Praying and Working for Justice: Racialization." Radical.net. January 14, 2018. https://radical.net/sermon/praying-and-working-for-justice-racialization.

Platt, David. "United By Hope Part 3: Four Steps To Full Life." Sermon. McLean Bible Church, Vienna, Virginia. October 4, 2020. https://mcleanbible.org/sermons/United-by%20Hope/87.

Reid, J. K. S. (trans. from French) in *Geneva Confession, 1536* by John Calvin. London: John Knox Press, 1954.

Rothman, Lily. "Why It Took So Long for the World to See How Phnom Penh Fell." Time.com. April 17, 2015. https://time.com/3814193/anniversary-phnom-penh.

Ryle, J.C. *Holiness*. Mulberry: Sovereign Grace Publishers, 2001.

Sanger, Margaret. "The Wickedness of Creating Large Families." Chapter 5 in *Woman and the New Race* (1920). http://www.bartleby.com/1013.

Schaeffer, Francis. *How Shall We Then Live*. Wheaton: Crossway, 2005.

Schaff, Philip. *History of the Christian Church Vol. I-VIII*. Peabody: Hendrickson Publishers, 2011.

Schwartz, Matthew. "Trump Tells Agencies To End Trainings On 'White Privilege' And 'Critical Race Theory.'" NPR.org. September 5, 2020. https://www.npr.org/2020/09/05/910053496/trump-tells-agencies-to-end-trainings-on-white-privilege-and-critical-race-theory.

Sensoy, Ozlen and Robin DiAngelo. *Is Everyone Really Equal?: An Introduction to Key Concepts in Social Justice Education 1st edition*. New York: Teachers College Press, 2012.

Sensoy, Ozlen and Robin DiAngelo. *Is Everyone Really Equal? An Introduction to Key Concepts in Social Justice Education 2nd edition*. New York and London: Teachers College Press, 2017.

Sey, Samuel. "Black Liberation Theology and Woke Christianity." Slow to Write.com. May 5, 2018. https://slowtowrite.com/black-liberation-theology-and-woke-christianity.

Shedd, William G. T. *Dogmatic Theology, Third edition*. Phillipsburg: Presbyterian and Reformed Publishing Company, 2003.

Shenvi, Neil and Sawyer, Pat. "Engaging Critical Race Theory and the Social Justice Movement," *Journal of Christian Legal Thought*, 10, No. 1 (2020).

Shrier, Abigail. *Irreversible Damage: The Transgender Craze Seducing Our Daughters*. Washington, D.C.: Regnery Publishing, 2020.

Smart, Robert Davis, Michael A.G. Haykin; et al. *Pentecostal Outpourings: Revival and the Reformed Tradition*. Grand Rapids: Reformation Heritage Books, 2016.

Smith, Samuel. "Matt Chandler: Church has mostly 'refused to participate' on race, 'turned over' inheritance." Christian Post.com. June 10, 2020. https://www.christianpost.com/news/matt-chandler-church-has-mostly-refused-to-participate-on-race-turned-over-inheritance.html.

Solzhenitsyn, Aleksandr. *The Gulag Archipelago 1918-1956 An Experiment in Literary Investigation*. New York: Harper & Row, 1985.

"Stain of Mohler 3." TheNewCalvinist. November 25, 2019. YouTube video. 1:04:36. https://www.youtube.com/watch?v=MIlnLU-vt_g.

"Statement on Social Justice & the Gospel, The." Statement on Social Justice. com. Accessed September 20, 2020. https://statementonsocialjustice.com/wp-content/uploads/2018/09/SSJG-FINAL.pdf.

Sunshine, Glenn S. *Slaying Leviathan: Limited Government and Resistance In the Christian Tradition*. Moscow: Canon Press, 2020.

Taunton, Larry. "Understanding What is Happening in America, Part II: The Pale Marxist Trojan Horse." Larry Alex Taunton.com. August 26, 2020. http://larryalextaunton.com/2020/08/understanding-what-is-happening-in-america-part-ii-the-pale-Marxist-trojan-horse.

Taylor, Charles. *A Secular Age*. Cambridge: Harvard University Press, 2007.

Thompson, Sherwood. *Encyclopedia of Diversity and Social Justice*. London: Rowman & Littlefield, 2015.

"Tim Keller and Progressive Evangelicalism." Enemies Within the Church. com. Accessed September 8, 2020. https://enemieswithinthechurch. com/2020/08/22/tim-keller-and-progressive-evangelicalism.

Trewhella, Matthew J. *The Doctrine of the Lesser Magistrates: A Proper Resistance to Tyranny and a Repudiation of Unlimited Obedience to Civil Government.* Create Space Independent Publishing Platform, 2013.

Trueman, Carl R. *The Rise and Triumph of the Modern Self, Cultural Amnesia, Expressive Individualism, and the Road to Sexual Revolution,* Wheaton: Crossway, 2020.

Weaver, Richard. *Idea's Have Consequences.* London: The University of Chicago, 1948.

Webster, D.D. "Liberation Theology." In *Evangelical Dictionary of Theology Second Edition.* Grand Rapids: Baker Academic, 2001.

Wellum, Stephen J. "Editorial: The Urgent Need for a Theological Anthropology Today." *Southern Baptist Theological Journal. 13. No. 2* (Summer 2009).

Westminster Divines. "The Westminster Confession of Faith (1647)." Ligonier Ministries online. Accessed October 3, 2020. https://www.ligonier. org/learn/articles/westminster-confession-faith.

"What We Believe." Black Lives Matter.com. Accessed September 12, 2020. https://blacklivesmatter.com/what-we-believe.

"Whistleblower: 'Dangerous' theology taught at Al Mohler's SBTS seminary." Capstone Report.com. Accessed October 2, 2020. https://capstonereport. com/2020/05/18/whistleblower-dangerous-theology-taught-at-al-mohlers-sbts-seminary/34410.

White, James. "Woke Religion with Tim Keller, Fulgentius of Ruspe on the Hypostatic Union." Alpha and Omega Ministries. August 4, 2020. 01:17:43. https://www.aomin.org/aoblog/exegesis/woke-religion-with-tim-keller-fulgentius-of-ruspe-on-the-hypostatic-union.

Whitefield, George. *The Works of the Reverend George Whitefield.* London.

Williams, Jarvis and Kevin Jones. *Erasing the Sin of Racism from the Southern Baptist Convention.* Nashville: B&H, 2017.

Winn, Peter Winn. "Q&A: The Homosexual Agenda." CitizenLink.com. July 25, 2003, https://web.archive.org/web/20080612003916/http://www.citizenlink.org/CLFeatures/A000000562.cfm.

Woods, Curtis. *"The Literary Reception of the Spirituality of Phillis Wheatley (1753-1784): An Afrosensitive Reading.* Ph.D. Dissertation. Southern Baptist Theological Seminary. 2018. https://repository.sbts.edu/bitstream/handle/10392/5714/Woods_sbts_0207D_10471.pdf?sequence=1&isAllowed=y.

"Word Foundations INSIGHTS AND COMMENTARY FROM A BIBLICAL PERSPECTIVE." Accessed October 3, 2020. https://www.wordfoundations.com/pastor-tom-ascol-seeks-to-amend-resolution-9.

Worthen, Molly. "Can Black Evangelicals Save the Whole Movement?," New York Times.com. April 20, 2019. https://www.nytimes.com/2019/04/20/opinion/sunday/black-evangelicals-diversity.html.

Zockler, Otto. *Geschichte der Beziehungen Zwischen Theologie Und Naturwissenschaft.* Gutersloh: C. Bertelsmann, 1877-79, II.

For more information about

Wes Carpenter
and
Woke Religion
please visit:

@theologyconvos

For more information about
AMBASSADOR INTERNATIONAL
please visit:

www.ambassador-international.com
@AmbassadorIntl
www.facebook.com/AmbassadorIntl

If you enjoyed this book, please consider leaving us a review on
Amazon, Goodreads, or our website.

More from Ambassador International

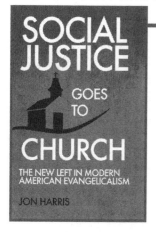

Social Justice Goes to Church: The New Left in Modern American Evangelicalism answers, from a historical perspective, the vital question, "Why are American evangelicals moving Left?"

Author Douglas Kruger traces the unfolding ideology from its dark genesis (the French Revolution and subsequent terror) through its various incarnations—Marxism, relativism, post-modernism, and all the way to today's identity-politics. He points out the flaws, fallacies, and in many cases, the body-counts these ideologies have wracked up. Become a master at identifying, debunking, and dismantling dangerous ideas.

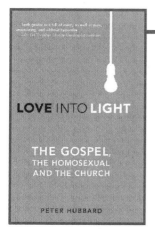

Sadly the church has often been afraid to talk about homosexuality. Many Christians feel confused and divided between the call to love and the call for truth. And many who struggle with unwanted same-sex attraction feel alone and alienated by the church.

Written from the heart of a pastor with a love for people and a sensitivity to our culture, *Love Into Light* is your next step toward becoming more faithfully and helpfully engaged with people in your families, in your church and in your neighborhood.

Made in the USA
Columbia, SC
07 December 2022

72905110R00178